Crossing the Mainstream

Crossing the Mainstream

Multicultural Perspectives in Teaching Literature

Eileen Iscoff Oliver
Washington State University

National Council of Teachers of English
1111 W. Kenyon Road, Urbana, Illinois 61801-1096

Grateful acknowledgment is made to the *Arizona English Bulletin* for permission to reprint portions of Eileen Iscoff Oliver's essay "Successful Writing Programs and Methods of Assessment for Non-mainstream Students" (Spring 1992).

Grateful acknowledgment is also made to Alfred A. Knopf, Inc., for permission to reprint "Harlem (Dream Deferred)" from *The Panther and the Lash* by Langston Hughes. Copyright 1951 by Langston Hughes.

Manuscript Editor: Michael Himick

Staff Editors: Marlo Welshons and Michelle Sanden Johlas

Cover Designer: Victoria Martin Pohlmann

Interior Book Designer: Doug Burnett

NCTE Stock Number 09721-3050

It is the policy of NCTE in its journals and other publications to provide a forum for the open discussion of ideas concerning the content and the teaching of English and the language arts. Publicity accorded to any particular point of view does not imply endorsement by the Executive Committee, the Board of Directors, or the membership at large, except in announcements of policy, where such endorsement is clearly specified.

Library of Congress Cataloging-in-Publication Data
Oliver, Eileen Iscoff.
    Crossing the mainstream : multicultural perspectives in teaching literature / Eileen Iscoff Oliver.
      p. cm.
    Includes bibliographical references.
    ISBN 0-8141-0972-1 : $19.95
    1. American literature—Minority authors—Study and teaching.
  2. Pluralism (Social sciences) in literature—Study and teaching.
  3. Literature and society—United States—Study and teaching.
  4. Ethnic groups in literature—Study and teaching. 5. Minorities in literature—Study and teaching. 6. Culture in literature—Study and teaching. I. Title.
  PS153.M56045 1994
  807' . 1'273—dc20

                                              94-14634
                                                 CIP

In memory of Ben,
who taught me to love the whole world and everybody in it,
especially the children.

———————

For Reva,
whose gentle strength has guided me, Liane,
and the rest of her children for three generations;

and for Emma and Joe,
for whom all the children of the world are like flowers,
every one different, every one beautiful.

———————

To Bernie,
whose flame blazes through the darkness
so that tomorrow's children will be able to see;

and to Kenny, J.J., Rachel, and Deborah,
who are constant reminders that learning about our children
is a never-ending labor of love.

Contents

Preface

U nfortunately, some of us continue to teach the same canonical works we have used for decades, missing out on all of the excellent literature that has been, for one reason or another, excluded from the traditional canon. In the meantime, our students find less and less relevance in what they are reading, and those who are marginalized by current curricula become even more alienated as they continue through school. My purpose in writing *Crossing the Mainstream* is to bring attention to these issues by examining ways in which we can expand our canon to include diversity in our curricular choices.

This book is separated into three sections. Part I, "Multicultural Literature for Whom?" attempts to develop a rationale for expanding the canon to include multicultural literature in everyone's educational experience. It also confronts the issue of censorship, which many of us struggle with when introducing new literature into restricted curricula. Part II, "Curricular Challenges: Beyond Eurocentric Values," begins the task of cataloging the multitude of literary works that might be included in the new repertoire. It also explores the complicated process of learning critical analyses quite different from those most of us received in our own educations. Finally, Part III, "Teaching Strategies for Multicultural Literature," gives examples of how multicultural works can be incorporated into literature courses.

Readers should be aware of some semantic problems as they approach this text. As various terms and phrases come in and out of fashion, some labels enjoy long lives, while others quickly become obsolete. Thus, although I use labels like *mainstream* and *nonmainstream* literature and *multicultural* education, the politics of terminology renders these terms precarious. An issue of propriety, one must be careful when using references that may not be acceptable to all readers. Nonetheless, I fear that no matter what terminology I use, someone will find it offensive. Or perhaps my terms will be obsolete by the time the ink dries on the page. Recognizing this semantic trap, I offer the following discussions using what, at this time, seem to be acceptable terms based on my research into the work of many educators and people of letters. Although terms like *mainstream* and *nonmainstream*, *multicultural*, *pluralistic*, and *diverse* seem appropriate to me today, my apologies to readers who find them disagreeable now or in the future. I hope the tone of this book presents my work as a beginning effort in what I expect to be a long, long task in which many of us will be engaged.

And because I venture into areas where my expertise is limited, I have called upon friends and colleagues to assist me. I would therefore like to express my special appreciation to Shelli Fowler, Alex Kuo, Rory Ong, Ricardo Sanchez, and Marian Sciachitano, who prevented me from going too far astray. Their expertise was invaluable. Also, many thanks to Jeanne Richeson, whose patience and efficiency facilitated my efforts.

I am certain that this book leaves out a lot. It is, however, only a start. Perhaps it will help stimulate and support an ongoing dialogue about multicultural literature. Perhaps it will generate ideas and provide motivation for change where there has been little. It will, I hope, invite readers to work together to find new and better ways to introduce an ever-changing student body to what has heretofore been either unacknowledged or undervalued.

I Multicultural Literature for Whom?

1 Literature for Students of Color: On the Outside Looking In

Years ago, when I first read Louise Rosenblatt's classic *Literature as Exploration*, I was struck by her discussion of "relevance" and the teenage reader. Not only does she tell us that students' spontaneous response is the first step to their understanding and awareness of literature, but she also underscores the detrimental effects that irrelevant selections have on the positive reading experiences of nonmainstream students. Her example of the outrageous mismatch between students and the literature they read has stuck with me ever since:

> During a reorganization of education on the Indian reservations
> some years ago, it was discovered that in some classes the Indian
> boys and girls were being required to read Restoration comedies.
> (Rosenblatt 1976, 57)

Imagine! Kids looking out windows, staring at walls, their heads on desks—lost. And the English teacher at the front of the classroom, forging ahead, dragging her languishing charges along with her—or so she thinks. This picture might give us all a laugh if it weren't so painfully recognizable. Whether we want to acknowledge it or not, many of our students nationwide suffer the same classroom tortures. In fact, according to Rosenblatt, the plight of the Native American students in her example "differs only in degree from the average American child's relation to much of the literature he [or she] reads in [the] . . . classroom" (57).

After twenty-five years of teaching in high schools, community colleges, correctional facilities, and universities, I can see that Rosenblatt's scenario is the rule rather than the exception, even today. I have taught in California, Texas, New York, Minnesota, and Washington in classes labeled "upper-middle," "blue collar," and "inner-city." Unfortunately, restricted reading experiences exist everywhere. Theoretically, we have made great strides in "multiculturalizing" the literature we consider valuable and appropriate for secondary students. But the fact remains that vast numbers of them are still reading majority writers almost exclusively (Applebee 1989), a situation that is considered anathema in current research in reader response, literature for high school students, cross-cultural awareness, and multicultural education.

The great gap between what we preach—that readers respond to work that relates to their own lives—and what we practice—the same tired selections from outdated anthologies—pervades school systems throughout the United States. And not without consequence. According to Beach and Marshall (1991), African American students,

> particularly those in inner-city schools, have difficulty identify-
> ing with the cultural perspectives of the dominant culture . . .
> when they are daily experiencing quite a different cultural world.
> Thus, if their study of literature . . . excludes African-American
> perspectives, they may perceive an enormous gap between the
> school culture and their home culture. (445)

As obvious as all this sounds, the teaching of irrelevant literature and the alienation of nonmainstream students persists.

I am constantly reminded of this situation by my former students. Recently, I received a late night call from Sandy, who was having a problem with her class. I told her we could work on it and encouraged her to visit me. The next day Sandy came directly from school, where she had obviously "been through the mill." This once composed, self-assured, top-notch student was completely frazzled. As she described her situation, it became clear to me that her students were utterly bored with, even alienated by, the work they were doing.

Sandy's class was typical of many in our inner-city schools, with no real "majority" population. Of her thirty-three students, some were African Americans, some were Asian Americans, some were Latino/as, and a few were European Americans. Some were recent arrivals from other countries with a minimal grasp of English, and several were repeating the sophomore-level class as juniors and seniors. Moreover, the class was at the end of the day. My first question was "What are they reading?" "World literature," Sandy answered. "*The Odyssey*, excerpts from *The Divine Comedy, Macbeth, Cyrano, Hedda Gabler*." Say no more!

I'm not discrediting these great works. We don't want to water down our cultural heritage by leaving out the masterpieces. But unless we figure out a better way to teach these classics, we might as well acknowledge that we've already lost many of our students and admit that we're just going through the motions. Teaching these works to a dying audience is not teaching them at all, and we owe our students—not to mention Shakespeare and Dante—more than that. What we're missing is the "connection." If students aren't motivated by literature, they won't read. Yet if they can discover in literature ideas and experiences relevant to their own lives, they'll astound us.

I once taught in a "continuation" school outside San Francisco. The tiny student body was made up of kids who had been kicked out of one of the six comprehensive high schools in the district. There was no "majority" population. Within our ranks we had truants, runaways, strong-armed robbers, and chemical dependents. At least half of the students were periodically visited by probation officers checking up on their cases. In short, this was a tough crowd to please.

When I first arrived, I naively stocked my room with all of the "appropriate classics" and adolescent literature that I had previously taught in a large, traditionally focused comprehensive school. I showed my treasures to the reading teacher, who also maintained the "library" next door. She smiled politely and said that she hoped the students would enjoy my books. But Fran knew that the students wouldn't respond positively to my choices. So did the other teachers who had worked with these kids. And after seeing my selections collect dust on the shelves, I knew too. These students had no interest—initially at least—in reading what I thought was great literature. They first had to discover literature—their literature—on their own.

For example, I gave Gordon Parks's *The Learning Tree* to Bobby, an obviously hostile African American student who made no bones about not wanting to be in school. He sat down and read until the end of the period. The next day, Bobby came in, handed me the book, and told me that he had finished it and wanted another. Vicki, a Mexican American student, a chronic truant, and a runaway, was from an abusive family and pretty much earned her living on the streets. I gave her *Carmen*, a story about a girl in similar straits. She finished the book by the end of the day. I could relate many more stories about students with terrible academic records who, when given the chance to read material they found relevant, read book after book, softened their attitudes about school, and became willing to write and speak about what they were reading.

If one of the purposes of "teaching" literature is to "help more students engage successfully with print" (Tchudi and Mitchell 1989, 110), then we must provide our students with selections they will enjoy and help them to develop positive attitudes about what they read. We must make sure that their reading experiences, initially at least, provide them with both the opportunity to identify with the characters they read about and the opportunity to expand their worlds through the vicarious adventures that stories offer.

Reading for Identification

Kiah (1985) notes:

> In a pluralistic society where racial, cultural, and social diversities abound, each group eventually develops traditions and special interests. Within each group are exhibited mutually shared experiences that are unique to and characteristic of people of the relatively same background. It is the sharing of these experiences that provides a cohesiveness, or feeling of togetherness, to a particular group. These experiences become crucial and salient to the members of the groups as they strive to maintain and preserve that which gives them a sense of worth and self-identification. (286)

It is not surprising, then, that English teachers are able to find literature that students can identify with fairly well for those students who are most like them. Demographically, I'm talking about mainstream students who like to read, whose family environments are conducive to literary experiences, and who are relatively successful in school. We are much less successful, however, with students who are different, who did not grow up in middle-class families, who live in homes where reading experiences are not valued, or who come from nontraditional family settings.

In 1990, as part of an outreach program at St. Cloud State University in Minnesota, I invited ten high school students of color to visit my junior-level "Literature for Teaching" class. This experience would allow my students—almost all of whom were Midwestern, mainstream students who thought of non-Nordic, non-Germanic peoples as "ethnic"—to interact, mostly for the very first time, with students who were different from themselves. I will never forget the frozen looks on my students' faces when those ten African American, Asian American, and Mexican American high school students walked into the room. Although I knew that the European American students would be somewhat uncomfortable, I was startled by their response: they looked scared!

I explained to the visiting students that our class was composed of prospective high school teachers and that they, as high school students, were obviously experts on this topic. I also explained that I had prepared a series of questions for them. Their responses to these questions were enlightening. The visiting students were explicit in telling their audience about how they were able to "get around" assignments that they didn't like, giving detailed examples of how they could call their friends and share answers, "scam" the teacher by listening to what he or she thought was important and then parroting it back, or use any of the other little tricks that many of us have come grudgingly to know over the years.

What was most informative, however, was the visiting students' response to my question about their favorite books. One student said, with great poise, that he didn't like anything the teacher "made" them read because she never told them why they had to learn these books, only that "they were assigned" and that "there was no choice." I asked him if he had read any of them. "No," was his response. I then asked if he had read anything that semester. "Well, I just finished *The Autobiography of Malcolm X*." (This event occurred prior to the renewed interest in Malcolm X generated by Spike Lee's film.) "How was it?" I asked. "Great! I loved it." Since I felt that this was as important a text to understanding twentieth-century America as most others we require our students to read, I asked my own students how many of them had read it. Answer: none. "What else?" I pressed. "Ralph Ellison's *Invisible Man?*" Again, I polled my students. Three of them had read it, admitting collectively that they had a difficult time with it. It had been hard to understand. "Why?" our high schooler asked.

Our guests then went on to share some of their other positive reading experiences, mentioning multiethnic titles like *A Boat to Nowhere*, *The House on Mango Street*, and *Love Medicine*. They also talked about books more commonly found in the canon of high school literature: *To Kill a Mockingbird, Huckleberry Finn, Lord of the Flies*, even *Hamlet*. I asked, "What was it about these books that you liked?" Their positive responses seemed to center around a particular teacher, Mr. Ender, and the fact that he didn't "set in stone" the books that everybody had to read. From what they were saying, the students responded favorably to this teacher because he allowed them great latitude, because he guided their selections rather than making them, and because he included in his suggestions many multiethnic authors.

Unfortunately, we do not have enough Mr. Enders in our schools. Students are too often given limited choices of what they can read, and the selections are often uninviting, particularly to nonmainstream students. As Scott (1988) writes, schools must "change or modify materials so that the content includes experiences and knowledge familiar both to nonmainstream groups and mainstream groups" (31). Continuing to ignore the literatures of diverse groups is not only unrealistic and unscholarly, but also offensive to the students we teach. In a country whose demographics have changed drastically in the last few decades, it makes no sense to deny our students a look at the world through the eyes of all of its artists.

Expanding Our Worlds through Literature

Discussions about expanding the literary canon to include multicultural perspectives tend to ignore the flip-side of the argument. That is, good literature—"the classics," so to speak—should be taught to everybody. Somehow, when we talk about using multiethnic literature for nonmainstream groups, some get the impression that mainstream literature is for mainstream groups. This assumption ushers in an entirely different set of misconceptions about what people should have the opportunity to read.

I often require teachers to read Maya Angelou's *I Know Why the Caged Bird Sings* (1969). It's surprising how many of them have not read this book, which is great for high school students. I focus on Angelou's description of what books meant to her while growing up in Stamps, Arkansas:

> During these years in Stamps, I met and fell in love with William Shakespeare. He was my first white love. Although I enjoyed and respected Kipling, Poe, Butler, Thackeray, and Henley, I saved my young and loyal passion for Paul Laurence Dunbar, Langston Hughes, James Weldon Johnson, and W. E. B. Du Bois' "Litany at Atlanta." But it was Shakespeare who said, "When in disgrace with fortune and men's eyes." It was a state with which I felt myself most familiar. (11)

Doesn't every English teacher dream of having a student like Maya, a student who loves literature—and "the classics" at that? But she didn't develop this interest by having her teacher ram literature down her throat. Actually, Angelou's whole story is about how this poet/linguist/ essayist/dancer/singer/civil rights activist learned to love language and create works of art by being allowed, in one way or another, to find a voice of her own. Of course, Maya had Mrs. Flowers, the woman who taught this diffident little girl to like herself, the world, and what it had to offer. Mrs. Flowers, the "aristocrat of Black Stamps," was, according to Angelou, "the lady who threw me my first life line" (77), the woman who introduced her to books.

Classic examples of African Americans who must "steal" the privilege of learning how to read go far back into our history. For example, Frederick Douglass (1845) speaks of first being taught to read by his owner, Mrs. Auld. Yet Auld's husband, upon learning of such "dangerous" activity, forbade her from continuing, warning her that nothing good could come from having a literate slave. Douglass describes how he then cleverly enticed his white contemporaries into completing the task that Mrs. Auld had begun.

In a poignant passage in *Black Boy* (1945), a very popular book among high school students, Richard Wright explains how he used his boss's library card to check out books, since African Americans were not allowed to use the library. He describes his fascination with H. L. Mencken's work and with the world of fiction as literature unfolded before him:

> [Mencken] was using words as a weapon, using them as one would use a club. Could words be weapons? (272)

> Reading was like a drug, a dope. The novels created moods in which I lived for days. (273)

And in reading Dreiser's *Sister Carrie*, Wright thinks of his own mother and her suffering (274).

I mention these writers not only for the power and beauty of their work, but also because the significance of literature in their early lives is an important lesson for nonmainstream students. A few years ago, I heard Maya Angelou (1990) speak to a group of students in Minnesota. In short, she told them to "go to the library." She talked about a number of mainstream artists whom she encouraged everyone to read. She also laced into her discussion Harlem Renaissance writers like Countee Cullen and Langston Hughes. Telling her audience that "poetry and music are responsible for keeping us erect," she harkened back to her life in Stamps, Arkansas, where, discovering Shakespeare, she knew that "he wrote for me." She also named Turgenev and Achebe, saying that they too wrote for her. "And," she said, dramatically underscoring her words as only Maya Angelou can do, "*I am worth it!*"

Angelou's message here is that authors—mainstream and nonmainstream—write for all of us. Yet to say this is not to deny the importance of including nonmainstream literature in the literary canon. We need all points of view. In 1991, I attended a MELUS (Multi-Ethnic Literature of the United States) conference in Minneapolis and had the opportunity to hear Paul Lauter, editor of *The Heath Anthology of American Literature* (1990), speak about the nature and conception of this new text. He outlined the principles of the multiethnic, gender-fair approach that the editors took. Explaining that these principles would inform all subsequent Heath texts, Lauter (1991) said:

> The most profound change that has occurred during the past twenty years is . . . that literature can no longer be divided into "mainstream" and "marginal". . . . Unfortunately for most readers, [though,] because women and ethnic writers have been so seldom anthologized, coming to know their work—and to understand its significance, especially if it deviates from what have

become accepted patterns of literary representation—has been difficult.

Riding home from the MELUS meetings, I asked my colleague Judy Foster about *The Heath Anthology*, which she was using in her American literature course. She responded enthusiastically, explaining that, for her, the Heath text "changes the whole focus of what we consider to be American literature." She offered several examples of what she meant. Reading the slave narratives of Frederick Douglass and Harriet Ann Jacobs, she said, gave new meaning to what students up to now have thought of as nineteenth-century American rhetoric. And she compared the "fanfare and attention" of Thoreau's "Civil Disobedience" to Angelina Grimke's "Appeal to the Christian Women of the South." "Here's a woman," Judy claimed, "who wrote to Christian women all over the South, telling them to 'break the rules,' encouraging them to help free slaves, to teach them to read, and to speak out against this sin against God and man. And hardly any of our students had heard of her until the Lauter text came out."

I now have my own copy of *The Heath Anthology*, and I can see why Judy was so enthusiastic about it. James Banks (1991) has noted that its publication was a significant milestone in the struggle for multiethnic literature. "This collection," Banks has said, "embodies the concepts of multiethnic studies and most certainly will influence subsequent collections."

One of the most destructive features of maintaining the literary canon as a white, male-dominated corpus is the denial of the existence of other literary works. Thus, students of color and others who do not fit into the mainstream are always on the outside looking in. They are required to read books about people they often perceive as oppressors. They seldom have the opportunity to see that they too possess a literary heritage worthy of study. In a later chapter, I will discuss some of the reasons we hold so stubbornly to the current canon. For now, I will simply say that we must look beyond what were considered literary masterpieces when many of us were undergraduates. To deny students their heritage because we know little about it, to portray the "Eurocentric slice" of cultural literacy as the only one there is because we aren't familiar with others as well, is not just ignorant on our part; it is also a cruel method of keeping many of our students from self-actualizing through literary experiences they can relate to. As Bennett (1986) writes:

> Literature and artistic achievements by one's own people provide sources of identity and pride within the individual, and sources of respect from others. They can help expand students' readiness

for empathy. Self-knowledge, self-acceptance, and security are necessary before people can understand and accept others with whom they may disagree. (197–98)

The growing momentum for curriculum reform will, I hope, no longer allow the literature of "others" to be marginalized as it has been for so many years. For one thing, more and more scholars are "discovering" it. For another, more and more students are demanding it. As students of literature, we should all thirst for material we have been deprived of for so long. Everyone—the many students of color across our country and everybody else—is entitled to know the history and pain and beauty of the world as it has been recorded by artists who come from all of the strands that make up American literary society. It is for all of us that I write this book. May we read, learn, and grow from these experiences and teach our students to do the same.

2 The Culturally Deprived American Majority

Allan Bloom (1987) tells us that the American mind is closing. He objects to the increasing openness of modern theory, to the egalitarian acceptance of contemporary social critics, and to the inclusion of multicultural identities and political stances, all of which he claims has brought about the decline of intellectual thought on college campuses nationwide. Calling for a return to classical literature and traditional models, Bloom denounces the democratization of disciplines that he believes has overtaken our intellectual communities. Instead of applauding the relativistic nature in which modern intellectuals "take in" and analyze new ideas, he is critical of their "lack of attention" to the traditional models of Western thought.

But Professor Bloom is mistaken in his assertion that the academy's potential for change and willingness to learn new approaches is bad. In decrying what has been lost, Bloom fails to acknowledge and make room for what has been recognized as valid and relevant in a changing world. To ignore reality, or worse, to deny it, is not only unproductive, but also unethical. We do not practice deceit in education—at least we shouldn't—especially when it relates to the marginalization of people.

Holding fast to old traditions is no longer a viable option. New evidence has entered the public domain. A few years ago, after information about Columbus's annihilation of the Arawak Indians gained some recognition, a teacher asked me whether it might not be better to avoid mentioning this fact to students, who, after all, thought of Columbus as a hero. She was suggesting that we withhold evidence to protect the image of this American icon. But how, in good conscience, can we do that?

Further, the recognition and inclusion of other disciplines and other perspectives are not responsible for the myopia that Bloom sees in the minds of students today. Rather, the downward trend in American intellectual thought has more to do with students' lack of interest in an irrelevant curriculum.

In "Illiberal Education" (1991), another so-called "preserver of the traditions," Dinesh D'Souza, laments the immunity that "champions of minority interests" have, "even when they make excessive or outlandish claims with racial connotations" (52). For instance:

> The African-American scholar Leonard Jeffries claims in class that whites are biologically inferior to blacks and that the "ultimate culmination" of the white value system is Nazi Germany. (54)

An interesting point of view. D'Souza continues by citing sociologist Becky Thompson, who begins her course on race, class, and gender

> with the feminist principle that in a racist, classist, and sexist society we have all swallowed oppressive ways of being, whether intentionally or not. Specifically, this means that it is not open to debate whether a white student is racist or a male student is sexist. S/he simply is. Rather, the focus is on the social forces that keep these distortions in place. (54)

Both of these perspectives almost guarantee student engagement. Either would be a great point from which to begin a stimulating discussion on racism or sexism. So what is D'Souza afraid of? Our mission as educators is to make students think. Shouldn't they be presented with nontraditional points of view in order to make use of their critical thinking abilities? Besides, are these theories so outlandish? Think of the status of women a hundred years ago. Consider the three-fifths clause in our Constitution and the institution of slavery in general. Think of the degeneracy of the Nazi regime. Think of the audience Shockley and Jensen have had. We should not privilege certain theoretical outbursts and then not listen to divergent positions.

Besides, I think D'Souza overestimates the power of the professor's opinion. Students do not automatically accept a new concept—especially one that doesn't fit into their previously constructed schema—just because a teacher or a professor presents them with it. At least my students do not. In fact, it is my observation that most students are generally quite parochial in their thinking. It takes a lot to move them off dead center.

E. D. Hirsch, Jr. (1987), the much-maligned proponent of cultural literacy, had a good idea. No one disputes the value of world knowledge, a strong literary background, and shared information from one's culture. We all wish our students had these qualities. But when Hirsch puts the responsibility for failure on "faulty theories promulgated in our schools of education and accepted by educational policymakers" (110), he is way out of line. The school is central to the success of students, but we cannot discount everything else. And to suggest that Hirsch's program of cultural literacy would solve the ills of our nation's schools is an affront and discredits many hardworking teachers.

Whose Culture Is It, Anyway?

Defining the relevance of cultural literacy, Mullican (1991) asks, "Whose culture? Whose literacy? All of us are culturally illiterate to a degree, since none of us knows everything" (246). He then describes a poem about the Beatles that one of his students wrote, a poem that he found difficult to understand because he lacked the proper background. I am reminded of the paper on the musical group Metallica that one of my own students wrote. I was clearly the most ignorant member of his peer response group.

Every semester I conduct an experiment in my teaching methods class. I ask students to list the ten most important works every educated person must read. When they finish, I put them in groups and ask them to come up with a single list. After much negotiation and lots of conversation about "this has to stay" and "that has to go," they put their choices on the chalkboard. We then look at the six or so lists and compare. Of course, no two lists are ever the same. What we determine is that there is no specific literary canon.

Evidently, the sixty K–college English teachers who met at the 1987 English Coalition Conference in Maryland agree (Elbow 1990). This group convened in an attempt to identify the direction of the teaching of English and the language arts. One of the speakers, E. D. Hirsch, Jr., recommended plot summaries, terms, and information. The group balked at his emphasis, however, and sought less restrictive guidelines. Following Hirsch, Shirley Brice Heath spoke to the group and reflected on "conditions of nourishment and challenge . . . not just . . . skills or scores or grades" (Elbow 1990, 18).

As we develop our own literary canons, we must be sure that what we are doing is not culturally biased. Rita Kissen (1989), for instance, comments on the cultural biases that the preservice teachers in her course "Children's Literature of Emerging Nations" harbored, biases they did not even recognize that they had:

> Their world view was strongly ethnocentric, exalting competition and individualism, permeated with racism and sexism, and embodying what I have come to call "technophilia," the assumption that technology is an absolute good and that human beings are meant to control rather than reverence nature. (212)

The changing demographics of the American population make it essential that we move toward a more diverse outlook regarding the literature that we teach in our classes. I say this not just because we will soon have a "majority minority" population, but because mainstream students will be "culturally deprived" if we do not. And that puts the responsibility on teachers to provide a wide variety of reading selections from the best traditional and contemporary writers we have. What exactly is the literary canon? Raymond (1990) tells us that "all human experience can be a worthy subject of literature, and that our traditional exclusions merely impoverish ourselves and our students" (82).

Eliminating Myths of Hate

We *can* make a difference. Every educator knows the power of good teaching. We also know that racism, homophobia, ableism, sexism, and other forms of discrimination are destroying our students' learning environments. Discrimination affects not only those who have been marginalized, but everyone else as well. Because many of us perceive the world monolithically, we jeopardize ourselves and our future in a number of ways. As teachers, we must begin to look at the realities behind the surface of ethnocentric behavior and work harder to eradicate some of our most dangerous biases.

The issue of affirmative action, for example, is one of the most volatile of all the topics I have encountered in the classroom. Though students usually try to be "politically correct" about racism and sexism, all hell breaks loose whenever the subject of college admissions, scholarships, or job potential crops up. One student, convinced that he had not been admitted to West Point because "his place" was "taken" by "a minority, probably a female," wrote, "It is unfortunate to think that a fully qualified student was denied admission to a deserved position at West Point merely because of race and sex." This attitude, I believe, is representative of the backlash created by myths and misinformation about affirmative action, which has become the automatic scapegoat of anyone who did not get his or her anticipated job, promotion, scholarship, or college acceptance letter.

What we need to understand is that scapegoating doesn't just affect those who bear the brunt of the hostility and bitterness it creates. It also harms those who use it as an excuse, because it gets in the way as they try to face up to their own limitations. And parents who do not accept their children's limitations, who choose instead to find scapegoats for lost scholarships or college rejection letters, only reinforce their children's misperceptions.

Discrimination and ignorance affect us all. Yet we can make a difference using literature as a tool because it allows us to live vicariously through the characters we read about. Bennett (1990) writes:

> As painful as it may be, children and young adults must face facts about the racist past. Under the guidance of knowledgeable and caring teachers, minorities and nonminorities can gain insight into a social context that helps explain current patterns of poverty, protest, and apathy as well as interracial isolation, stereotypes, misconceptions, and conflict. (303)

For students to do so, however, for students to "face facts about the racist past," educators must examine both what they teach and how they teach it.

Banks (1989) tells us that most school material is taught from a middle- or upper-class white male perspective, which limits students' ability to perceive concepts and issues from other perspectives. "Consequently," he writes, "students gain only a limited conception of the development of the nation and the world" (20–21). And Bennett (1990) demonstrates that misconceptions and stereotypes often start with the literature and textbooks we use. She writes:

> According to Banfield of the Council on Interracial Books for Children, racism in textbooks is usually most evident in five important ways: the historical perspective; the characterization of Third World peoples; the manner in which their customs and traditions are depicted; the terminology used to describe the peoples and their culture and the type of language ascribed to them; and the nature of their illustrations. (76)

The negative views students often have of Africans, for example, frequently start with the misinformation, stereotyping, and mystification found in textbooks. These misconceptions, Bennett says, worsen similar stereotypes about African Americans and "feed the doctrine of white supremacy" by perpetuating myths about the inferiority of black people (75–76). And when we analyze the meaning of expressions such as "blackening" someone's character, giving someone "a black eye" (a mark of shame), or calling someone a "blackguard" (Robert B. Moore, cited in Bennett 1990, 76), understanding how racism perpetuates itself through literature becomes elementary.

Though it often makes us uncomfortable, teachers must accept some of the responsibility for perpetuating myths and misperceptions. Do we recognize that stereotypic language and images exist in much of the literature we teach? Do we confront these issues? Or do we avoid teaching the material because it might get us into trouble? We too must "face facts about the racist past" if we are to make a difference.

Take *The Merchant of Venice*, for instance. Thomas McKendy (1990) suggests that "a careful look at Shakespeare's prejudices and their roots can teach students not only about historical attitudes, but about their own unacknowledged assumptions as well" (18). He tells us that an analysis of the "Hath not a Jew eyes?" speech is not enough to absolve Shakespeare of anti-Semitic thought. By using our own culture's attitudes toward Gypsies, McKendy illustrates that Shakespeare in his time probably knew as little about Jews as students today know about Gypsies. Thus, he writes strictly from a stereotypic view. McKendy writes:

> [Shakespeare had] most likely never seen nor spoken with a Jew. . . . He would have known that Jews on the continent were often money lenders, a profession closed to Christians . . . and that these money lenders were despised . . . [but] Jews for Shakespeare, like Gypsies for my students, were a somewhat exotic and largely unknown people. They were perhaps an abstraction to him, and as such he was probably no more hostile to them than my students are to Gypsies. . . . None of this, however, precluded Shakespeare from including an offensive and degrading picture of a Jew when he needed a two-dimensional villain for his play. (20)

McKendy concludes by telling us that we should not trivialize this bias: "In our own country, such casual stereotypes have almost certainly smoothed the way for more vicious prejudices, for the persecution and slaughter of Jews, Gypsies, and others" (21).

Diversity in Literature . . .

. . . When There Are No Students of Color in the Class

Sometimes teachers tell me that they don't need to teach ethnic literature because there aren't any minority students in their classes. Wrong! That's all the more reason to incorporate such literature into their canon. The changing demographics of this country demand that we expand the heretofore Eurocentric, male-dominated canon to broaden the perspectives of "majority" readers. The corollary to Maya Angelou's assertion that Shakespeare wrote for her is that Richard Wright wrote for Suzie Q. Smith living in Centraltown, U.S.A. And if Suzie can read and appreciate the works of great artists of color, perhaps she will become less narrow in her thinking, better able to identify with those outside her immediate community, and more successful in preparing herself for life in America.

In addition, there is just so much more out there than the literature that has been traditionally taught. Teachers shouldn't miss out on the opportunity to add some excellent literature to their canons. To assume that good literature comes only out of the European American classical tradition is both arrogant and ignorant.

... When There Are a Few Students of Color in the Class

Sometimes teachers ask me what literature they should teach when there are one or two students of color in their classes. These teachers are the brave ones. I fear that most teachers who feel uncomfortable with ethnic issues simply avoid teaching "sensitive" literature altogether. My first response to those who do raise the issue is to encourage them by telling them that there is no one answer to their dilemma, any more than there is ever one solution to any teaching situation. What teachers must do is expect a variety of responses from students of color, just as they would from everyone else. I have had students from ethnic minorities who were happy to contribute to class discussions relevant to their ethnicity. Others were not and remained silent. I have had some who felt empowered by the activity. I have had others who were defensive.

There are no rules. Yet I have always tried to be sensitive to any material being read and discussed that might be misconstrued. I speak to students individually when I think that the literature we are reading may be more closely tied to them than to others. I think I can sense if a student is uncomfortable. If a student does seem uneasy, I might privately mention to the student that if there is some part of the literature that he or she finds personally relevant, he or she should feel free to add to our discussions. I have had a variety of results with these reassurances. Sometimes students feel empowered enough to contribute as "an expert" on a foreign language or dialect or community issue, perhaps sharing an anecdote about "what it was like when my older brother tried to get a job and was turned down because of his limited English." Sometimes students remain silent but tell me privately that the questions I ask in class are important to them. I have had students who say nothing until the end of the course and then thank me for "bringing a lot of that stuff out in the open." Majority students do the same. We need to realize that young people are often much more open than we think. Sometimes our own fear keeps us from doing what we think is right.

What I try not to do is make inaccurate assumptions. I never assume that just because Cindy is a Lakota Indian from South Dakota, that she somehow represents the voice of the Laguna Indian from the Southwest that Leslie Silko writes about in *Ceremony*. Even though Jesse, an upper-middle-class member of the honors orchestra whose parents are professors, is African American, he does not share the oppression of poverty and isolation that Richard Wright describes in *Black Boy*. I never ask students to act as spokespeople for their race, gender, sexual orientation, religion, whatever.

I do make an attempt to let students see what life is like from other points of view. A short essay that I like to use for this purpose is Brent Staples's "Night Walker" (1986), a narrative about a very tall African American newswriter who likes to take walks at night. Seeing him approach, people move to the other side of the street; women clutch their purses; car locks click quickly as he passes. To put people at ease and thus ward off such unnecessary and unpleasant insults, he carries the *Wall Street Journal* under his arm while he walks and whistles opera music. Not only is this a great model for students' own narratives, but many also learn something about aspects of life they had never before considered. Often their realization prompts an African American male in the class to contribute his own experience, much to their surprise. "We never thought of that" is frequently the reply.

Another very good short piece is Michael Dorris's "For the Indians, No Thanksgiving" (1988), in which he depicts the now institutionalized feast as "the last full meal" for reservation Indians, who

> reside in among the most impoverished counties in the nation.
> They constitute the ethnic group at the wrong peak of every scale:
> most undernourished, most short-lived, least educated, least
> healthy. (201)

This essay always prompts a number of students to pursue excellent related research questions. I have also had two Native American students—one Shoshone, one Choctaw and Chippewa—share some moving stories about their parents' experiences and their families' history during class discussions of Dorris's work.

... When the Class Is Racially Mixed

Just because a school is racially mixed is no guarantee that all of its students will be treated fairly. I have taught in places where teachers have established a genuine atmosphere of sharing, where people appreciate one another's culture, and where students seem well able to interact fairly with members of other ethnicities. Yet I have also been in situations that encouraged just the reverse. In fact, one negative effect of integrating schools twenty-five or so years ago was that many of the students of color who were bused into mainstream schools wound up in lower-level classes for a variety of reasons other than ability or potential. And the effects of the internal segregation resulting from tracked classes persist in many schools even today.

As a college supervisor of preservice teachers, I have sometimes questioned the expectations that both they and their cooperating teachers have held for some of their students. Once, in Sacramento, California, a cooperating teacher told me that "when you get a certain number of a 'certain kind' of student, you can't really do anything with the class." I responded that I would have to find a more positive role model for my student teacher. He answered, "Well, there *are* some liberals left who still believe they can make a difference."

Even in the best of situations, we still face the perplexing question of whether or not we should use literature that may be offensive to students of color. That is, if a work of literature is objectionable because of some aspect that may be perceived as racist, should we throw it out? Peter Smagorinsky (1992) says "No," but we must use

> a greater sensitivity in our teaching that reflects our recognition that the experiences of some of our students may not enable a dispassionate reading. In this light we would need to be very open-minded in listening to student responses and try to work constructively with them. If *Huck Finn* is truly a great book then students should have great experiences with it. I don't think this is possible unless we treat the book emotionally as well as intellectually. (226)

This position, however, does not go uncontested. Dr. Ernece B. Kelly of the City University of New York points out that it is

> a notion which is more acceptable to racial majority (white) teachers than to minority ones. I'd propose that white teachers read a book which offends them because it paints a picture of their race or class or ethnic group which is likely to cause pain or humiliation or the like. That might enable them to experience these feelings and to discover if they become defensive during that experience and if they, in fact, might not be ultimately inclined to discourage use of that book. In short, I think this view is premised on an underestimation of the emotional/psychological damage that books such as *The Adventures of Huckleberry Finn*, with its use of "nigger" and other demeaning characteristics, are likely to have on minority readers.

The question, then, is not so easily answered. We do not want to give up our "classics," but there are many other excellent books available for our students. My advice is for teachers to select their literature carefully, making informed choices about what their students should read.

Using Literature to Discover Our "Sameness"

In developing her rationale for teaching multiethnic literature, Bedrosian (1987) points to

> the steady influx of immigrants to this country and the need for ... apparently assimilated students, many of whom will soon be

> working professionally with these immigrants, to understand the
> social and psychological demands of adjustment. (125)

Thus, in teaching a course in multiethnic literature, Bedrosian responds
to the need students have to learn about other cultures. Yet she also
allows her students to rediscover who they themselves are. She points
out what should be an obvious irony in defining the term *multicultural*
with respect to the American population, for who, except the Native
American, is not from a different culture? As Bedrosian's students explore the literatures of their own cultures in her class, they discover that
"despite their breadth of attitude, despite the varying quality, each story
and poem, essay and play, center[s] on universal issues—family, work,
separation—that [are] directly accessible to everybody" (132). They learn
that people are more alike than different.

In teaching a diverse selection of folktales, fables, myths, and legends, we can help students apply their reading to present values, develop their social sensitivity, expand their knowledge of geography and
history, and "broaden their appreciation for literary techniques used by
authors from different cultural backgrounds" (Norton 1990, 29). Much
of the literature of diverse writers contains the issues every one goes
through. A young adult who reads Alice Childress's *Rainbow Jordan*, for
example, does not have to be African American to relate to its exploration of a fourteen-year-old girl's feelings of alienation. There is no "mainstream," if you really think about it.

In his article "Revising the Literature Curriculum for a Pluralist
Society," Cox (1988) offers some excellent advice for including diverse
literature along with the regular "staples" of our canon. Encouraging
teachers to use student input in selecting materials, he suggests that we
help "our students see themselves as members of several interlocking
communities" (30). We thus need to know each other.

As the country undergoes the tremendous demographic changes
described in the next chapter, teachers must expand what heretofore
was the standard canon to include realistic pluralistic perspectives. If
we don't, we will be consciously excluding a huge section of our population. We will also be missing out on some wonderful literature.

3 Changing Demographics in America

Harlem (Dream Deferred)*

What happens to a dream deferred?

> Does it dry up
> like a raisin in the sun?
> Or fester like a sore—
> And then run?
> Does it stink like rotten meat?
> Or crust and sugar over—
> like a syrupy sweet?
>
> Maybe it just sags
> like a heavy load.
>
> *Or does it explode?*

Langston Hughes

I wrote this chapter in June 1992, in the aftermath of the Rodney King affair. Like many Americans, I watched the country rip apart once again, just as we knew it would once the verdict came in from the jury. Sadly, those of us old enough to remember the Watts riots of the sixties watched it happen all over again. And once again we listened to the mixed views of our students and colleagues.

Coincidentally, I had just given this Langston Hughes poem to my African American literature class, explaining it as a metaphor for many of the works we were reading. Perhaps if we begin to listen to writers like Langston Hughes, and Nikki Giovanni and Ricardo Sanchez and Leslie Silko and Frank Chin and James Baldwin, we won't keep making the same mistakes. Maybe we can avoid another Rodney King horror. Indeed, Hughes's description of the effects of the deferred dream explains many events in our history. What happens to people when they are oppressed? When their goals are thwarted? What happens to a dream deferred?

The literature is full of examples of the ways in which people are shaped by oppression. The numerous accounts from Japanese American writers about the internment of American citizens during World War II, for instance, attest to the cruel treatment of Japanese Americans in this country. Or open any chapter of *Bury My Heart at Wounded Knee* and read the same ugly mistake repeated again and again against Native Americans. We don't learn our lessons from the past.

Divide and Conquer

Perhaps the most disturbing part of these latest events is that while hostility increases between diverse groups, the majority power structure goes on, business as usual. But that's nothing new. It's called "divide and conquer." Minority groups in this country have often been at each other's throats as each group struggles to find its way up the socioeconomic ladder. We see this phenomenon in the struggles of the Southeast Asian, Mexican, and Central American groups now entering the United States in a steady stream. We've seen it before in the early struggles of southern and eastern European, Jewish, Irish, Chinese, and Japanese immigrants. Some of these groups look less like the dominant group than others; they do not blend in as easily and thus have more to contend with. But then African Americans have known that all along.

As Henry explains (1990), "minority groups often feel keenly competitive" (30). Latino leaders feel that the demands of African American groups often render the needs of the Latino community less important. Blacks feel that the growth of Asian and Latino groups has weakened the potential for gain in African American communities. And women's groups—not necessarily concerned with the specific needs of women of color—have become powerful by virtue of their numbers and strong affirmative action guidelines. Often we are fighting for the same little piece of the pie. Divide and conquer! A dangerous strategy that works. And it's getting more vicious.

Do racial majority students understand the conditions under which many of our citizens entered this country? My observation is that they do not. As educators, we must work actively against the continuing barriers that many students of color deal with on a regular basis. And literature, I believe, can help us in this endeavor.

Teachers' Perceptions

In an increasingly disturbing environment, teachers have a definite role. We must work actively to change the perceptions that many of our students have regarding the developing polarization of this nation. It's our job. Churches have been unsuccessful. Families often perpetuate existing myths. And most communities don't provide much guidance. If we can't effect change in our schools, then where will it happen? We *can* make a difference.

First, though, we need to be realistic about our efforts to increase the number of teachers from diverse backgrounds, because we're not getting very far. I applaud NCTE's efforts via "Teachers for the Dream" and programs like it. But as Zeichner (1992) notes, "teachers in the U.S. and students preparing to become teachers are mostly white, Anglo, monolingual women." Add to this profile the characteristics of the prototypical English teacher, who loves books, has been exposed to "the classics" of the English and American literary canon, has had success with writing and with being a student in general, and who dreams of imparting these fine qualities to a group of adoring students. But the world is not like us. These are the very characteristics that cause people to make comments like "I'd better watch how I speak" or "English! Ugh! That was my worst subject." The faster we recognize this, the faster our students are going to tolerate us and, perhaps, learn that we do have something to offer them.

Most students don't play by our rules. I once supervised a student teacher—a lovely young Texan who talked about "the help" at home—who told me that she had given a boy an "F" on his paper and "He didn't even care!" I responded, "Why should he? He's not graduating. He's only in class because his probation officer told him he either goes to school or to jail. He chose school." The student teacher was shocked. The point here is that even though most of us "English types" are cut from a pretty standard mold, the students we teach are increasingly different—and that's great, if we don't louse it up. When preservice teachers tell me that they want to teach in an area similar to the middle-class, homogeneous one "they came from" or "in an academically oriented school where kids really want to learn," I counsel them out of our program. Not only do I find this attitude repulsive, but I also consider it unrealistic.

Who Are the Americans?

The more this country grows, the more diverse it gets. And that's the most exciting thing to happen in education in a long time. Our population continues to shift, to look different, to have different values. Fifteen years ago I had never heard of the Hmong people. Yet today, according to Walker-Moffatt (1992), there are 100,000 Hmong Americans, who as a group are quite distinct from other Southeast Asian Americans. And the impact of the Hmongs on school districts is significant in many urban areas, from Minneapolis, Minnesota, to Merced, California.

A whole array of diverse groups exists in the United States today, groups that can be defined in terms of race, ethnic background, economic conditions, physical diversity, sexual preference, household makeup, same-sex family partners, students or family members affected by AIDS, students affected by family suicide, students affected by sexual or other physical or mental abuse, and who knows what else. The following data are thus general measures, scanty in large part and certainly not inclusive of all groups. Most have to do with white/black/Latino comparisons in particular, because those have been the groups measured most often over time. Even so, the statistics for Latinos (called Hispanics in the reported study) and blacks are continually footnoted with explanations such as "Hispanics may be of any race" or "Black numbers include Hispanic" (OERI 1991, 26). To me, such caveats mean that the lines we use to consider distinct groups are, in fact, very, very blurred.

In addition to these limitations, other problems exist. Data for Asian Americans, for example, are often misleading because the "designation . . . 'Asian-Americans' . . . encompasses so many different peoples as to be rendered virtually meaningless" (Mizokawa 1992). According to Mizokawa, while groups do identify in the aggregate, it's for political reasons having little to do with educational goals. Mizokawa points to the same difficulty in using Native American labels:

> The classification of a person as a "Native-American" aggregates . . . Shoshones, Hopis, Apaches, Cree, Sioux, Navahos, Swinomish, Arapaho, and a myriad other peoples.

With over five hundred separate Indian nations recognized by the U.S. government and many more bands applying for official status, how can we even talk about "a" group? Further confounding this analysis, many young Native Americans are hesitant to identify themselves publicly at all for fear of being discriminated against.

Despite the difficulties we face in trying to get an accurate demographic analysis, we do know this. According to William Henry (1990):

> In the 21st century—and that's not far off—racial and ethnic groups in the U.S. will outnumber whites for the first time. The "browning of America" will alter everything in society, from politics and education to industry, values, and culture. (28)

Indeed, this "browning of America" will have a profound effect on school enrollments. According to Zeichner (1992), by the year 2020, 40 percent of the nation's school-age youth will be children of color.

We have a lot of work to do if we're going to be ready for the future. As Geneva Gay (1989) tells us, although there has been some progress in educational attainment among ethnic minorities over the last twenty years, dropout rates among nonmainstream groups are still a major problem. While African Americans have increased their average years in school from 8.0 in 1970 to 12.0 in 1985, whites have gone from 10.9 to 12.5 in the same period. The dropout rate for blacks in 1985 was 12.6 percent, which is still higher than the 10.3 percent reported for whites. In California, Latinos are reported to have the highest dropout rate of all ethnic groups; in some districts as many as 40 percent leave school before the tenth grade. The dropout rate for Mexican Americans and Puerto Ricans has reached 50 percent in some places, and in areas like Chicago and New York it exceeds 70 percent. Dropout rates for Native Americans are not reported as systematically, but there are indications that the educational status of Native Americans is even worse than that of the groups cited above (169–70).

A look at success rates for Asian Americans is also deceiving. Though they are often considered high achievers in secondary and higher education, Gay points out that there is "immense diversity of the Asian-American subgroups." She also points to major issues such as "the serious language and adjustment problems that recent refugees and new immigrants encounter" and "the disparity between educational attainment and income" (171).

Further, if we look at college costs—tuition, room, board, etc.— we see that charges rose 31 percent at public four-year colleges and 51 percent at private colleges between 1979–80 and 1989–90, with public and private colleges listing an average cost of approximately $5,000 and $12,500 respectively (OERI 1991, 51). Given the financial data for nonmainstream families, it is not difficult to see that minority populations have fewer opportunities in higher education. Additionally, in spite of the push for diversity at colleges and universities, large attrition rates for minority students tell us that alienation and a variety of other factors lessen these students' chances of earning a degree.

We need to consider other data as well. In *Youth Indicators 1991: Trends in the Well-Being of American Youth*, the U.S. Department of Education's Office of Educational Research and Improvement (OERI) offers a number of comparative data regarding family, income, and education. According to this research, the percentage of single-parent families in the United States grew from 11 percent in 1970 to 22 percent in 1989. And this estimate reaches 28 percent for Latino families and 54 percent for African American families (OERI 1991, 28–29). These figures mean that, on average, at least every fifth student in our class is from a nonmainstream group.

The OERI also reports that while the average American family had an income of $34,200 per year in 1989, and while white families operated on $35,975 per year, the average incomes of Latino and African American families were $23,446 and $20,209 respectively (OERI 1991, 35). Also, 19 percent of all families lived "in poverty" in 1989. Of the families in this group, 51 percent had a woman as the head-of-household, 36 percent were Hispanic, and 43 percent were African American (OERI 1991, 39). Other data show that 54 percent of the children living in households where a woman was head were raised on an income of less than $10,000 (OERI 1991, 37). And "despite such high poverty rates, most unmarried women with children work" (OERI 1991, 4).

Mental and physical health conditions have also changed over the last few years. These changes have affected not only the lives of the victims, but their family members as well. The number of reported cases of AIDS for 15- to 24-year-olds quadrupled between 1985 (379 cases) and 1989 (1,586 cases). And suicide is one of the five leading causes of death in adolescence (OERI 1991, 117). We need to take such figures into account as we consider just who the students that populate our classrooms are.

The Inequality of Education

A lot can be learned from these data. First, we must acknowledge that there are gross inequities in our schools. Something is wrong with a system when children come from disparate conditions and are yet expected to perform equally. When a child comes to school hungry, or comes after witnessing or experiencing abuse at home, can we expect the same performance as we do from other students in the class? When a nonmainstream student comes to class and hears and reads only about the inferiority of his or her race or ethnic group, can we expect the same response to, say, Jack London or Charles Dickens? When a student enters a college or university program in which nothing relates to his or her culture, can we expect a high degree of motivation toward the curricular choices that we make?

Indeed, only a fool would say that education is equal in this country. The environments that exist in some of our schools are shocking for even the most seasoned teacher. My friend Claire, for instance, who earned a doctorate in education from Stanford, once told me why she quit teaching English in what she described as "a pretty rough New York City school." She confided:

> I could take just about anything. I'm six-feet tall, from a pretty bad neighborhood, and not afraid of much. One day I called the office to have the armed guard come to my room, unlock my door, and escort a student to the bathroom and then back to class. Instead, he escorted her to the bathroom, raped her, and beat her so badly she had to go to the hospital. That day I turned in my resignation. I couldn't take it anymore.

In her article "Ethnic Minorities and Educational Equality" (1989), Geneva Gay says that though there was steady progress in educational equality during the 1970s and early 1980s, these gains were "minimized by an unsympathetic national administration and a general social climate of conservatism toward social service programs" (169). She illustrates the result:

> 750,000 economically deprived children cut from federal assistance programs
>
> relaxation of antidiscrimination requirements for schools receiving federal funds
>
> new funding for rural and private schools; less for urban and inner-city schools
>
> drastic cuts in bilingual, migrant, Native American, and women's equity funding and programs
>
> steady decline in minority college enrollment and completion

In addition, Gay notes that schools continue to be racially segregated. Urban schools continue to have less money, fewer resources, poorer facilities, more inexperienced teachers, and higher staff turnover. And in integrated schools, students are often tracked, resulting in a disproportionate enrollment of minority students in lower-ability classes and lower minority enrollment in academic courses (174). This fact tells us a lot about disproportionate college enrollment and attrition rates, as students in higher tracks are better prepared and thus more successful in college.

Moving into the Twenty-First Century

As teachers of literature, we can make several important changes that will end up benefiting all of our students. First, we can introduce diverse literature. Bringing in the literature of an individual's group—whatever that group is—validates that individual. Further, it gives the members of that group an advantage that many, perhaps most, other students have on a regular basis. Lots of literature from diverse groups exists. Lots more is coming. We have an explosion of pluralistic literature to look forward to, and we will all be enriched as a result.

Also, we shouldn't count on generalities when dealing with students. They don't work. Stereotypes are dangerous, difficult to break, and hard to make up for once they are exposed. Stereotypes are offensive, no matter what.

A few years ago I went to a panel discussion led by "Asian American women students." I was anxious to finally get the "Asian" perspective on school, women's issues, cultural values, and the like. The panel consisted of an American-born Japanese-Caucasian college student in her first year of studies at an exclusive private school in the Midwest, a recently arrived Hmong refugee attending junior college in an ESL program, a forty-year-old Chinese woman from Hong Kong who had lived in America for about ten years and was currently working on a Ph.D., a Vietnamese student who had come to the United States as a child with her parents over fifteen years ago, and an Indian student from Calcutta attending medical school. The "Asian" perspective? You bet! Just like the "American" perspective. What I learned that day was never to make assumptions about any group of people until listening to their stories, their needs, and their goals.

Finally, Marian Wright Edelman, activist for children's rights, has a message for those who do not want to recognize diversity: "You don't have to like black and brown children. You just need to recognize that we need them economically" (*Essence* Awards, 29 May 1992). Shouldn't we know that? Shouldn't we be teaching that and much more? Shouldn't we be using literature to illustrate the value of every human being?

I love the United Negro College Fund's slogan: "A mind is a terrible thing to waste." Somewhere out there, there may be a mind that will solve the mystery of cancer or of AIDS. Somewhere there's a person who might change the world. But are these individuals languishing in schools that do not provide them with the tools they need to advance? Are their campuses too dangerous for them to devote themselves to their studies? Are these students from families living below the poverty line, where the $5000 per year needed to attend college is beyond reach?

Many of my students like to rebut this line of reasoning by telling me that there are lots of minority scholarships and that everyone has an equal chance to attend college. My response: Hogwash! Not everyone who deserves a scholarship gets one. Not everyone who gets a scholarship can free himself or herself from family obligations to get there. Not everyone who gets there can survive in an unfriendly or expensive environment. Not everyone who survives is admitted to or survives graduate school. Not everyone who survives graduate school is awarded the position that he or she deserves.

Most of the students I have who plan to become teachers know about suffering, oppression, and injustice through books and lectures or perhaps from observing someone else's experience. Almost never have they experienced bias or malice firsthand. And I'm glad that's the case. But if it weren't for the attention that we try to place on these issues, most of our students wouldn't know about them at all.

Our job is to provide the best possible educational experience for our students. But we've already heard that. We must also be sensitive to their needs. We must know who they are and where they come from and what we have to give them for them to succeed. Teachers who think they can effect a change in all of their students are naive. We can't. But we must recognize the potential that is being wasted and try to give as many of our students as we can the best opportunity possible. We *can* make a difference.

4 Expanding the Canon through Perceptions of Diversity and the American Dream: An Experiment

C ross-cultural studies in teaching literature continue to be problematic, not only because most of us lack more global exposure, but also because we share a common reticence to venture into what, for many, will be unknown territory. Thus, most of us who cut our teeth on Eurocentric models of literary criticism continue to teach our students in the same manner. Yet to me, real cultural literacy in a multiethnic world means that an educated person must know something about the lives and literatures of the peoples that make up the macroculture.

Few would dispute that nonmainstream students benefit in many ways from the infusion of multiethnic courses. But in our zeal to provide for "minority" populations, we tend to neglect what we might fairly identify as the "culturally deprived" group: the racial majority students who are typically educated in homogeneous environments, devoid of knowledge of and exposure to the diversity that makes up the fabric of our nation's rich culture.

Studying Diversity and the American Dream

When teaching at a university in central Minnesota, far from the "big cities" of the nation, I found that my students' understanding of the immigrant experience in America was two or three generations old. For these students, to be "different" was to be non-Catholic, non-Protestant, non-Scandinavian, non-German, non-rural. During our discussions of current issues such as immigration and changing demographics, my students always made a distinction between "us" and "them" when referring to nonmainstream groups, with whom they had experienced little interaction and of whom they had little understanding.

Troubled by their perceptions, I designed my honors English course to provide a wider range of literature for these students, many of whom would soon fulfill their general education requirements and never take another literature course. Since the primary goal of the first-year class was to teach students to collect data and prepare a research paper, focusing on the history and literatures of nonmainstream groups seemed appropriate. Students were to select their own areas of literary analysis based on the notion that the literature of a pluralistic society is diverse. Research would include relevant historical and cultural background, identification of appropriate characteristics of artistic excellence, and evaluation of the treated literature through the application of recognized criteria.

Since the course was designed to get students to examine the literature of diversity and to explore the concept of "difference" and how it impacts on achieving the American dream, we looked at issues of equality, immigration, assimilation, and alternative lifestyles from the perspective of those outside the mainstream. Our text was Colombo, Cullen, and Lisle's collection *Rereading America* (1989), a centerpiece from which students could branch out into their individual research areas. This text provided excellent insight into many nontraditional groups and gave rise to lively discussions, many of which were intermingled with various discoveries from the students' individual readings.

Initial class discussions reminded me of Kissen's (1989) description of the xenophobia from which many mainstream students suffer. Though my class was composed of honors students, bright and already successful in their academic pursuits, these individuals were also from very traditional rural backgrounds and were often myopic in their perception of nontraditional groups. Native Americans, for instance, were invisible to these students. Although one of the largest populations of Ojibway people in the country is located in Minnesota, and although the Mille Lacs Reservation was less than forty-five minutes away from the campus, no one mentioned this nation of people in any of our discussions of local diverse cultures until I finally identified them myself.

My students tended to think of themselves as "the real Americans." When I asked them to talk about their own family histories, many of them shared stories of migration and pioneering, of the discrimination faced by their grandparents and great-grandparents because of "improper" languaging abilities, and of traditional religious and social customs. Yet they clearly saw no relationship between their families' personal experiences and those of more recent immigrant populations.

In presenting course requirements, I told my students that I hoped that our text would stimulate ideas and interests that would ultimately help them select a nonmainstream group for study. I asked them to choose their areas of literary analysis based on the notion that the literature of a pluralistic society is diverse and that nonmainstream work deserves a place in the macroculture's literary canon. All of the students were required to investigate the relevant historical and cultural background of the group they selected and to give periodic progress reports on information such as the group's reasons for migration, the history of the people in America, and the individual characteristics of their literature. The students' second task was to read and provide information on the literature of authors within the group they had selected. Finally, students would present their findings in groups based on some common aspect of their individual work.

Selection of Topics

Students selected topics based on a list of suggestions provided by me, the reference librarian with whom we worked, and several provocative essays from our reading collection. Some found specific authors; others picked groups. Our class list of selected topics was impressive:

Asian American writers

Chinese American writers

Japanese American writers

Soviet dissidents and immigrants

The homeless

Chicano literature

Native American women

Native American literatures

The Ojibway

Nineteenth-century immigrant women

African American women

The black experience in the changing South (1940–1969)

Black writers of the depression

Malcolm X and Martin Luther King, Jr.

W. E. B. Du Bois and Richard Wright

Women out of the mainstream

Toward the end of the quarter, we viewed the film *El Norte*, the story of a brother and sister from Central America who struggle to come to the United States only to meet with misery and disaster. A tragic representation of the dreams and disillusionment that possess so many immigrants, this film had a profound effect on my students. The class also saw the movie *Glory*, the story of the first African American regiment to fight in the Civil War. Historically based and fascinating in its characterization, the film provided poignant examples of what some call "fulfillment" and of the perspective that many nonmainstream people have on the American dream.

Final Presentations

At the end of the quarter, students presented their research and literary analyses. Grouping them loosely according to their topics, I asked them to pull together, under some consistent theme, the experiences and the literatures of the groups and authors whose literature they had read. I also requested that each group present a question to the class, and I informed the students that these questions would appear on the final exam.

This was the real test. Had students grown as a result of their experience, or had my efforts been in vain? Can we actually accomplish cross-cultural approaches to understanding and recognizing literature? Or should we be satisfied with doing the best we can with what we've already got? These questions and several others plagued me as we approached our final days together.

What students presented far surpassed my expectations. Those who had worked on women's literature traced oppression through the eyes of women using Anne Moody's *Coming of Age in Mississippi*, Toni Morrison's *The Bluest Eye*, Alice Walker's *The Color Purple*, Ignatia Broker's *Night Flying Woman*, and Sandra Cisneros's *The House on Mango Street*. Treating the nineteenth-century immigrant experience, they presented Rose Cohen's *Out of the Shadow*, Gro Svendsen's *Frontier Mother*, and Marie Hall Ets's *Rosa*. Identifying women out of the mainstream, they presented Kate Chopin's *The Awakening* and Sylvia Plath's *The Bell Jar* and other works from these two writers. We learned, through accompanying historical documentation and authors' accounts, about the differences and similarities of nonmainstream women, about the relative absence of sexism in the "old way of living" in the Ojibway community, and about the prejudices that northern European women had before coming to America.

The group centered around the lives and literatures of African Americans picked as their theme "Methods of Survival by African Americans." This group discussed W. E. B. Du Bois and Richard Wright and their efforts to fight discrimination through communism, the work and ideas of Harlem Renaissance writers Langston Hughes and Zora Neale Hurston, the religious teachings of Martin Luther King, Jr., and the struggles of Malcolm X, contrasting the beliefs, intellectual development, and successes of all these twentieth-century figures.

The group loosely connected around the topic of Asian Americans proved to be, in many ways, the most diverse group, both chronologically and geographically. Drawing from the histories and writings of several Japanese, Chinese, Filipino, and Southeast Asian authors, this group treated the class to discussions of such books as *Aiiieeeee! An Anthology of Asian-American Writers*, Louis Chu's *Eat a Bowl of Tea*, Maxine Hong Kingston's *The Woman Warrior*, Yoshiko Uchida's *Desert Exile*, Mine Okubo's *Citizen 13660*, Joy Kogawa's *Obasan, Woman in the Woods*, and *A Choice of Dreams*, John Okada's *No-No Boy*, Carlos Bulosan's *America Is in the Heart*, and Maureen Crane Wartski's *A Boat to Nowhere*. Rounding out this group was my "resistant dissident" report on Soviet writers using Elena Bonner's *Alone Together*, Andrei Sakharov's *Progress, Coexistence, and Intellectual Freedom*, Aleksandr Solzhenitsyn's *One Day in the Life of Ivan Denisovich*, and Anatoly and Avital Shcharansky's *The Journey Home*.

By far the toughest assignment, or so I thought, belonged to a group consisting of one student who chose to look at the military history of the Lakota land his grandfather had claimed. In the course of his research, he read John Neihardt's *Black Elk Speaks*, Paul Radin's edited book *The Autobiography of a Winnebago Indian*, Dee Brown's *Bury My Heart at Wounded Knee*, N. Scott Momaday's *House Made of Dawn* and *The Way to Rainy Mountain*, and Nancy Wood's edited collection *War Cry on a Prayer Feather*. The student studying the Native Americans of the northern Midwest provided a three-page bibliography including all of Louise Erdrich's work, Ignatia Broker's *Night Flying Woman*, Jim Northrup's prose collection *Walking the Rez Road*, and numerous Ojibway poems, short stories, and historical documents. Chicano literature reviewed included Rudolfo Anaya's *Bless Me, Ultima*, the poetry of Gary Soto, and Sandra Cisneros's *The House on Mango Street*. The plight of the homeless was examined using Jonathan Kozol's *Rachel and Her Children*, a collection of poetry written by members of a San Francisco homeless shelter entitled *Out of the Rain*, and the Steinbeck classic *The Grapes of Wrath*. After much thought, this group chose as their theme "The suffering, pain, and indignation of certain groups can never be fully understood by people of privilege."

Assessing Student Outcomes

The institutional goal of this course was to expose students to research techniques through data collection in an effort to teach them the skills needed to write a term paper. In that I think the course was successful. My students read far more, used wider and more varied resources, and secured much more assistance from the library staff than I expected they would. In their evaluations, most of the students expressed surprise at the enthusiasm they felt for conducting their own research. Many said they felt much more comfortable with the prospect of working on their own in the future.

My own goal for the course, however, was to provide an opportunity for students to learn something about the lives and literatures of nonmainstream groups. How close did I come to achieving this goal? One student began her presentation on African American women by telling us:

> When I first started this project, I'm embarrassed to say . . . that I thought it wasn't going to be worth my time . . . that the literature of uneducated black women would not have much to say to me. How wrong I was! The reading I've done has allowed me into their lives and I'm much the better person for it. These women have endured and overcome far more than any of us will ever experience.

Another student said that she was glad to have chosen Native American women, commenting, "They write so well. They really have a lot to say." (At which point another class member quickly corrected her, pointing out that her surprise displayed some residual stereotyping, to which the first speaker uneasily agreed. We all still have much to learn.)

In their class evaluations, students commented:

> You tried hard to make us think about things we otherwise wouldn't have.

> This class has opened my mind to different people's cultures. Living in central Minnesota makes it difficult to experience cultural diversity.

> Very beneficial. . . . I learned much about my topic . . . and through others' presentations, [got] an overview of the real American society. . . . Everyone should be exposed to this material.

> We incorporated the research with the literature in an interesting and informative manner. . . . I learned a lot about our society and reasons for discrimination and prejudice. It helped me look at literature I would otherwise not have known.

> I learned about minority groups through our readings and our individual research projects. I enjoyed the literature read and feel closer to my subject. I feel that some of my racial prejudice disappeared.

Only one student took exception to the "freedom of thought" we tried to practice in class:

> I did learn some new perspectives towards minority groups, but I didn't like the ideas that were seemingly forced on me when the class discussed homosexuals. This is a personal issue and views depend on personal background, religion, etc. I feel strongly about this and did not appreciate being told my views were wrong because they are not.

I regret that I did not detect this hostility during our discussion and deal with it more successfully.

On the face of it, students accomplished much more than I had anticipated. Still, these classroom victories are not without problems. I thus conclude this narrative by providing some suggestions to those interested in teaching such a course. First, recognize that you do not have to be an expert on all the literatures of the world. I certainly was not, though I worried early in the quarter that I would shortchange my students because of this weakness. Nonetheless, the readings and research of the students, along with my efforts to fill in the gaps, proved more than adequate for their projects.

Next, realize that topics will be uneven and dependent on library holdings, interlibrary loan conditions, local (and sometimes private) sources of materials, and the will of your students. Although our campus was well equipped with information about and the works of earlier recognized men and women of letters, our searches for more current nonmainstream writers produced meager results. Students must accept these conditions as the nature of research and understand that perseverance yields rewards. They will also discover the advantage of collaboration when resources are scarce.

Finally, my biggest fear: that venturing into new territories where students were, in many ways, educating themselves might reinforce some of the negative stereotypes and prejudices they already harbored. Perhaps my "hammer over the head" approach to learning about others would backfire and create a class full of confirmed bigots—and I would be responsible. Many times I held my breath and hoped that my efforts would bring positive results. But when I looked over their final papers and read their class assessments, my faith in exposing learners to quality literature and letting them make up their own minds was restored.

If we give students the opportunity to see the world through the eyes of others, we are giving them a look at the American dream from everyone's point of view. In our efforts to expand the literary canon to provide a more realistic look at what American writers have to say, we discover for our students—and for ourselves—a vastly unappreciated yet wonderfully broad-based literature.

5 Censorship in the Classroom: Fighting Back

Your choice of reading material for my daughter is in bad tast and I have told
her to have nothing more to do with this dirty book. I was never Told to read
this kind of book why should my daughter be forced to read it. You will see
her grads do not suffer as a results of my orders.

I received my first complaint from a parent in 1968—the year I began teaching—in response to Richard Wright's *Black Boy*. I was so naive in those days that it never occurred to me that anyone would criticize this wonderful book. In retrospect, I believe that I was also very lucky, given the explosion of censorship that has been visited upon us in the last two decades. Even though I had a few unpleasant moments, had to humble myself for the benefit of my less-than-liberal-minded principal, and had a column written about me in the local newspaper entitled "Teacher Teaches Dirty Language," I got off pretty easy. The matter was resolved when my principal managed to pacify the irate parent with stories from "the old neighborhood" and I agreed to allow his daughter to read another book. What the girl's father didn't realize, though, was that this was the first book I had succeeded in getting Mary to read. In fact, she finished the book early, only then showing her father "the dirty part."

When I came to this school—forty minutes away from San Francisco, "The City That Knows How"—I was shocked by the bigotry and racism I heard from my students. Raised in an all-white, working-class community, the student body had had little contact with people of color and manifested the sort of ugly stereotypes that I assumed would be endemic only in a more isolated population, not in one just minutes away from a major multiethnic area. Attempting to discuss these issues with them was a waste of time. It became clear to me almost immediately that I might as well drop the discussion. Since they were obviously arguing from such an emotional position, my preaching would certainly backfire.

Nevertheless, my department did agree to let me order *Black Boy*, Wright's autobiographical account of oppression and racism. As beautifully written as it is compelling, the book has become a staple in many high school literature classes. Since Wright's story ends when he is about the same age as were my ninth-grade students, I thought it would be a perfect novel for them. And it was. Not only did everyone keep up with the assignments, they also read ahead, discussed the novel enthusiastically—even in other classes—and wrote wonderful expressions of their feelings.

In the book, Richard is bitten by a dog. The wound festers, and nobody does anything about it. My students couldn't stand it. They carried on and complained, and when I said, "Well, after all, why should his boss do anything for him? Richard's black," they had a fit. I was thrilled. *Black Boy* had transformed my students' feelings. "I never knew," they said. "I guess I never thought about how it would be." This experience became the cornerstone upon which my belief in the value of literature was built.

And then I received the letter from Mary's father. Typical of the process in such complaints, Mary had showed her father a line out of context, one containing the words "nigger bitch." He objected to the word *bitch!* But it didn't matter. The book was already a huge success with the students.

Since my early years in teaching, censorship has grown to epidemic proportions all over the country. Today, the number of banned books and those which are being brought into question is increasing at a frightening pace. Indeed, according to the National Coalition Against Censorship (1987):

> For some people in the United States today, books have become the enemy. In one book banning controversy in Florida, a parent saw her child's seventh grade classroom and lamented, "It's like walking into a B. Dalton bookstore with desks. There are books just lining the walls." (1)

Although rare only a couple of decades ago, censorship is now a tremendous problem. And because of recent court rulings, it threatens to grow stronger.

Currently, I try very hard to arm the preservice teachers in my methods courses with as much ammunition as I can without frightening them. I try equally hard to dissuade them from avoiding anything controversial, another result of the current reign of terror. In fact, as educators, we must constantly ask ourselves, to what degree does the threat of censorship affect our teaching of literature?

Unfortunately, the impact of censorship is enormous. When Chaucer's "The Miller's Tale" is targeted because of its "crass humor"

(NCAC 1987, 8), when works by Shakespeare, Sophocles, Dante, Hemingway, Dickens, Orwell, and other authors are pulled from shelves because of their "vulgarity" (NCAC 1987, 9), when *Ms.*, *Lysistrata*, much of the work of Judy Blume and Robert Cormier, "The Lottery," *The Learning Tree*, and *Black Boy* "go on trial," every one of us engaged in the teaching of literature needs to stand at attention. The stories of Edgar Allen Poe and Herman Melville have been attacked for being "depressing," "not morally uplifting," and "not Bible-based." Steinbeck has been condemned in toto because of his commitment to "extreme liberal causes" (Simmons 1991, 7–8). And since young adult literature looks at "the difficult issues, the tough words, the ambiguous endings . . . censorship seems to go hand in glove" with this new genre (Christenbury and Small 1991, 1).

It is often difficult to be objective when we are faced with such repressive attitudes. An emotional topic, the question of who has the right to tell us what we should teach evokes strong reactions from English educators. When I discuss censorship issues with preservice teachers, they often ask me about the responsibilities involved in selecting texts and about getting approval from parents. I always ask them about their last trip to the dentist: "Did you tell your dentist how to pull your teeth or what kind of anesthetic to administer to you?" "No," they say. "Then why," I ask them, "would we as teachers—if we know what we're doing—ask parents which books we should teach their children? We're the experts. Not them. Though they are entitled to have a voice in what we propose for their children, it is not their job to plan curriculum or choose materials. It's ours."

To be fair, though, we owe it to our accusers to try to see this issue from their perspective. We need to recognize our censors and understand who they are. Recently, I looked at Mayher's review (1990) of *Storm in the Mountains*, Moffett's account of the controversy over his *Interaction* series and several other texts that many of the citizens in Kanawha County, West Virginia, opposed. Using the voices of the protesters, Moffett presents the controversy from the perspective of "mountaineer fundamentalists" who do not want their children exposed to other points of view (Mayher 1990, 83).

Censorship comes from all over, from the left as well as the right, from people in favor of human rights as well as from what we might ungenerously call the "lunatic fringe." The unfortunate reality is that those who oppose our ability and freedom to choose for our students those books we think best are people who believe that they are justified in their pursuit. Indeed, in "A Profile in Censorship," Raines (1986) describes the censors of school material as "perfectly ordinary men and women who view themselves as exemplary parents and citizens or, at the very least, as patriotic, responsible, and caring people whose only motive is to protect their children and defend the Republic" (37).

Still, the extremes to which parents will go in their efforts to "protect" their children are hard to fathom. The much-maligned *Impressions* series was attacked by some Yucaipa, California, parents who saw "the hand of Satan himself" in stories like "Beauty and the Beast" (Meade 1990, 38). Such parents appear to be searching for books to complain about. Take another case. At the end of a Frank Modell story called "One Zillion Valentines,"

> one little boy gives another little boy a valentine card. Then, on the next page, there is an old traditional rhyme, called "Lavender's Blue." One of the lines reads: "And we shall be gay, dilly dilly, and we shall both dance". . . . Some of the parents . . . put the two together and came up with [a perception that the book] amounts to a classroom endorsement of male homosexuality. They say the juxtaposition has to be more than circumstantial. (Meade 1990, 40)

There have been some gains made in this battle between educators and censors. But even those get lost when we examine the large number of complaints coming from every direction. Although the 1982 Supreme Court decision *Board of Education, Island Trees v. Pico* held that it is unconstitutional for school boards to ban books "simply because they dislike the ideas contained in these books" (NCAC 1987, 1), censorship continues. In fact, in the 1988–89 school year, censorship issues surfaced in forty-two states (Marilyn Elias, cited in Bjorklun 1990). Marilyn Elias cites the *Hazelwood School District v. Kuhlmeier* 1988 Supreme Court decision as the impetus for the increased number of incidents. At issue in the Hazelwood case were the contents of two articles in the school newspaper that the principal thought inappropriate. The court's decision gave school officials "considerable control" over such school materials (Bjorklun 1990, 38).

Citing as examples Mel and Norma Gabler, founders of Educational Research Analysts of Longview, Texas, and Parents of New York United, the organization responsible for the Island Trees battle, McDonald (1991) warns educators against the organized efforts of national, state, and local groups, groups that have already had significant effects on the selection of books in our schools (552). And if we drop multicultural literature into this mire, we are really in a fix. As Buchanan (1988) notes, "opponents of pluralism and tolerance in public education" have already proved ready to level accusations of "secular humanism," "globalism," and "situational ethics" against educators who introduce multicultural literature into the classroom. Further, I have seen many a multicultural title passed over because of "language unbefitting to our students." It's more likely, though, that curriculum coordinators and teachers use "objectionable language" as an excuse not to have to deal with some other uncomfortable issues.

The roots of such avoidance are well documented in the history of teaching English in this country. Prominent English educators in the early sixties believed that high school literature anthologies should reflect "the very best ever thought and written in the spirit of the humanistic tradition and the Anglo-American heritage" (Applebee 1974, 172). At this same time, however, scholars like James B. Conant were exposing, through books such as *The American High School Today* (1959) and *Slums and Suburbs* (1961), "the astonishing inequities in the quality of education for urban and suburban youth" (Applebee 1974, 226). Others concerned with the nonmainstream subculture of poverty, like Kohl, Kozol, Herndon, and Hentoff, wrote shocking accounts of the conditions in many of our nation's schools. And the Task Force on Teaching English to the Disadvantaged called for more relevant language experiences and "appropriate imaginative literature" (Applebee 1974, 226–27). Yet multicultural perspectives and nonmainstream works, by their very definition, come into conflict with those that are valued in the mainstream as "the very best of our Anglo-American heritage."

Censors often make several assumptions about the meaning of texts that dictate their responses. According to McDonald (1991), censors often take fictional texts literally and believe that books should be used as moral models. They believe that "objectionable behavior" observed in the actions of characters will have an adverse effect on teenage readers, who cannot make up their own minds and must thus be protected. Censors also often believe that education should be "value-free," and they therefore disapprove of any exposure to human values in texts. Unfortunately, this proscription targets many contemporary, especially young adult and multiethnic, novels, which often raise questions about values that have traditionally gone unquestioned (550–52). Major objections also occur with books containing "bad language." Yet here McDonald writes:

> Burress suggests that "bad language" hides the real motives of many critics and cites as evidence the fact that *one third of the objections were to books by ethnic writers, suggesting that censorship derives from racist motives.* (551; my emphasis).

The Big Three Plus One

Aside from racist attitudes, what drives the engine of censorship? Basically, as Julian Thompson (1991) suggests, it's the "Big Three Plus One": censors object to (1) vulgar language, (2) sexual activity, and (3) anti-establishment attitudes; plus, we censor ourselves through our own avoidance. Applebee (1974) seems to validate much of this theory in his discussion of censorship in the late forties, when objections to literature "focused on one of two issues: political ideology or sex" and the threat of communism "became the excuse for a widespread wave of restriction of instructional materials" (204).

1. Vulgar Language

Parents who fear that their children will suffer adverse effects from vulgar language have not set foot on a junior or senior high school campus in the last twenty-five years. As one who has frequented hallways, gyms, parking lots, and cafeterias in schools all over this country, I can attest to the fact that my vocabulary of "blue" words has grown extraordinarily from the experience. If parent-protesters stood outside classrooms during passing period or—dare I suggest it?—went into a bathroom during school hours, they would never complain again about vulgarity in literature. In fact, I would bet money that many of the children whose parents are complaining the loudest use the most offensive language of all. And those who don't have heard it all anyway. From what, exactly, do parents think they are protecting their children?

2. Sexual Activity

Are they kidding? In this country? Where teenage pregnancy is so prominent—among all socioeconomic groups? Where teenage suicide has reached epidemic proportions? Where the majority of children come from "broken" homes and child abuse is rampant? Where a shockingly large percentage of adolescents have been sexually active since their early teens? Are we really worried about sexual activity in novels? Do we really think that kids get these ideas from books? We ought to be grateful to authors like Judy Blume, Robert Cormier, Maya Angelou, and J. D. Salinger for providing students with some useful information and the knowledge that they are not alone.

3. Anti-establishment Attitudes

I think Thompson (1991) says it all here:

Even though numbers 1 and 2 are often cited as the response for the banning (or avoiding) of a young adult book, I suspect it's number 3 that activates the censors fastest and most furiously. Holden Caulfield's sense that adults have sold out, become a bunch of phonies—well, that idea's completely unacceptable to members of the grown-ups' union. (2)

Plus Avoidance

In discussing "levels" of censorship, Thompson (1991) calls attention to what is probably the most serious issue regarding the exclusion of literary pieces in our schools. The most newsworthy cases, he says, are the Salman Rushdies, which occur only sporadically. The next level of cases are the ones we've been talking about: the banning of titles as a result of parental or group complaint. This kind of censorship occurred 172 times in 42 states during the 1988–89 school year (Marilyn Elias, cited in Bjorklun 1990). But the most troublesome level is the one Thompson calls "censorship by avoidance." According to Thompson, "This kind of censorship takes place whenever teachers decide they won't require (or suggest) a book, because they fear the consequences" (2).

Using the charge of "secular humanism" as a threat (Davis 1986, 67), censors cause teachers to censor themselves. It's called "the chill factor." No complaints have to be made; teachers, fearing their communities, the ideologies of parents, or the conservatism of the school system, simply choose not to use certain materials. Said one teacher, "There are many books that I would buy unhesitatingly for an urban area that I do not consider for purchase here." Sometimes the self-censorship is more subtle. Some school districts use materials that have been altered, with the "objectionable" pages or words left out. Others occasionally withdraw funds so that "questionable" materials cannot be purchased (NCTE 1978, 5). Yet the result of such reluctance to offend is always the same: the spectrum of texts that we are willing to present to our students continues to narrow.

I believe that this "censorship of avoidance" occurs all the time, either consciously or unconsciously. Many teachers would rather choose an acceptable book than face what may become a very unpleasant experience. I've seen this with colleagues in department meetings called to order texts, when preservice teachers ask their cooperating teachers what materials they can teach, and in the early days, even in my own behavior. After a few incidents such as the one over *Black Boy*, I asked myself whether or not it would be worth teaching or recommending a particular book or series, wondering from whom or where the next complaint would come. There is no telling how many times teachers pass over books that they think would be of value to their students in order to avoid a controversy.

Yet as Davis (1986) points out, this "self-censorship means reading and selecting literature through someone else's eyes and with someone else's values" (66). McDonald (1991) similarly points out that teachers who censor themselves begin to doubt their ability to make decisions and begin to form attitudes about literature based on outside pressure (554–55). Teachers aren't the only ones affected, though. We have to remember that our avoidance limits students' access to a wide range of ideas and experiences, which, in turn, infringes upon their right to read.

Indeed, what of our responsibilities to our students? Isn't it our obligation to provide them with the tools for learning? Doesn't this mean we should provide them with a wide range of materials and information? Shouldn't we encourage them to think critically about what they learn and to develop their own ideas based on the information they have? But how can they do this if we limit their access? We may find that what we teach is unpopular or doesn't even agree with our personal precepts, but students should be exposed to all the information. As Christenbury and Small (1991) point out, "In the best of young adult literature, which addresses the difficult issues, the tough words, the ambiguous endings, we and our students have a chance to confront reality and to consider ethical choices" (1).

Selection or Censorship?

The issue here should not be to eliminate "bad" literature, but to select the best materials available based on responsible guidelines. Take the film industry as an example. In my opinion, many, many movies are not worth the two hours they take to see. Still, I neither can nor want to eliminate these movies by fiat; that would be censorship. But wouldn't it be wonderful if our students could develop a more critical ability to decide what is worth their time and what is not? That is, if we can teach students to evaluate what they see, then perhaps we wouldn't have such a glut of substandard movies on the market. The same goes for literature. There's a lot of "good stuff" out there and a lot of bad. Wouldn't it be great if we could help students make the distinctions for themselves?

In dealing with the question of "selection," NCTE's 1982 "Statement on Censorship and Professional Guidelines" makes some important distinctions:

Censorship	Professional Guidelines
Eliminate books with unhappy endings.	Include some books with unhappy endings to give a varied view of life.
Review your classroom library and eliminate books that include stereotypes.	Review your library. Add books that portray groups in nonstereotypical ways.
Do not accept "policeman." Insist that students write "police officer."	Encourage such nonlimiting alternatives as "police officer," "officer of the law," and "law enforcer."
Drug abuse is a menace to students. Eliminate all books that portray drug abuse.	Include at appropriate grade levels books to help students understand the personal and social consequences of drug abuse.
Remove this book. The language includes profanity.	Determine whether the profanity is integral to portrayal of character and development of theme in the book.

Selection becomes crucial when using books with stereotypical characters. According to Kiah (1985), many young adult novels about African American teenagers introduce but do not resolve existing social problems. She cites, as an example, *A Hero Ain't Nothin' But a Sandwich* by Alice Childress, saying that Childress "is no doubt exercising an iconoclastic approach to the writing of fiction for teenage readers by presenting this open-ended story and thereby forcing the readers to come to grips with their own set of values" (294). Kiah also cites Frank Bonham's books, which "abound with stories on organized gang behavior and fighting gangs, phenomena that are not representative of the total black community" (294). To balance the presentation of the African American experience when using books like these, Kiah suggests that teachers highlight positive aspects of the black community, such as characteristics of the extended family and its shared responsibility for children and financial support (295).

I agree with Kiah regarding the need for a wide range of experiences for readers. Both Childress's and Bonham's books were always very popular among my high school students. When properly taught, books such as these allow students of all groups to "walk in the shoes" of characters under severely stressful conditions. They give readers the opportunity not only to identify with others, but also to gain some understanding of other worlds through vicarious experience. Should we really limit materials that have such potential? We simply need to be careful in how we present them.

In "Stereotypes of American Indians in Adolescent Literature," Carver (1988) presents a number of interesting titles for classroom use. She also points out instances where stereotyping exists, inadvertently or otherwise. She points to the "Tonto English" and inappropriate use of the word *squaw* in Elizabeth George Speare's *The Sign of the Beaver* (27), the lack of positive role models among full-blood characters in Jon Hassler's *Jemmy* (29), and the incorrect use of the term *Eskimo* in Jean Craighead George's *Julie of the Wolves* (30). Does she mean that we should eliminate these otherwise popular and well-written novels? I doubt it. If so, then I suppose we should eliminate *The Merchant of Venice* for its anti-Semitism and *Huckleberry Finn* for its racism. Instead, we can use these books to point out to students that sometimes improprieties and biases exist even in the most highly regarded literature.

Since one of the goals of the English class is almost always "to develop critical thinking skills," why not make censorship and selection issues a learning tool? Many teachers are already confronting censorship issues in the classroom. For instance, Carole Williams (1988) designed a unit examining censorship in which she had high school seniors respond to a Phyllis Schlaffly article attacking journal writing. In their responses, students moved away from their original emotional reactions toward rational, clear, well-organized responses. And in looking at their district's censorship policies, the students discovered their own biases and the "need to examine, contemplate, challenge, assimilate, and participate in the experience that literature affords" (68).

Elsewhere, Reimer and Brock (1988), using several novels that are often censored, planned a unit that began with a staged incident in which the principal burst into the room and demanded the return of the unacceptable books. This dramatic "prelesson" was followed by student research into censorship, writing, and verbal sharing of ideas. The students were greatly involved in all of these activities and no doubt wound up with a heightened awareness of themselves and their positions.

Finally, Frangedis (1988) uses "close textual analysis and candid discussion" to deal with the controversial aspects of *Catcher in the Rye*. Her approach is to portray Holden Caulfield as a troubled, sympathetic character who has fine human qualities. She doesn't avoid the novel's controversial points; she and her students discuss the profanity, atheism, and sexual promiscuity included in the novel. In doing so, Frangedis demonstrates that "a tactful, sensitive approach . . . will enable students . . . to understand . . . our troubled hero . . . [and] the issue of censorship in general, which actually affects them more than it affects teachers" (75).

Proactive Measures to Confront Censorship

But what can we say to teachers who are consciously or unconsciously eliminating books because they fear reprisals? How can we arm them so that they can teach what they think is worthwhile and not what their communities dictate? Although there may not be a definitive answer to this question, there are steps that we can take that will facilitate our efforts to secure the freedom to make our own decisions about what we will teach. As Christenbury and Small (1991) write:

> Armed with book rationales, a materials selection policy, and a procedure for dealing with challenged books, we can battle the censors. We will not, it is sure, always win, but we can raise the flag and, perhaps, end the days of lonely fighters. (1)

First, however, a few principles:

We and our students have rights. The Minnesota Department of Education (1985) writes:

> The freedoms to teach, to learn, and to express ideas without fear of censorship are fundamental rights held by public school teachers and students as well as by all other citizens. These freedoms, expressed and guaranteed in the First Amendment to the U.S. Constitution, must be preserved in the teaching/learning process in a society of diverse beliefs and viewpoints and shared freedoms. Public schools must promote an atmosphere of free inquiry and a view of subject matter reflecting a broad range of ideas so that students are prepared for responsible citizenship.

Note, however, that the Minnesota Department of Education goes on to say that "criticism of educational resources and teaching methods and the advocacy of additional educational resources are also essential First Amendment rights of students, faculty, parents, and other members of the community." Free debate, yes. Censorship, no.

Teachers should be empowered to teach as they see fit. We should not have to look over our shoulders. Many organizations exist to support the freedom to teach and the freedom to learn. The ALAN Intellectual Freedom Committee, for example, exists to defend the First Amendment, provide assistance for teachers, promote free access to information, and work with other anti-censorship organizations (Sacco 1991, 6–7). And many committees and organizations have prepared statements—such as NCTE's statement on students' right to read—to assist teachers.

We need to stick to the principles that we as educators stand for. But to do that successfully, we have to develop strategies to deal with censorship and to be prepared for it when it comes. NCTE (1978) describes a number of steps teachers can take *before* they are confronted with censorship:

Keep abreast of recent issues and court decisions regarding censorship. If we do our homework, we won't be caught unprepared. Small and Weiss (1991) describe a number of committees and organizations designed specifically to deal with censorship. NCTE's Standing Committee Against Censorship, for instance, coordinates "requests for information and for assistance from affiliates and individual members" through NCTE's director of affiliate and membership services. Several publications also assist teachers with regular updates on censorship, including *School Library Journal, English Journal,* the *Newsletter on Intellectual Freedom,* and *Censorship News,* the newsletter of the National Coalition Against Censorship.

Before beginning a unit or book, develop a rationale for teaching materials. We should always know why we are teaching a particular lesson, unit, or literary piece. If material is worth teaching, there's a reason for it. We should be able to justify the importance of the work to anyone.

Check into or develop department, school, or district procedures for handling censorship. Today most districts are prepared to handle censorship cases. Teachers should become familiar with—or, if they do not exist, create—local preview forms for the acquisition and reconsideration of materials, local policy on district review, the local library's bill of rights, local policy on the freedom to view films, procedures for submitting a rationale for use to the department or district, complaint procedures, and other district policies.

Enlist department support. Too many times teachers are "out there by themselves" when their departments should be supporting them. Indeed, although this should never happen, some of our worst censors might turn out to be our colleagues. But even if getting full consensus among our peers is impossible, I'd muster as much support as I could if I were about to begin a controversial piece, especially if I were in a community where censorship was prevalent. Besides, we never know what's possible until we try.

Keep administrators informed and get their support. Though Simmons (1991) writes that administrators' "track record in supporting their teachers in time of parental challenge is spotty indeed" (7), the more we can share curricular theory and research and other information with administrators, the less threatened and more supportive they will be when censorship issues arise. After my few early "scrapes," I learned to go first to my department chair and then to the principal with a rationale and all other information that I felt would facilitate my case before beginning a controversial piece. Not only was my principal much more willing to assist, but I also think he was flattered that I would spend time informing him of my plans. Another advantage is that I was able to keep him abreast of any exciting activities that took place in my class.

Get community support. NCTE (1978) suggests that one way to develop community support for materials is to have a professional get-together twice a year, during which school personnel meet to talk about new materials. Another suggestion is to plan activities for special events like National Hispanic Heritage Week (September), Trick or Treat for UNICEF (October), and Black History Month (February). NCTE also suggests having a media week during which local newspapers and radio and television stations are contacted in order to acquaint people with the resources in the district. The Council writes:

> Remember, the press, more than any other single element in your community, is concerned with the preservation of First Amendment rights. In time of trouble, the press can be your strongest ally. (13)

Notify parents. After being "stung," I took some precautions that eliminated the attacks I encountered in my first year. I began each semester with a letter to parents, welcoming them, telling them that I looked forward to a wonderful semester with their children, and mentioning several of the activities that I had planned for the term. I also wrote that I had made plans for the students to read "a number of exciting books and other materials." I cautioned parents, however, that "if at any time you would prefer that your child not read one of our selections, just let me know and I will be glad to offer an alternative assignment which you would find more suitable." Parents were asked to sign this letter, and students were required to return it. I kept these "permission slips" in my top drawer. I do not know whether students ceased to show their parents what they were reading for fear they would complain or whether parents felt less empowered to attack, but I never received any more complaints about materials in the eight years that I taught at that school.

Be confident. Teachers make the best decisions for their students. Although parents have the right to declare a particular literary work "unsuitable" for their child, the judgment regarding materials rests with the teacher. The teacher, not the parent, is in the best position to provide broad-based reading experiences.

Censorship has grown at a frightening pace. I wish I could say that if we all followed the steps articulated above, we could eliminate all of our problems. Yet that simply isn't being realistic. The increase in censorship cases does not bode well for English educators, and we must prepare for what I fear will be an increasing burden on us all.

As I describe the various precautions that we can take to prevent the unfortunate results reported in the journals, I am reminded that despite all of these efforts, the battle, in those cases in which it cannot be avoided, will still be an arduous one. After their long, hard struggle to keep the *Responding* series intact in Washington County, Virginia, Raines (1986) reports that the English teachers began to wonder whether the fight was worth it. "We were being worn down," he notes. Community support was waning, the materials were being compromised, and, in fact, over the next few years the series disappeared altogether. The effects of the controversy, Raines wrote, "will be crippling to this school system for many years to come" (43). His conclusion:

> Even when school officials have done everything that NCTE and other professional organizations recommend, even when school leaders are logical and fair and consistent, even when teachers have goodness and truth on their side, the censors frequently prevail. (44)

Perhaps what makes this issue even more pernicious is the fact that the censors will not only frequently prevail, but sometimes they'll even divide us in the process. A particularly discouraging example of this effect involved teacher Claudia Johnson, who fought to restore a text called *The Humanities: Cultural Roots and Continuities* in Lake City, Florida. She lost support, was ostracized by colleagues, friends, and neighbors, and was secretly told by some that they feared they would be verbally or physically abused if they supported her.

If we are to maintain some standards of freedom in our curriculum, we must fight against this kind of abuse and intimidation. We must work together, or we will fight alone—and lose. Simmons (1991) writes, "Maybe that's the grimmest lesson to be learned from recent censorship events. They've divided us and damn well may conquer" (8).

6 Multiethnic Literature for Mainstream Teachers: Another Experiment

When I signed up for this class, I had little idea of what even to expect. All I knew was that I did need some English credits. You have turned me on to the importance of and desire to teach ethnic literature. Since our district has done very little in this area, I anticipate that I will be the main person responsible for encouraging and helping others in this endeavor.

Some of the strategies that we use on our younger students don't work with adults. That's why I decided to try a "topics" course on multiethnic literature with some teachers a few years ago. Since this area has not been fully accepted into the mainstream of the typical English education curriculum, I thought that such an approach would give teachers working on masters' degrees an opportunity to explore areas that have received little attention.

A big obstacle for English instructors, even those of us who want to "multiculturalize" our curriculum, is that we have so little time. All those papers to grade! The lessons to prepare! The meetings to attend! All those demands made upon us by our administrators and our students! Who has time for new literary pursuits? So, we often stick with the "tried and true." Even with the not-so-true.

My colleagues and I often commiserate about the irony of our profession. We chose this field because of our love of language and literature, but, as a result of our choice, we have no time to read. I saw my "topics" class as an opportunity for teachers to spend some "captured" time reading literature they probably hadn't read before. What English teacher could resist? The description of the course follows:

Seminar in Teaching Multiethnic Literature

For junior and senior high school teachers, this course will allow participants to increase their awareness of cultural pluralism within the context of teaching literature. Readings and research will examine ways to incorporate nonmainstream authors, poets, and playwrights into the curriculum. Students will read several multiethnic selections, pursue a specific area of literary analysis, and explore the notion that the literature of a pluralistic society should be reflected in what we teach. Materials and instructional strategies will be developed, compiled, and shared. Censorship will be discussed.

When I introduced my objectives for the course, I explained that my goal was for students to take advantage of the opportunity to read various literary works and to analyze ways in which they could use such pieces to expand the canon they were already using. Thus, students of the course were expected to:

identify the concepts of cultural pluralism and ethnoviolence as they relate to students

evaluate the usefulness of multicultural literature in the English class

analyze several works from nonmainstream writers

develop strategies for expanding the generally accepted canon to include multiethnic literature

create and present units of literary study based on the concept of diversity

Yet as our first discussion of "cultural pluralism" revealed, most students were unclear as to what exactly the expression even meant. Students had enrolled for the most part because mine was one of the few courses in English available that would count toward either their master's degree or an incremental step up their district's pay scale. At least half of the students commuted long distances after having taught all day and found the Monday night slot to be the most workable for their already busy schedules. What students lacked in knowledge, however, they made up for in their willingness to give this multicultural thing a shot. No one resisted, and no one asked if the topic was worth studying for an entire quarter. Thus, we began the course together with no negative baggage to drag along with us.

Our discussions began with some very general observations, ones which, quite frankly, surprised me. Although several of the class members had been teaching for many years, few had heard of any of the authors we were going to read. Even fewer had used any of the books in their classes. A few were familiar with Wright or Angelou or maybe even Anaya. But none of them had thought extensively about the importance of using multiethnic literature in the classroom for both mainstream and nonmainstream students. And when I took a verbal inventory of how much or how little students knew about and made use of issues of cultural pluralism, several commented that they hadn't really done much in this area, nor had they thought much about its importance. Many said that since they were involved mostly with racial majority students, these hadn't been major concerns for them.

One teacher shared that although she had used works like *To Kill a Mockingbird* (sometimes criticized because of the helpless victimization of Tom Robinson and the romanticized heroism of Atticus Finch) when she had one or two African American students in her class, her tendency was to avoid using this book because of some "delicate issues." Another said that he had always felt unprepared to teach African American literature because he was not black. Someone else, however, responded to this admission by pointing out that if we followed that logic, only those who belonged to a particular group would be allowed to teach the literature of that group. "That pretty much wipes out most of the great works," he decided. Another student said that she would be glad to teach Native American literature, but that there wasn't enough available. Yet someone else responded that she had just taken a course in Native American literature and that "there was a ton. We just don't have access to publishers."

Little by little our discussion yielded an author here and a poet there, until it was agreed that perhaps there were a number of writers that we needed to learn about. At this point, one young man admitted that he felt intimidated by our discussion because he recognized very few of the names that had been mentioned. Yet that was our beginning: an admission that we didn't know all there was to know. From there, we just needed to be willing to learn.

Although our course would focus on multiethnic literature, we started by defining the notion of cultural diversity. Our concept of this country's diversity should include all groups, and teachers should always be cognizant that the makeup of such groups changes drastically and unpredictably. Our country is shifting demographically all the time; in a few decades, our definition of what constitutes a "minority" will be significantly different. Further, lifestyle characteristics should also figure importantly into any concept of our cultural diversity.

In focusing on multiethnic literature for my class, I underscored the fact that reading six books written by authors representing four groups—African American, Native American, Mexican American, and Japanese Canadian—was a far cry from being multiethnic. This was just a first step, nothing more. These readings would merely be a starting point from which students could pursue their own fields of interest.

Each week, students read a novel and wrote a short piece based on their impressions of the work and their ideas for incorporating it into the existing canon. Each person brought copies of their work for everyone else in the class. We began with Richard Wright's *Black Boy,* a favorite of mine. Because I love this book and have had such great success with it, I was both interested in and surprised by students' responses, some of which were tentative. Although everyone seemed to be very positive about their own experience reading *Black Boy,* some were worried about the "appropriateness" of the book. Pointing out the few sections where language and sex rear their ugly heads, several teachers felt that the book "would be appropriate for a mature, moderate-to-high ability eleventh-grade English class." I took exception, explaining that I had used it with a "lower-level," ninth-grade group over twenty years ago. Though I did have trouble with one parent, my teaching of the book was still a great success.

Despite their concern, students were quick to praise the book for its compelling description and beautiful language, agreeing that Wright was, indeed, a great artist. One student enthusiastically wrote:

> This novel left me at a loss for words. It is a well-written, true story of a boy who, though unjustly inflicted with terror and pain, survives. It is a story that students would never forget.

I was also impressed with the collection of stylistic, symbolic, and thematic notes that class members made in their responses.

During these first few weeks, I spent some time talking about ethnoviolence, a disease that has been alive and well in this country for a long time. Despite these discussions, students found *Black Boy* oppressive. And, in spite of Maya Angelou's great joy and inspiration, they found much of our next book, *I Know Why the Caged Bird Sings,* oppressive as well. Fancy that! People who have been oppressed writing about oppression! I hadn't realized that students would find these themes so surprising. It reminded me of how far away many of us are from understanding others.

Many teachers are afraid to teach controversial texts, and members of this class were no exception. One student wrote:

> I would not use *Caged Bird* as a whole-class novel. There is too strong a potential for controversy. As I began the novel, I thought I had a strong possibility for our eighth-grade buying list; but the molestation scene brought a sinking feeling. I knew what was going to unfold between Maya and Mr. Freeman and I knew that it meant that the book was out. I didn't want to read on. . . . Perhaps this is a cowardly attitude. After all, if things like this happen, ought not they be discussed? I agree that that's only right, but my opinion is almost irrelevant. Even if students could handle it, I'm not certain my fellow teachers or the administration would.

> Also, I'm sure some parents would object. Since there are other good African-American novels appropriate for this grade level, I would choose one less controversial.

Well, maybe she's right. But I explained to the class that I had also used this book years ago and that I had not had any problem with it. In fact, I pointed out that since we are now uncovering so many cases of child abuse—physical and emotional—perhaps this book would provide comfort and awareness to some of our young readers.

One class member, Terráce Evans, wasn't shrinking from controversy. She saw in Angelou's book an opportunity for her students, all of whom were from "mainstream, middle America":

> Marguerite Johnson's experiences are similar to those experiences most readers lived and felt in their own growing up years. Angelou is able to see the laughter, the struggle, and the learning that are all a part of the "becoming" process. From her struggles with religion, family, and transience, and her disciplined outlook on physical beauty, sex, death, and education, we can hear the strains of the music this "bird" sings as we "listen" to our own pasts.

Angelou's work made such an impact on Terráce that she decided to teach it along with her staple, *To Kill a Mockingbird*. Coming from a school district with strong restrictions on what materials teachers could use, she secured permission from her department chair and her principal prior to teaching *Caged Bird*. I heard from Terráce about six months ago. Her unit had been a great success. In fact, she was honored with a state teaching award for excellence because of her efforts with this project. Terráce's experience proves that we will never know what successes we might have until we try.

Some teachers in the class were concerned that mainstream readers might get the impression that all African Americans suffer from the kind of oppression that Wright and Angelou describe. That's a good point, one that has been raised before. My response is that there are numerous other selections from which to choose. For my money, however, I'd rather err on the serious side than on the side that allows us to believe that most people of color today have no problem attaining equal rights. In my opinion, too many students think that way already.

We ended this section of the course with a discussion of Molefi Asante's (1987) theory of Afrocentricity, which gives the mainstream, Eurocentric modus operandi a run for its money. Although Asante has been attacked recently for his model, I believe that his "read" of history and the development of the African continent makes as much sense as the Eurocentric traditions that we have always been taught in our histories of Western civilization.

Next we focused on Native Americans. Our discussion of the attrition rates for the Native American children in our schools shocked even some of the teachers who had a few Native American students in their classes from time to time. Raising issues of alienation and hopelessness, we discussed whether "the culture of school" might not in fact be a hostile environment for Native American students.

We then read Ignatia Broker's *Night Flying Woman*, the narrative account of Oona (Night Flying Woman), a great-great-grandmother who tells the tale of the Ojibway, pushed from the East Coast to the northern Midwest, losing their long-established way of life along the way. This tale is all too familiar. It relates to a multitude of Native Americans, both as individuals and as sovereign nations.

Most students agreed that they could teach this book to almost any class because it is short and easily read. One student, however, was troubled by what she perceived as a lack of emotion. "I couldn't stand this book," she wrote. "It's so heartless, so emotionless. After all Oona and her family suffer, she never shows any feeling." Yet someone else pointed out to this student that she had missed the strongest part of the book: "Don't you see the emotion in her descriptions? The environment mourns this human tragedy . . . the trees, the winds. . . . Broker uses nature to depict her great sorrow at what is happening to her people." The first student was surprised at this observation. "I guess I'll have to go back and look at it again," she said.

I believe that the reason that students often miss the depth of Broker's message is that they are often unaware of the values of Native American literature. Looking at the literature through Eurocentric eyes, they miss the aesthetic quality because they do not understand it. If we are to evaluate—and appreciate—nonmainstream literature, we need to become aware of nonmainstream perspectives on art.

When we came to Canadian writer Joy Kogawa's *Obasan*, another favorite of mine, we had to redefine our understanding of "Asian Americans." Is a seventh-generation American Chinese the same culturally— or in any other way—as a Cambodian refugee who arrived here last year? Is a Filipino resident of San Francisco the same ethnically as a Hmong resident of Minneapolis? We decided that the term *Asian American* was so broad it could hardly be used at all. We compared it to the term *European American*, which could describe peoples ranging from the French to the Polish, from the Swedish to the Spanish.

Most students responded positively to the artistry of *Obasan*. In many places the book reads like poetry; for me, it is breathtaking. This book could be used in so many ways for so many themes. Many of my students agreed. One wrote, "Kogawa is a keen observer of life, and she writes with almost microscopic detail." Another commented, "I found Joy Kogawa's novel *Obasan* to be an enlightening and unique journey through a world of ignorance and prejudice, seen through the eyes of a child that wished to love."

Once again, there were dissenters. One student wrote:

> I thought the beginning was terribly slow. I really had to force myself to keep reading and stop counting pages until the "real story" began. I was not at all comfortable with the writing style of the present-day narrator and never felt truly engaged in the conflicts she was experiencing as an adult. Perhaps this is because I know so little about the culture, the history, the traits, and the values of the people. The meaning of her dreams eluded me, and the metaphoric language was ineffective. I was frustrated by it and felt like I was reading through a fog or had just taken some mind-altering drug. The transitions in time seemed clumsy and were confusing, and the present-day sections were intrusive.

I disagree. This student's remarks were clearly out of sync with the majority of students in the class. Further, her comments on all of the books were fairly consistent. The further the writing got from mainstream style and content, the less she liked it.

When we came to Rudolfo Anaya's *Bless Me, Ultima,* the story of a young boy growing up in the Southwest, this same student complained about the abundance of Spanish words, which she said made the book more difficult for her to read. Several of us were surprised by her comments, especially since she taught in a school with a significant Mexican American population and had told us about the culture clashes that had recently taken place. At this point, I began making comparisons between these students and the much younger ones from my undergraduate honors class. Further, I began developing my own biases about teaching teachers.

Other impressions from students surprised me. The religious mysticism in *Ultima* was, for some, frightening. One student said that she had nightmares about the story and found the whole thing so disturbing that she couldn't do anything more with the book. I was astounded. It had never occurred to me that the book would have such an effect. Her feelings, however, were validated by another very seasoned teacher who said that he too found these passages very disturbing. We thus had a lengthy discussion about magical realism, a literary form brought to us by Colombian-born Gabriel García Márquez and other

Mexican and South American writers. Still, another student was struck by the violence and death experienced and/or observed by the young hero, Antonio. This blending of fantasy and harsh reality had not affected me so personally. I simply was not prepared for these responses.

Another student, however, who identified herself as German Catholic, said:

> There is nothing more gratifying than to read something in a story that is familiar to the reader; it validates your own experiences. While growing up Catholic and attending a Catholic school, I experienced the power of wearing a scapula, and in the homes of many of my friends, there was a shrine to the Virgin Mary like the one in the Marez home. And, I know how Tony felt the first time he stepped into the confessional. And, I too experienced the depression that comes with fasting and strict penance during Lent. This made the story very meaningful to me.

Finally, this response:

> I'm not sure how to explain this or why it is so, but of all the books we have read, this seemed first a novel, then a multicultural novel. This would be a strong recommendation for its use in the classroom. As we strive to make our curricula more culturally diverse, I believe it is wise to avoid using all "reactionary" pieces . . . pieces that focus mainly on the oppressed minority's response to their treatment by the Anglo majority. We risk creating the impression that these groups have nothing else to say.

I do agree with this last statement. It is important that we give students a variety of materials. And they do exist.

The last book that we looked at as a class was *The House on Mango Street* by Sandra Cisneros. Once again, we were not without controversy. The book is, as one student described it, "a statement about being a Mexican American female in an urban and impoverished neighborhood where the only chance for escape seems to be marriage." Although many felt that the book could be used at a variety of grade levels, others felt that it portrayed negative stereotypes of young Mexican American women. One student said that he had certain notions of this group that were reinforced by the book: girls, standing in doorways, wearing a lot of makeup, waiting for whoever might take them away from this oppressive existence.

Yet this statement was contested by someone who had just gone to a book-signing by Sandra Cisneros. "No," she told us, "Cisneros said that her characters are drawn very purposefully, very true to life. She knows exactly what effect she's having on her readers. She wants you to see her characters as they are." Another student added, "And who are they? For some of the women who marry, life is mundane, limiting, and abusive. They spend their days gazing out the window. Some of the women have been abandoned. Some fear their husbands. Some who still live with their parents fear their fathers." Another student wrote:

> *The House on Mango Street* provides justification for the use of multicultural literature in the English classroom in that it represents, even celebrates, our differences and our individuality, while showing us those things that link us as human beings.

After we had read and discussed this series of books, students chose areas in which to read and conduct research. Just as in the long-term assignment I gave to my undergraduate honors students, members of this graduate class were to gather background information on the authors and groups they were studying, read widely from the literature of their chosen topics, and review critical analyses that had been written by others in the field. In addition, these teachers were expected to provide their colleagues with suggestions for implementing these multiethnic works in their established curricula.

While students were preparing for their presentations, we talked about several other issues, including retention/attrition rates for nonmainstream students, problems that class members had in relating to what had been discussed in class, the negative stereotypes perpetuated in the media and their influence on the perceptions of our students (or, for that matter, on the perceptions of our peers), the need for interdisciplinary cooperation in teaching literature, and anything else anybody felt was important.

By this time, we were ready for individual presentations. Although somewhat uneven, many were the source of some wonderful ideas and materials that I and several of my students have since used quite successfully. One student took the standard themes already used by many teachers and presented strategies for incorporating multiethnic literature. Another student provided excellent background in Japanese-American relations for the past four generations, great material for those interested in using *Obasan* or any of the short stories and plays that the student reviewed. Several people offered wonderful ideas and resources for incorporating oral histories, folklore, fairy tales, and myths into the Eurocentric model we have all become so familiar with. Since students are often required to read and learn about the origins of Western culture, it would be an easy matter to add traditions from other groups. In all, by pooling our resources, we came up with strategies, materials, and background that would have been almost impossible to compile individually.

Just as I had in my undergraduate honors course, I held my breath the entire semester wondering whether I had made the case for expanding the literary canon better or worse. At the end of the semester, however, students expressed feelings of gratitude for our work together. Most of them told me that this was a whole new area for them, that prior to the class, they had known very little about cultural diversity and its place in the English curriculum. Several agreed that now that they had been introduced to these issues, their teaching would never be the same. They were aware of multiethnic literature and the importance of including it in the canon of works we present to our students. Some said that they had not realized that they had kept such good literature out of their classes simply because it might be controversial. Although a few were a little scared, they were going to "get up the courage" to speak out against the censorship that existed in their schools. One student said, "I offer all of you a challenge. I challenge each one of you to vow to use nonmainstream authors, teach your students their value both aesthetically and ethnically, and five years from now look back and evaluate whether or not you have made a difference."

I did not, of course, make converts out of them all. Some are probably teaching as they had been teaching all along. Others might have made only minor changes. But I feel confident that some are now more empowered to fight for the literature they believe in at department and faculty meetings. Many had become committed to change and talked about bringing up these issues with their colleagues. In my experience, moving faculty is sometimes more difficult than influencing students or parents. But if we are willing to accept these challenges, we *can* make a difference.

7 Dealing with Ableism, Ageism, Sexism, and Homophobia: "Otherness"

I once heard author/poet/critic/publisher Ishmael Reed (1991) speak on the topic "multiculturalism." He said that the term has become too common, too popularized, too used. I agree in part. The terms *multicultural* and *nonmainstream* have been greatly abused. Indeed, as a member of faculties in several states, I have witnessed horrific examples of racist, sexist, ageist, and homophobic behavior carried out in the name of diversity.

The most obvious misuse of the word *multicultural* is when it is used synonymously with *multiethnic*. Ethnicity is just one subset of the multicultural experience. Though ethnicity—especially race—is often the most obvious kind of difference among citizens of the United States, many more aspects of "otherness" exist. These further aspects are what carry multiculturalism beyond the bounds of ethnicity and into a broader sphere.

"Otherness"

Most would agree that *multiethnic* refers to a multitude of regional, religious, and racial groups. But *multicultural* is an even broader term. Besides the multitude of ethnicities, multiculturalism must include any nonmainstream group with characteristics of "otherness."

Being different is not particularly valued in this culture, especially not among young people. In their quest to "fit in," students strive to be like others. Just look at the costumery on a high school campus. Stand in the hallway during passing period in a typical high school, and you can't miss the various personae: the jocks, the preppies, the stoners. Indeed, you can often tell what a student's desired image is just by the clothes he or she wears. Although I have no scientific justification for these observations, I first made note of this phenomenon in my early years of teaching and have watched it operate ever since.

Students who do not "fit in" to a particular group are often excluded by their peers. Thus, the discrimination faced by many people is not necessarily racist, anti-Semitic, or the like, though heaven knows we have plenty of that. Unfortunately, bias doesn't stop there. Still, most adolescents outgrow their "differentness" and become part of the general population. But many others in the United States endure continued bias because of ableism, ageism, sexism, and homophobia. I have had discussions with many students and colleagues about all of these issues, and I am sorry to say that they are not all sympathetic.

I must confess my own errant ways. As I reflect on my own teaching, I believe that I have always been conscious of ethnic, religious, and racial issues, and I have tried to ensure that my students have had positive, direct experiences in these areas. Like so many other teachers, my efforts were no doubt limited by ignorance, time constraints, and perhaps weariness. I could have searched more actively for works by and about different groups of people. But the effort was there. I am not sure, however, that I have always addressed the problems created by other forms of prejudice. When it comes to these other issues, my report card isn't so good:

Evaluation: Eileen Oliver's Sensitivity to and Literary Treatment of Ableism, Ageism, Sexism, and Homophobia

Ableism: Poor

Ageism: Poor

Sexism: Fair

Homophobia: Good

To tell the truth, I'm a little reluctant to go on after having given myself this assessment. It appears that I haven't established a very good record in any of these areas until very recently. I have a feeling, however, that I'm not alone. It's only recently that questions have been raised about many of these issues, and only recently that a plethora of literature about them has been put—with a little digging—into the public domain. Yet literature about all of these issues is available, and teachers should take advantage of it. Though we may not have had an exemplary record in the past, we can increase our own understanding of these issues now.

Ableism

As a high school teacher in the years before much of the development in special education, I didn't realize that I had students who might now fit into this category. I did, however, have a number of students over the years who I thought of as behavior problems—students who couldn't sit still, who "performed" whenever I would allow it, who were sullen, depressed, or angry, students whom I now realize probably had various emotional or learning disabilities. Yet in the the past, these students were often relegated to the "X" group, our euphemistic name for remedial classes. In all the years I taught, I don't think I ever recommended to have a student put into an "X" class. It was like going to jail. Once students were there, there wasn't much they could do to climb out.

When I transferred to the district's continuation school, I learned much more about emotional and learning disabilities. Many of the kids who ended up there had distinct characteristics that I would now recognize as indicative of these impairments. I've always wondered what might have happened to them had we been able to address their needs in the large comprehensive high school *before* they did poorly in school, developed truant behavior, or got into trouble.

Sometimes family members suffer too. Jennifer, a student in a teacher education program at Syracuse, had an older brother, John, who had been labeled "developmentally disabled." As his condition worsened, the family decided that he could not be left alone anymore. At twenty-three, Jennifer felt that she couldn't leave home, that she had a responsibility to her family and to John. The family did not dissuade her from this position. Though her studies suffered and she began missing work, she was convinced that she should do more for her brother and that taking any time for herself would be selfish. Yet when I spoke to a counselor at the facility that often treated John, it was apparent that Jennifer's staying home would not improve her brother's condition.

Unfortunately, neither I nor the dean of students could convince her of that, and Jennifer almost buried herself in guilt, responsibility, and self-doubt. Recently, I got a letter from Jennifer telling me that she had finally moved out; her family had "let her go." Her brother had been placed in a special home, and she was now a special education teacher. Her tone sounded more positive than ever before. But it had taken a *long* time.

Once a new student's mother came to talk to me about her son Joe, whom she described as having dyslexia, a term used by physicians to describe a number of different disabling conditions. She explained to me that Joe had spent ten years in special schools and was only now being mainstreamed into a regular high school. In describing his disability, she explained that while it might take a "regular" student forty-five minutes to complete an assignment, Joe would need at least thirty minutes more to process all the information. When I told her that Joe could always take his work home at night and finish it with her, she began to cry. Horrified that I had said the wrong thing, I apologized, asking her what she would like to have happen. She apologized for her tears and told me that she had just visited the history teacher, who told her that "Joe could take as long as everyone else and not a minute more." Clearly, there is need for more literature and information by and about people with learning disabilities, for teachers as well as for students.

What we must remember about students with certain physical impairments is that they are in no other way disabled. One of my students, Bernadette, was legally blind and worked with a resource teacher. She had a special typewriter, and while the other students wrote, she typed, which didn't seem to bother anyone. Though I wanted her to feel as much a part of the class as anyone else, it never occurred to me to find books that she might identify with or to ask her to share her expertise and special abilities. Bernadette was outgoing, friendly, and eager to participate in all school activities. She would have loved to become a resource for the rest of the class.

So much literature exists that could help kids in their quest to belong. My cousin Cindy, who now has three wonderful children of her own, was diagnosed with scoliosis at age thirteen. She had to wear a brace from neck to thigh and a mouthpiece to put her jaw into the correct position. She was devastated. It didn't matter how much she was told that this wasn't permanent, that she would need the brace for only a year or two. Maybe reading some literature about others in her situation would have helped. I wish I had been able to recommend some at the time.

We must remember, though, that trying to make students with disabilities "feel like everyone else" is as unrealistic as asking teachers "not to see color," as asking them "to treat everyone the same." That's impossible. It's also insulting. In a pluralistic society, we should both accept people as a part of the larger community and acknowledge their uniqueness.

I learned this lesson from Professor Mark Seng of the University of Texas at Austin while taking his class on learning theory. At the start of the class, Dr. Seng asked if someone would take notes for Brian, a blind student. Since no one raised a hand, and since I was a bit older (and wiser?) than most of the others, I volunteered. I have never taken such good notes for any class before or since. My success in the class was greatly enhanced by the responsibility I felt toward Brian, and I have capitalized on this experience ever since by setting up similar cross-tutoring situations in my own classes.

What I learned most in this class—besides learning theory, that is—was Dr. Seng's approach to relating to people with disabilities. Once, in a discussion about the importance of visual, auditory, and kinesthetic perception, Professor Seng turned to Brian and said, "Well, Brian, I guess you can tell us about the necessity for various compensating skills." I froze. How could he openly point out Brian's blindness like that? How could he single out this poor man and call attention to his disability? To my surprise, Brian launched into a fascinating treatise on the importance of skills compensation, a system which, I learned, we all take advantage of in one way or another.

Another time, while discussing the importance of various inventions, Seng turned to Cheryl, a student in a wheelchair, and said, "I'll bet the discovery of the wheel is an important one for you, huh Cheryl?" Again, I was horrified. He was holding up her disability for all of us to consider—right in front of her. But Cheryl grinned and said, "You bet! Where would I be without these wheels?"

Some time after these discussions, I spoke to Dr. Seng, telling him that he had taught me a great deal about facing what had been for me a difficult question. He pointed to an award he had received from a local organization of disabled people. The plaque was in recognition for his fair and sensitive treatment of the disabled.

Fortunately, kids today do not seem to be as "hung up" as I was. My daughter Rachel, for instance, had a severely disabled student named Sandy in her fifth-grade class. Sandy was very bright. She was a member of the Brownie troop and a participant in the choir. The students took turns wheeling Sandy to lunch and to the playground. They read to her and helped her with her materials and her lessons. We have come a long way since I was in school.

Nonetheless, we have a long way to go before people with disabilities will have equal access to the opportunities the rest of us take for granted. Many of the stereotypes that make people with disabilities endure unfair bias still persist. In conducting an activity to portray the insidiousness of these stereotypes, Davis (1989) found that while her six-year-old students found few distinctions between racial groups, they did display certain biases in their perceptions of people with disabilities. Students were presented with two pictures: the first of a girl sitting in a chair and the second of a girl in a wheelchair. When asked "Who is the better student?" twenty-nine chose the girl sitting in the chair, six said the girl in the wheelchair, and seven were unsure.

Relating findings from Biklen and Bogdan (1977), Margolis and Shapiro (1987) tell us that to rid ourselves of these stereotypes, we must first recognize those that exist in our literature. They point out that like sexism and racism, negative stereotypes of disabilities abound. We have, for example, the villainy of Captain Hook, Richard III, and Captain Ahab, the piteous Tiny Tim, and Lenny of Steinbeck's *Of Mice and Men*. Pointing to the subliminal messages of inferiority and evil that these famous literary characters convey, Margolis and Shapiro argue that since we learn our values from such literature, we are giving negative messages to our students about disability.

We must teach our students to recognize the symbolic nature of literary instances of physical abnormality, to recognize, for instance, Richard III's physical deformity as a representation of his evil and ruthlessness, Philip's clubfoot in W. Somerset Maugham's *Of Human Bondage* as a symbol of his psychological bondage, and Quasimodo's disfigurement as a sign of his intellectual limitations. Further, we should determine where stereotypes originate. Biklen and Bogdan (1977) point out:

> In fairy tales, there is the malicious Rumpelstiltskin and the mean witch (who "leans upon a crutch") in *Hansel and Gretel*. Classic children's literature has exploited this stereotype to the hilt. Take Stevenson's *Treasure Island*. In evoking the terror and suspense that mark this book's opening pages, the key elements are the disabled characters Black Dog and Pew. The former is introduced as a "tallow-faced man, wanting two fingers." This minor disability sets a tone that is built up when the second man is described as that "hunched and eyeless creature". . . . In addition, when Long John Silver is introduced as a good guy, there is only a casual mention of the fact that he has a wooden leg. Later, when his treachery is revealed, the references to his "timber" leg become ominous and foreboding. (7)

Finally, characters with disabilities should be integrated in a positive way with others, not like Tiny Tim or Clara from *Heidi*. Margolis and Shapiro (1987) recommend positive books like *The Story of My Life* by Helen Keller or *Joni* by Joni Eareckson and biographies of people like Franklin Roosevelt, Beethoven, Stevie Wonder, and Thomas Edison.

There are a number of ways in which we can include representations of people with disabilities in our canon. I have recently learned, for instance, about the Association for Theatre and Disability, which, along with the American Alliance for Theatre and Education, put on a conference for artists and educators entitled "Theatre: The Art of Inclusion" (1992). With workshops, demonstrations, and performances on such topics as "literacy for a multicultural society," "innovative strategies for directors," and "exploring curriculum subjects through drama," conferences like this one steadily advance the diversity of our drama.

Ageism

Who knows where our stereotypic thinking comes from? Even those who think they are blameless discover their own biases from time to time. A few years ago, for instance, I realized that I was making a terrible generalization about older adults. Whenever I spoke to someone with grey hair, I raised my voice. I had to be told several times by people with whom I was speaking that I did not have to shout, that they were not hearing-impaired.

There is an easy explanation for my behavior. My father had a hearing problem for many years. In fact, this impairment runs in our family. I have been speaking loudly to my aunts and uncles since I was a little girl. As their ability to hear got progressively worse, my volume increased accordingly. My tendency to speak loudly to anyone with grey hair is thus based on my experience with older adults who don't hear very well. Still, it's unfair of me to assume that all older adults need me to shout at them.

This misinformed behavior was inadvertent and certainly not malicious. Yet a look at the general treatment of older adults in this country shows that our behavior is not always so innocent. Occasionally the media shocks us with stories about abusive treatment of older adults. Indeed, the treatment that older adults receive in the dominant group in this country is sometimes less than exemplary.

The respect and position that older adults receive varies from culture to culture. Anna, a former colleague of mine whose heritage is both African American and Native American, once told me that she didn't think "white people" treated their elders very well. "In my culture," she told me, "we care for our elders; we revere them." The literature is full of examples of the love and respect that older adults receive in many nonmainstream cultures. Examining alternatives to mainstream treatment of elders is thus a fine opportunity to include multicultural literature in our classes.

Numerous literary examples attest to the value, strength, and dignity of older adults. Two major figures in Toni Morrison's *Beloved*, Baby Suggs and Stamp Paid, emerge heroically for their strength and courage in adversity. Pat Mora's poem "1910" creates a regal Doña Luz. Ultima, the curandera of *Bless Me, Ultima*, provides strength, hope, and healing to those who trust her. Loyalty to grandparents is never questioned in Richler's "The Summer My Grandmother Was Going to Die." Oona, the great-great-grandmother of *Night Flying Woman*, carries with her the wisdom of the old way amidst the ravages of cultural annihilation. And a former student of mine once did a unit on older adults using

Hemingway's *The Old Man and the Sea*, a series of articles on the Grey Panthers, and the films *The Whales of August* and *On Golden Pond*.

Sexism

Although we're a long, long way from achieving equality between the sexes, at least we're talking on an institutional level about the issues of women's studies, women's representation, and women's literature in our schools. This then is a good time for making changes in our curriculum to accommodate the many wonderful women authors, essayists, and poets who have been overlooked in the past.

In looking over the Educational Testing Service's "Advanced Placement Course Description for English," Patricia Lake (1988) noticed that only thirteen of the eighty-five authors suggested as models were women. She thus writes:

> I can only infer that there have been no women either interested in politics or able to express themselves articulately about political concerns, and only one who wrote biographical or historical material of merit. . . . Here, too, the implication is that *no* women wrote drama worth studying. (What happened to Lillian Hellman?). . . . Only three women poets . . . (Where is Pulitzer Prize–winning Gwendolyn Brooks?) And only three women wrote expository literature of note. (Where is Mary Wollstonecraft or Charlotte Perkins Gilman?) (36)

To put women writers back into the canon, Lisa Moore (1989) suggests pairing male and female writers. Pairing Dickinson's #288 ("I'm Nobody! Who are you?") with Whitman's "Song of Myself," for instance, evoked lively discussions from her students. Pairing Angelou's *I Know Why the Caged Bird Sings* with Richard Wright's *Black Boy* made for another successful unit. Moore continues:

> The more you think about writers or pieces of literature one-on-one, the more pairings will come to your mind. . . . How about *My Antonia* beside *Huckleberry Finn?* How about two carnival/initiation stories: Flannery O'Connor's "Temple of the Holy Ghost" and John Updike's "You'll Never Know Dear"? . . . I've always wanted to study Adrienne Rich's "Fish" beside Hemingway's *The Old Man and the Sea.* Sophisticated students may appreciate Edith Wharton's "Journey," about a woman on a train ride with her dying husband, coupled with Raymond Carver's "Compartment," about a man on a train ride to visit his son. If *Anne Frank: The Diary of a Young Girl* is not going over as well as it used to, try pairing it with Uri Lev's *Island on Bird Street.* Younger readers might enjoy the pairing of two wilderness survival stories: Scott O'Dell's *Island of the Blue Dolphins* and Jean Craighead

George's *Julie of the Wolves.* Carolyn Chute's *Beans of Egypt, Maine* has been critically compared with Faulkner's Snopes family— would they work one-on-one in the classroom? (38)

Andrew Barker (1989), however, points out that under some strategies, adding more writing by women means dropping writing by men, which, for him, means "putting *Huckleberry Finn* aside to make room for Sarah Orne Jewett, Charlotte Perkins Gilman, and Kate Chopin" (39). Barker suggests instead that in addition to "classics" like Miller's *Death of a Salesman,* Hemingway's Nick Adams stories, and Faulkner's "Bear," which allow boys to "make connections" with their own lives, we use works about girls growing up as well. Harper Lee's *To Kill a Mockingbird,* Carson McCullers's *The Member of the Wedding,* and Bobbie Ann Mason's *In Country* come to mind.

Our goal in adding women writers to the canon ought to be to bring even more excellent literature into the mainstream. And this is easy to do. For example, my African American literature course has, coincidentally, as many female writers as male writers. (While I'd like to take credit for that, I must thank Alex Kuo, professor of English at Washington State University, for sharing his syllabus with me.) Yet including Harriet Wilson, Zora Neale Hurston, Alice Walker, Toni Morrison, and the collection *Breaking Ice,* edited by Terry McMillan, is no gesture to please women. To leave out these artists would simply be excluding some of the best.

At least one of my students, however, saw in my selections a "slightly feminist slant." My response to that student: "Tough!" Good writers, men and women, should be presented for their talents. And unless we believe that women's writing is not as significant as men's, then women should be represented without regard to numbers.

Recently, a teacher told me that she would love to use more women's literature in her classes, but that there was not enough from which to choose. I brought her my copy of Sandra Gilbert and Susan Gubar's 2,400-page collection *The Norton Anthology of Literature by Women* (1985). This excellent publication begins with Dame Julian of Norwich, who was born in 1342, attesting to the fact that women have been writing for a long time and in great volume. Edith Blicksilver's *The Ethnic American Woman: Problems, Protests, Lifestyle* (1978) offers choices like Joan Baez Harris, Shirley Chisolm, Gwendolyn Brooks, Toni Cade Bambara, Diana Chang, Angela de Hoyos, Nikki Giovanni, Joy Harjo, Maxine Hong Kingston, Monica Krawczyk, Emma Lazarus, Mary McCarthy, Janice Mirikitani, Nicholasa Mohr, Grace Paley, Adrienne Rich, Marina Rivera, Muriel Rukeyser, Buffy Sainte-Marie, Ntozake

Shange, Leslie Silko, Berry Smith, May Swenson, Alice Walker, Margaret Walker, and Hisaye Yamamoto. Those who say that they "just can't find any 'ethnic' women writers" should start here!

Before leaving this subject, I would like to mention one more issue, one which has gotten me into trouble with a few of my feminist colleagues. While I believe that current feminist figures have looked carefully into this problem, we cannot deny that, historically, the feminist movement has been no friend to women of color. Bell Hooks's essay "Racism and Feminism" (1981) is a disturbing description of the active, sometimes violent, racism demonstrated by some of the earlier proponents of women's rights.

Hooks's words echoed in my head quite recently when I attended a meeting of faculty women. The university was conducting a search to fill a vacant administrative position. I was appalled to hear comments like "We want to make sure this position is given to a woman. Naming a person of color would limit *our* opportunities." Although we would like to think that all groups are working toward a mutual equality, this simply isn't always the case. Indeed, I believe that a large part of our responsibility as educators is to help students from the various groups in our culture sort out these issues so that we won't all continue to fight for the same little piece of the pie.

One final note: While studying Hooks's essay, teachers might want to point out that one of the most outspoken advocates of women's rights in the early years was Frederick Douglass, the former slave and prominent civil rights leader. Sojourner Truth's "Ain't I a Woman?" (1851) also fits well into this theme.

Homophobia: The Equal Opportunity Bias

Nowhere in the classroom, campus, or community have I witnessed hostility, resentment, or anger as virulent as that which is directed at the gay and lesbian community. I am sorry to say that some of the nastiest, most mean-spirited, and utterly hurtful remarks that have ever been uttered in my presence have been about gays. I have heard such unkind remarks from just about every racial and ethnic group I have been around, as well as from faculty members, school administrators (both high school and college), and even a city mayor. When it comes to gay and lesbian issues, we seem to bar no holds.

Let's start with young teenagers, who are at their worst when it comes to their attitudes about homosexuality. Since at this age kids are having a hard enough time defining their own identities and sexualities, many don't seem to have the strength of character to be generous to others. Further, even if they did, to defend gay and lesbian rights might somehow reflect on what they think others think of them. I have had several students, both male and female, in high school and in college, tell me privately that even though they agreed with me when we discussed these issues in class, they felt uncomfortable speaking in affirmation lest anyone think they were gay.

It is very difficult to empower students to speak freely under these conditions. Thus, we must bring good material into the classroom to assist students in their thinking about these matters. Regardless of what an individual's religious or moral philosophy happens to be, no one has the right to beat someone else to death with a baseball bat because of that person's sexual preference. This is an issue that needs to be discussed openly. When students resist the notion of tolerance, teachers must bring in examples of gay bashing and ask, Do you really condone this sort of behavior? Are you aware that such things go on in our country? Are you really willing to allow this hate and hostility to flourish if these are the results? I believe that every citizen of this country should answer these questions, and the best place to start is in the classroom.

Homophobia, like all prejudice, has an insidious way of warping people's perceptions. Take the case of Margarethe Cammermeyer. Colonel Cammermeyer was nominated for the position of chief nurse for the National Guard. A twenty-seven-year veteran of the military, she received the Bronze Star during the Vietnam War and was "selected from 34,000 nurses nationwide as 'VA Nurse of the Year' in 1985" ("Lesbian Has No Ill Will Toward Military," *Spokesman-Review and Spokane Chronicle,* 27 June 1992, B6). In a final security clearance before assuming the responsibilities of her new position, Colonel Cammermeyer answered truthfully when asked if she was a homosexual. Result: honorable discharge. Wouldn't this incident make a great cartoon strip?

> Frame one: A wounded U.S. soldier bleeding to death
>
> Frame two: Nurse Cammermeyer rushes to save him
>
> Frame three: Soldier asks if his rescuer is a lesbian
>
> Frame four: Nurse Cammermeyer responds "Yes"
>
> Frame five: Soldier rejects her aid and bleeds to death

Though I always offer it as a topic choice, students seldom want to work with the issue of homosexuality. This is so, I think, for many reasons, beginning with what they think others will think of them. I have had only one student pursue this topic extensively. That student was a very bright, very attractive young woman who had a very handsome boyfriend. She was very sure of herself and felt very confident not only about her academic ability, but about her sexuality as well. Phyllis's paper on homosexuality couldn't possibly shake anyone's image of her heterosexuality. She knew it, and so did everyone else.

Phyllis's research was excellent. First she gave an interesting account of the history of homosexuality in this country, citing a 1646 New Haven Colony law that made homosexuality a crime punishable by death. Then, after tracing the development of homophobia to the present, she discussed several literary works, beginning with Olga Broumas's poetry in *Beginning with O*. She continued with reviews of Audre Lorde's essay collection *A Burst of Light*, Tennessee Williams's *Cat on a Hot Tin Roof*, Alice Walker's *The Color Purple*, and Jane Rule's *Against the Season*, all of which have themes related directly or indirectly to the issue of homosexuality. In the end, I don't think Phyllis decided to become lesbian, nor do I think anyone in the class thought she would. What is important is that she learned some things, and so did the rest of us.

In her last meeting with me, Phyllis told me that she was glad that she had picked homosexuality as a research topic because she had never read about anything like it before. Further, she said that she had never thought about many of the issues gays and lesbians face. She wrote:

> I was very intrigued by these works because so many aspects of a homosexual's life were dealt with. The thought of homosexuals growing old and having to face the problems of losing their lovers doesn't come up very often . . . but the problems are still there. . . . With the help of writers like ones I studied, we have the opportunity to develop a better understanding of homosexuals, and with this understanding, homophobia can be lessened, and hopefully someday, eliminated altogether.

Whether teachers, administrators, and communities like it or not, a significant part of our population is gay. By ignoring this segment of our community, or worse, by denigrating these people, we force students who may be working out their own sexuality, or who have already determined their homosexuality, to sublimate, deny, hide, or feel less than equal. This is not what we're in the classroom to do.

What we are in the classroom to do is educate—all of our students on all of the issues. Many books are available that deal with the issue of homosexuality. In an interesting article on cross-cultural fiction, George Shannon (1988) recommends Nancy Garden's *Annie on My Mind*. In the book, the character Liza explains, "Even when I was little, I'd often felt as if I didn't quite fit in with most of the people around me; I'd felt isolated in some way that I never understood."

Someone once accused me of advocating homosexuality. I don't. Nor do I advocate being black, white, disabled, or old. People just are. What I do advocate, and what I believe is every teacher's responsibility, is that we make room for everyone, that we increase our tolerance of difference, and that, above all, we not create problems for others as a result of our own biases.

II Curricular Challenges: Beyond Eurocentric Values

8 Brainstorming a Canon

In a recent study of secondary schools, the National Center on Literature Teaching and Learning reported the following:

> Of the 11,579 individual selections reported in the public school
> sample . . . 81% were by male authors, 98% were by white (non-
> Hispanic) authors, and 99% were written within the United States
> (63%), United Kingdom (28%), or Western European (8%) tradi-
> tion. . . . In spite of efforts to broaden the canon over the past sev-
> eral decades, the study found only marginal increases in the per-
> centage of selections written by women (from 17% in 1963 to 19%
> in 1988) or by writers from alternative cultural traditions (from
> 0.6% to 2%). (Applebee 1992, 27–28)

Thus, despite the explosion of multicultural anthologies on the market,
schools haven't consistently welcomed nonmainstream perspectives into
their curricula. In fact, in analyzing five anthologies of U.S. literature
that schools often use, Pace (1992) found their selections to be

> unfortunately . . . not a chorus of multicultural voices. Of the 98
> writers represented in the textbook canon, 65 are white men, 16
> are white women, and 10 are black men. There are only four black
> women, and the two native Americans and single Chicano are
> males. There are no Asian Americans. (33)

This chapter offers suggestions for materials to use in a
multicultural curriculum, a variety of materials from a variety of groups.
Keep in mind, however, that I am by no means an expert in any of the
literatures I discuss. I do not claim to have the knowledge to present an
exhaustive representation of any particular group, genre, or category.
Instead, I offer only a list of titles that have come to my attention through
my own teaching and reading, through listening to colleagues, and
through soliciting suggestions from friends, former students, anyone
willing to talk to me. It's a preliminary list, not a definitive one.

I don't think that any of us can claim to know so much about
literature that we are able to make perfect judgments about someone's
reading practices. I have a great deal of respect for students of all backgrounds, ages, and abilities. If we give students the opportunity to evaluate books, they will have no trouble telling us whether they like them or
not. I have often asked my students to read various works and to offer
suggestions for others to follow. I "pick the brains" of many of my friends
as well. If they have literature that is working for them, then I want to
take advantage of those titles too.

I prefer to think of the compilation that follows as a brainstorming. That is, I have listed a number of works using much the same method we might use to gather any set of data or ideas that will later need to be sorted, grouped, organized, accepted or rejected, and so forth. I see this as a task that will take all of our efforts. And it's probably one we will never complete. But that's okay. The study of literature is organic. Some of the works I once taught I don't like anymore. Some of them I think I'll love forever. I've had to make room for new pieces by putting others aside—I'll probably take another look at them later. Some previously discarded works I've revived and welcomed back into my canon. In fact, when preservice teachers ask me what literature they should teach, I tell them that they should never feel that they *have* to teach anything. They should always choose works that they can be enthusiastic about and that they think will have some positive impact on their students' lives.

I have read many of the works that follow. Many, I have not. Some titles appear that I have only recently discovered and want to pursue. Many have been recommended by colleagues or by various publications. Others have been endorsed by NCTE or by other well-known state and national organizations. Instructors in communities, schools, or departments that are resistant to change or reluctant to add multicultural literature might want to seek out these endorsements, as the endorsement of a prominent organization might help to garner administrative or community support.

There are many groups that are not represented here at all. This void is not intentional. Rather, I simply haven't yet learned about the literatures of these groups. For some categories, there is a small representation. This paucity does not mean that there isn't more to be had. Again, it simply reflects my own lack of knowledge. Those who are looking for the literature of a particular group and who are disappointed with what I present should not be offended. Instead, I urge anyone with more titles and recommendations, or who has had a positive or negative experience with a book that he or she would like to share, to write to me (and others) with this information. We are all in this together, and unless we work collectively to bring attention to multicultural literature, those who want to maintain the status quo will continue to dominate—and our students will remain deprived.

One category of literature that I have practically eliminated from my list is literature written about a particular ethnic group by a mainstream writer. Although once widely accepted, this literature is no longer viewed by many as representative. That is, we should identify and value writers *from* the group we are reading about. To ignore them means that we do not think that they can speak for themselves, or that they are less talented, or that they do not exist.

For example, in my first few years of teaching, I used Conrad Richter's *The Light in the Forest,* which deals with cultural alienation and poses good questions for young people. I still like this novel and recommend it in the cross-cultural literature section of my list. But I have not listed it as a Native American work. Despite the fact that this book is often taught as an "Indian" novel, it was not written by a Native American author. If teachers want a Native American novel, there are plenty of Native American writers from which to choose.

I know that some will disagree with this position, saying that "a good book is a good book." I agree. But that isn't the point. Many years ago, I had a discussion with an African American educator who strongly objected to John Griffin's *Black Like Me,* a nonfiction account of a white man who ingests chemicals that turn his skin dark enough to "pass" as African American. He travels into the deep South to see what life is like for the black citizens living there. The book is the horrendous story of one harrowing event after another and of the cruel treatment he receives. When I discussed this work with my African American friend, I lauded it, saying that "all white people should read this book to get an idea of all the terrible things blacks endure on a daily basis." Her response: "Black sociologists, and, for that matter, black people in general, have been telling whites these things for years and nobody paid attention. Why does it take a white person to 'dress up' as a black man for people to get the message?" Why, indeed? I had no answer. I had never looked at it that way. I still like the book, but *Black Like Me* does not appear in the African American section of my list.

Nor does the epic poem of Chicano nationalism *I Am Joaquin* appear in the Mexican American section. Although I have used this poem in various courses over the years and admire it as a work of great significance, the authenticity of Corky Gonzales's authorship has lately been called into question by contemporary Chicano critics. Aside from the authors of certain nonfiction titles (documentaries, biographies, historical accounts, etc.), the authors, poets, playwrights, and filmmakers featured in my list are, to my knowledge, authentic voices from their communities.

Because of limitations of time and space, my list includes very few international titles. Except for a few favorites—like Joy Kogawa's *Obasan* and Sheila Gordon's *Waiting for the Rain*—and some specific recommendations—like a few titles from a list compiled by Jesse Perry

(1991)—I have stuck to the literature of the United States. This restriction means that a multitude of work about important topics like the Holocaust and apartheid had to be left out. Thus, such favorites as *Anne Frank: The Diary of a Young Girl,* though widely accepted in the canon, are not mentioned. Neither is Mark Mathabane's *Kaffir Boy,* an excellent work about life in South Africa. (For a compelling discussion of international literature, see Judith Peterson's article in the September 1992 issue of *English Journal.* In it she discusses some wonderful multicultural literature that goes beyond U.S. borders.)

Further, although I almost never believe in censorship, I must acknowledge that some of the works on my list might be offensive or objectionable to readers for a number of reasons, and teachers should be alerted to this possibility. And then they should make their own choices. I like the disclaimer issued in *Books for You: A Booklist for Senior High Students* (1985):

> In a few instances, you may find books whose subject matter or language may offend you, since some of the books we list contain unhappy endings, violence, sex, death, or obscenities. If such things offend you, then choose another book from among the hundreds listed. Our purpose is not to offend; on the other hand, we did not wish to exclude good books from this collection just because some individuals might find parts of them controversial or distasteful. (xi)

My sentiments exactly! Those who believe that there is any literature left in this world that will shock a teenager, we need to talk. Ditto for college students.

Stereotypes present a more difficult problem. My goal for this chapter was to gather up as many nonmainstream titles as I could get my hands on, to present them to teachers of literature, and to let them make up their own minds about what to present in their classes. In accomplishing this task, however, I risk including titles that some readers might find objectionable because of the manner in which certain characters are presented. For example, some teachers have found *The House on Mango Street* to be stereotypic. Without proper guidance, a literal-minded student reading Wright's *Native Son* might find reinforcement for some of the negative stereotypes he or she already labors under. Does this mean that I should take these superb works off my list? What other books might people find objectionable?

Recently, I spoke to a group of teachers at a conference and suggested some titles for multiethnic reading. A graduate student took exception to one title, saying that she had read it and thought that it did not represent a particular group in a positive light. I thanked her for her input and started to take it off my list. Then I thought about other titles that, given similar consideration, I really ought to remove. *Huck Finn* must go because of its racism. *The Merchant of Venice* is out because of its anti-Semitism. *Heart of Darkness* goes because of its mystification of Africa. Hey, wait a minute! Am I back in chapter 5? I thought we had finished with the censorship issue. Critics are right to point out that some multiethnic books are stereotypic (see Kiah 1985). Yet rather than excluding these titles, I believe that we should guide students' reading, pointing out and discussing negative qualities as we do, for example, the anti-Semitism in *The Merchant of Venice* or the stereotypic characters in William Armstrong's *Sounder* (Beach and Marshall 1991, 441).

In looking over my list, one colleague asked me why I hadn't grouped the works thematically, a method of categorizing sometimes useful in instruction. But most literature has so many possible themes that I felt that such a grouping would be too confusing. After considering various ways of categorizing the following materials, I decided on the most obvious classification: group identity. I hope this will be the easiest way to access the information for the greatest number of readers. Note, however, that although the main focus of this book is to highlight the literature of marginalized groups, I am by no means suggesting that teachers "ghettoize" these titles by group. Rather, these lists should be used as a resource for incorporating multicultural titles into the mainstream.

Finally, I am aware that some of the titles presented here are better than others. But that's true of all literature. And as the title of this chapter states, I am "brainstorming a canon." We all know that after brainstorming, a lot of hard work follows. For those interested in specific ideas and strategies for implementing some of these titles into their canon, chapter 12 presents a series of recommendations from educators who have used this literature successfully.

African American Literature

Literature by African Americans dates back to the early eighteenth century, with voices like Jupiter Hammon, Prince Hall, Olaudah Equiano, and Phillis Wheatley. Nineteenth-century slave narratives by Frederick Douglass and Harriet Ann Jacobs and the moving words of women like Sojourner Truth and Frances Ellen Watkins Harper are already included in many American literature classes. And the literature of the Harlem Renaissance, of the Black Arts Movement of the sixties, and of contemporary artists has received increasing recognition as scholars continue to discover what has been largely withheld in the past. Beach and Marshall (1991) write:

> The work of . . . writers such as Langston Hughes, Claude McCay, Gwendolyn Brooks, Lorraine Hansberry, Zora Neale Hurston, Richard Wright, Ralph Ellison, James Baldwin, Toni Morrison, Alice Walker, Nikki Giovanni, and August Wilson . . . represent major contributions to contemporary American literature. . . . And, poets such as Sonia Sanchez, Carolyn Rogers, June Jordan, Alice Walker, Audre Lorde, and Ntozake Shange portray the perspectives of African-American women, particularly their feminist struggle with patriarchal society.

Because such a plethora of African American writers exists, this list only touches the surface. For a further listing of young adult African American fiction, see Carolyn M. Corson's "YA Afro-American Fiction: An Update for Teachers" (1987).

Adoff, Arnold. *Celebrations: A New Anthology of Black American Poetry* (1977).

Angelou, Maya. *I Know Why the Caged Bird Sings* (1969). Angelou's autobiographic account of growing up in racist Stamps, Arkansas.

———. *Shaker, Why Don't You Sing?* (1983). Poetry.

———. *All God's Children Need Traveling Shoes* (1986). Another installment in Angelou's continuing autobiography.

———. *Now Sheba Sings the Song* (1987). Poetry.

Baldwin, James. *Go Tell It on the Mountain* (1953).

———. *Giovanni's Room* (1956).

———. *Nobody Knows My Name* (1961).

———. *Another Country* (1962).

———. *The Fire Next Time* (1963).

Bontemps, Arna. *Black Thunder* (1936). Harlem Renaissance writer's account of a slave's struggle for freedom, with overtones of the racism and poverty of the 1930s.

Cheatham, K. Follis. *Bring Home the Ghost* (1980). Set on the western frontier of the 1830s.

———. *The Best Way Out* (1982). A thirteen-year-old starts junior high school poorly, but learns, with special help, of his talents and of the value of family.

Childress, Alice. *A Hero Ain't Nothin' But a Sandwich* (1973).

———. *Rainbow Jordan* (1981). A girl adjusts to her mother's rejection and to life with her stepmother.

Cooper, J. California. *Homemade Love* (1986). Short stories.

Daughters of the Dust. Film by Julie Dash. A Gullah family from a sea island off the South Carolina–Georgia coast migrates north. Characters symbolize deities.

Ellison, Ralph. *Invisible Man* (1947). Blockbuster modernist novel about a young man searching for identity in a racist world.

Fuller, Charles. *A Soldier's Play* (1982). World War II story of murder in a segregated army.

Gaines, Ernest J. *The Autobiography of Miss Jane Pittman* (1971). Depicts the life of a woman who lives long enough to see freedom.

———. *A Gathering of Old Men* (1983). Several old men from the backwoods of Louisiana get a second chance.

Gates, Henry Louis, Jr., ed. *The Classic Slave Narratives* (1987). Personal narratives of Frederick Douglass, Olaudah Equiano, Harriet Jacobs, and Mary Prince.

Gilman, Michael. *Matthew Henson: Explorer* (1988). Biography of the explorer who accompanied Robert Peary to the North Pole.

Giovanni, Nikki. *Black Feeling, Black Talk* (1983). Twenty-six poems describing black experience.

Glory (1990). Film. Civil War story of the courage of the first African American regiment, suffering bigotry while fighting for their honor.

Glover, Vivian. *The First Fig Tree* (1987). Ellen, born into slavery, is not certain of the coming changes when Roosevelt declares war on Japan.

Guy, Rosa. *The Disappearance* (1979). An inner-city teen comes to live with a middle-class family and must solve a murder to save himself.

———. *New Guys around the Block* (1983). Sequel to *The Disappearance.*

———. *And I Heard a Bird Singing* (1987). Sequel to *New Guys around the Block.*

———. *The Ups and Downs of Carl Davis III* (1989).

Haley, Alex. *Roots* (1976). The struggle of black Americans as seen through one family's odyssey.

Hamilton, Virginia. *The House of Dies Drear* (1968).

———. *The Planet of Junior Brown* (1971).

———. *M. C. Higgins the Great* (1974).

———. *Arilla Sun Down* (1976).

———. *Sweet Whispers, Brother Rush* (1982).

———. *The Magical Adventures of Pretty Pearl* (1983).

———. *Willie Bea and the Time the Martians Landed* (1983).

———. *A Little Love* (1984).

———. *Junius Over Far* (1985).

———. *The People Could Fly: American Black Folktales* (1985).

———. *A White Romance* (1987).

Hansberry, Lorraine. *A Raisin in the Sun* (1959). Tragic play about a family torn apart through despair and misunderstanding.

Hansen, Joyce. *Home Boy* (1982). A young Caribbean boy moves to the South Bronx and gets into trouble defending himself against the taunts of others.

Haskins, James. *Black Dance in America: A History through Its People* (1990). The history of African American dance, from slaves forced to exercise to innovative contemporary dancers.

Himes, Chester. *Lonely Crusade* (1947). Tough look at the isolation and pressures facing the African American male.

———. *The Real Cool Killers* (1959).

———. *Cotton Comes to Harlem* (1965).

———. *A Rage in Harlem* (1965).

———. *Run Man Run* (1966).

———. *Blind Man with a Pistol* (1969).

Hunter, Kristin. *God Bless the Child* (1964).

———. *The Soul Brothers and Sister Lou* (1968).

———. *Lou in the Limelight* (1981). Girls in Las Vegas seeking fame are exploited until a surrogate mother helps.

Hurmence, Belinda. *Tough Tiffany* (1980). An eleven-year-old in rural North Carolina copes with her large family.

———. *A Girl Called Boy* (1982). An eleven-year-old girl dislikes her slave heritage until she goes back in time and is taken captive by slave traders.

———. *Tancy* (1984). A young girl searches for her mother and adjusts to freedom at end of the Civil War.

Hurston, Zora Neale. *Jonah's Gourd Vine* (1934).

———. *Mules and Men* (1935).

———. *Their Eyes Were Watching God* (1937). A young woman learns about life, love, and marriage in rural Florida.

Jacobs, Harriet. *Incidents in the Life of a Slave Girl, Written by Herself* (1861). Autobiographic account of the horrors of slavery.

Katz, William Loren. *Breaking the Chains: African-American Slave Resistance* (1990). Takes a look at slavery from the seventeenth century on, examining economic and historical causes, personal struggles, and the concept of freedom.

Lee, Spike. All films. Prophetic look at an America we often do not want to see.

Lester, Julius. *To Be a Slave* (1968). Compilation of reminiscences about life in slavery.

————. *This Strange New Feeling* (1981). Short stories based on the true accounts of three enslaved couples.

————. *Do Lord Remember Me* (1985). A reverend looks back on his long life.

Lyons, Mary E. *Sorrow's Kitchen: The Life and Folklore of Zora Neale Hurston* (1990). Biography of the woman who brought African American folklore to national attention.

Madhubuti, Haki R. *Black Men: Obsolete, Single, Dangerous?* (1990). Discussions of life now and in the future.

Marshall, Paule. *Brown Girl, Brownstones* (1959).

————. *Praisesong for the Widow* (1983). A woman inexplicably leaves on a cruise.

Mathis, Sharon Bell. *Brooklyn Story* (1970).

————. *Teacup Full of Roses* (1972).

————. *Listen for the Fig Tree* (1974).

————. *Cartwheels* (1977).

Mattox, Cheryl Warren, compiler and adaptor. *Shake It to the One That You Love the Best: Play Songs and Lullabies from Black Musical Traditions* (1989). African American history told through music and illustrations.

McCannon, Dindga. *Wilhemina Jones, Future Star* (1980). An eighteen-year-old deals with life in Harlem in the 1960s.

McKissack, Patricia, and Frederick McKissack. *A Long Hard Journey: The Story of the Pullman Porter* (1989). Explanation of the "tradition" of black porters and their labor union.

McMillan, Terry, ed. *Breaking Ice: An Anthology of Contemporary African-American Fiction* (1990). Five dozen authors of short stories.

Milton, Joyce. *Marching to Freedom: The Story of Martin Luther King, Jr.* (1987). Major events in the life of Dr. Martin Luther King, Jr.

Morrison, Toni. *The Bluest Eye* (1970).

————. *Sula* (1973).

————. *Song of Solomon* (1977).

————. *Tar Baby* (1981).

————. *Beloved* (1987).

————. *Jazz* (1992).

Myers, Walter Dean. *Fast Sam, Cool Clyde, and Stuff* (1975).

————. *It Ain't All for Nothin'* (1978).

————. *Hoops* (1981).

————. *The Legend of Tarik* (1981).

————. *Won't Know Till I Get There* (1982).

————. *Motown and Didi: A Love Story* (1984).

———. *The Outside Shot* (1984). Sequel to *Hoops*.

———. *Fallen Angels* (1988). A seventeen-year-old escapes Harlem for the horrors of Vietnam. For older readers.

———. *Malcolm X: By Any Means Necessary* (1993). Biography.

Naylor, Gloria. *The Women of Brewster Place* (1982). Women's struggles in the inner city.

———. *Mama Day* (1988).

Parks, Gordon. *The Learning Tree* (1963). A twelve-year-old boy learns about racial violence.

———. *To Smile in Autumn: A Memoir* (1979). Autobiography.

Reed, Ishmael. *Mumbo Jumbo* (1972).

———. *The Last Days of Louisiana Red* (1974).

———. *Japanese by Spring* (1993).

Sanfield, Steve. *The Adventures of High John the Conqueror* (1988). Sixteen tales about the legendary black slave and folk hero who found victory over bondage.

Shange, Ntozake. *For Colored Girls Who Have Considered Suicide, When the Rainbow Is Enuf* (1975).

———. *Spell #7: A Theater Piece in Two Acts* (1981).

———. *Betsey Brown* (1985). A teenager is caught between her father's interest in their African heritage and her mother's desire to fit into a white world.

Southerland, Ellease. *Let the Lion Eat Straw* (1979). Struggles of a woman in Brooklyn.

Tate, Eleanora E. *The Secret of Gumbo Grove* (1987). Raisin learns about black history and about the mystery of the famous person buried in the New Africa No. 9 Missionary Baptist Church Cemetery.

Taylor, Mildred D. *Roll of Thunder, Hear My Cry* (1976). Racism in rural Mississippi before and during the depression.

———. *Let the Circle Be Unbroken* (1981). Sequel to *Roll of Thunder, Hear My Cry*.

———. *The Road to Memphis* (1989).

Terry, Wallace. *Bloods: An Oral History of the Vietnam War by Black Veterans* (1984). Twenty veterans' accounts of heroism, racism, and the horror of war.

Thomas, Joyce Carol. *Marked by Fire* (1982). A young girl has to overcome the trauma of both a tornado and a physical assault.

———. *Bright Shadow* (1983). Sequel to *Marked by Fire*.

———. *Water Girl* (1986). A young girl wants to know why the injustices of the past were allowed to happen.

Walker, Alice. *In Love and Trouble: Stories of Black Women* (1973).

———. *The Color Purple* (1982). A woman's struggle through child abuse, poverty, and racism toward affirmation, friendship, and love.

———. *In Search of Our Mothers' Gardens: Womanist Prose* (1983).

Walter, Mildred Pitts. *The Girl on the Outside* (1982). Based on the Central High School integration fury in Little Rock, Arkansas, 1957. Portrays the fear and emotions of students on both sides.

———. *Because We Are* (1983). An honors student is transferred to a segregated school.

———. *Trouble's Child* (1985). A fourteen-year-old on an isolated island off the coast of Louisiana must make decisions about her future.

Washington, Mary Helen, ed. *Invented Lives: Narratives of Black Women, 1860–1960* (1987). Chronological anthology.

Wideman, John Edgar. *Damballah* (1981). Harsh tales set in Homewood, a Pittsburgh ghetto.

———. *Hiding Place* (1981). More Homewood tales.

———. *Sent for You Yesterday* (1983). More Homewood tales.

———. *Brothers and Keepers* (1984). Autobiographic account of two brothers.

Wilkins, Roy (with Tom Mathews). *Standing Fast: The Autobiography of Roy Wilkins* (1982). History of the civil rights movement, with attitudes and actions toward African Americans on the part of presidents from Roosevelt to Carter.

Wilkinson, Brenda. *Ludell's New York Time* (1980). A girl struggles with her new life in Harlem before returning to Georgia.

Williams, John A. *Africa: Her History, Lands, and People* (1962).

———. *The Man Who Cried I Am* (1967).

———. *Sons of Darkness, Sons of Light: A Novel of Some Probability* (1969).

———. *Captain Blackman* (1972).

———. *!Click Song* (1982).

———. *Jacob's Ladder* (1987).

Williams, Juan. *Eyes on the Prize: America's Civil Rights Years, 1954–1965* (1987). The history of the civil rights movement through stories and photographs. Also part of a superb PBS video series.

Wilson, Harriet E. *Our Nig; or, Sketches from the Life of a Free Black* (1859). Combination slave narrative and melodrama depicting the brutality of indentured servitude.

Wright, Richard. *Uncle Tom's Children* (1938). Short stories.

———. *Native Son* (1940). A story about racism and entrapment that shocked American sensibilities.

———. *Black Boy* (1945). Autobiographic story of Wright's youth.

X, Malcolm (with Alex Haley). *The Autobiography of Malcolm X* (1965).

Yarbrough, Camille. *The Shimmershine Queens* (1990). A young girl learns to glow with "shimmershine" and pride because of her African heritage.

Young, Al. *The Song Turning Back into Itself* (1971). Poetry.

––––. *Ask Me Now* (1980).

––––. *The Blues Don't Change* (1982).

––––. *Seduction by Light* (1988).

Asian American Literature

Until recently, Asian American literature got little attention. Yet writing by Asian Americans began at least seven generations ago and continues to thrive all over the country. Pioneering efforts to recognize this corpus of work have resulted in several popular anthologies. These anthologies have, in turn, ushered in an increasing interest in the poets, writers, and playwrights who, under the umbrella label "Asian American," represent a variety of ethnic and cultural groups. Below is a sampling of the literature available to those interested in pursuing this broad range of work.

General

Asian Women United of California, eds. *Making Waves: An Anthology of Writings by and about Asian American Women* (1989). Poems, memoirs, essays, and fiction from a woman's perspective.

Bruchac, Joseph, ed. *Breaking Silence: An Anthology of Contemporary Asian American Poets* (1983). Fifty poets, with autobiographic statements.

Chan, Jeffrey Paul, Frank Chin, Lawson Inada, and Shawn Wong, eds. *The Big Aiiieeeee! An Anthology of Chinese American and Japanese American Literature* (1991). Collection of short stories, poetry, historical documents, and other work.

Chin, Frank, Jeffrey Paul Chan, Lawson Inada, and Shawn Wong, eds. *Aiiieeeee! An Anthology of Asian-American Writers* (1974). Writings that challenge old stereotypes and "claim America" for Americans of Asian descent.

Chock, Eric, et al., eds. *Talk Story: An Anthology of Hawaii's Local Writers* (1978).

Chock, Eric, and Darrell Lum, eds. *The Best of Bamboo Ridge: The Hawaii Writers' Quarterly* (1986). Special issue.

Geok-lin, Shirley, Mayumi Tsutakawa, and M. Donnelly, eds. *The Forbidden Stitch: An Asian-American Women's Anthology* (1988). The poetry, prose, and art of new and established writers and artists.

Hagedorn, Jessica, ed. *Charlie Chan Is Dead: An Anthology of Contemporary Asian American Fiction* (1993).

Hongo, Garrett, ed. *The Open Boat: Poems from Asian America* (1993).

Hsu, Kai-yu, and Helen Palubinskas, eds. *Asian-American Authors* (1972). Stories and poems about Asian American identity, maternalism, and assimilation.

Cambodian

Crew, Linda. *Children of the River* (1989). Forced from Cambodia by the Khmer Rouge, a seventeen-year-old honors student tries to adjust to American customs and romance in Oregon.

Szymusiak, Molyda. *The Stones Cry Out: A Cambodian Childhood, 1975–1980* (1986). Autobiographic account of the horrors of war.

Chinese

Berssenbrugge, Mei-mei. *Fish Souls* (1971).

———. *Summits Move with the Tide* (1974).

———. *Random Possession* (1979).

———. *The Heat Bird* (1983).

———. *Empathy* (1989).

———. *Sphericity* (1993).

Chang, Diana. *The Frontiers of Love* (1956).

———. *The Only Game in Town* (1963).

———. *Eye to Eye* (1974).

Chin, Frank. *The Chickencoop Chinaman; and, The Year of the Dragon: Two Plays* (1981).

———. *The Chinaman Pacific & Frisco R.R. Co.* (1988). Short stories about Chinese American history and contemporary experiences.

———. *Donald Duk* (1991). Dream sequences of a young man seeking his identity.

Chin, Marilyn. *Dwarf Bamboo* (1987). Poetry on urban experiences.

Chu, Louis. *Eat a Bowl of Tea* (1961). A young couple faces the demands of adjusting to life in America.

Far, Sui-sin [Edith Maude Eaton]. "In the Land of the Free," "Leaves from the Mental Portfolio of an Eurasian," "The Story of One White Woman Who Married a Chinese," "Her Chinese Husband." Among the first works published by an Asian American author, Far's stories depict the exploitation suffered by her family.

A Great Wall (1987). Film. A Chinese American family learns about their history.

He Liyi. *The Spring of Butterflies and Other Folktales of China's Minority Peoples* (1986).

Hwang, David Henry. *Broken Promises: Four Plays* (1983).

———. *M. Butterfly* (1988).

———. *FOB and Other Plays* (1990).

Kingston, Maxine Hong. *The Woman Warrior: Memoirs of a Girlhood among Ghosts* (1976). A young woman finds identity through myth and reality.

———. *China Men* (1980).

———. *Tripmaster Monkey: His Fake Book* (1989).

Kuo, Alex. *The Window Tree* (1971). Poetry.

———. *New Letters from Hiroshima and Other Poems* (1974). Poetry.

———. *Changing the River* (1986). Powerful poetic images of life, land, emotion, and silence.

Lai, H. Mark, Genny Lim, and Judy Yung, eds. *Island: Poetry and History of Chinese Immigrants on Angel Island, 1910–1940* (1986).

Lau, Alan Chong. *Songs for Jadina* (1980). Poetry mingling life in California with that of "the nameless ones" who came before.

Lau, Carolyn. *Wode Shuofa: My Way of Speaking* (1988). Complex poems on Chinese tradition and American language.

Li Fei-kan. *The Family.*

Lo Kuan-chung. *Romance of the Three Kingdoms.*

Louie, David Wong. *Pangs of Love* (1991). Short stories.

Lowe, Pardee. *Father and Glorious Descendant* (1943). Early days in San Francisco's Chinatown.

Lum, Wing Tek. *Expounding the Doubtful Points* (1987). Poetry about familial and domestic experiences.

New Year (1987). Film by Valerie Soe. A fourth-generation Chinese American girl looks at negative stereotypes.

Ng, Fae Myenne. *Bone* (1992). Debut novel.

Nieh, Hua-ling. *Mulberry and Peach: Two Women of China* (1986). A tale about running from oppression.

Shih Nai-an. *Water Margin.*

Tan, Amy. *The Joy Luck Club* (1989). Short vignettes about women in pre-war China and their daughters growing up in California.

Wei, Katherine, and Terry Quinn. *Second Daughter: Growing Up in China, 1930–1949* (1984). Leaving China at age nineteen, a young woman gives a detailed account of rural and city life in China during the war.

Wong, Jade Snow. *Fifth Chinese Daughter* (1950). Autobiographic story of a young girl's attempt to reconcile ethnic pride with assimilation in the 1930s.

Wong, Nellie. *Dreams in Harrison Railroad Park* (1977). Poetry.

———. *The Death of Long Steam Lady* (1986). Poetry.

Wong, Shawn. *Homebase* (1979). A young man struggles with dual identity.

Yee, Paul. *Tales from Gold Mountain: Stories of the Chinese in the New World* (1989). Eight stories—with accompanying paintings—about the traditions, living conditions, dreams, and values of Chinese immigrants.

Yep, Laurence. *Dragonwings* (1975). A young boy and his father in early twentieth-century San Francisco attempt to make a flying machine.

———. *Child of the Owl* (1977). A young girl tries to adopt her grandmother's beliefs.

———. *Sea Glass* (1979). A young Chinese American boy faces prejudice in California.

———. *Dragon of the Lost Sea* (1982). A fantasy tale based on Chinese myth.

———. *The Mark Twain Murders* (1982). Mark Twain and a young friend attempt to investigate a murder.

———. *Dragon Steel* (1985). Fantasy tale of a dragon princess whose way is blocked by supernatural creatures.

———. *Mountain Light* (1985). An adventure story set in nineteenth-century China.

———. *Monster Makers, Inc.* (1986). Science fiction tale of a scientist's creation of mini-monsters.

Filipino

Bulosan, Carlos. *America Is in the Heart* (1946). A young man learns about the hardships of life in America.

Hagedorn, Jessica Tarahata. *Dogeaters* (1990). Difficult but rewarding novel about growing up in upper-middle-class Manila.

Santos, Bienvenido. *You Lovely People* (1966). A look at second-class citizenship and disappearing identity.

———. *Scent of Apples* (1979). Short stories.

Villanueva, Marianne. *Ginseng and Other Tales from Manila* (1991). Poignant stories about urban violence, rural poverty, and the courage of the Philippine people.

Hmong

Moore, Dave, ed. *Dark Sky, Dark Land: Stories of the Hmong Boy Scouts of Troop 100* (1989). From atrocities in Laos and Cambodia to difficulties in Eden Prairie, Minnesota.

Numrich, Charles H., ed. *Living Tapestries: Folktales of the Hmong* (1985).

Indian

Mukherjee, Bharati. *Jasmine* (1989). A Hindu woman in rural Iowa learns to adapt to a different world.

———. *The Middleman and Other Stories* (1988). Short stories.

Pevsner, Stella. *Lindsay, Lindsay, Fly Away Home* (1983). A sixteen-year-old must move from India to the United States to live with her aunt.

Japanese

Armor, John, and Peter Wright. *Manzanar* (1988). Photographs by Ansel Adams. Commentary by John Hersey. Description of life in Manzanar, a "relocation center" during World War II.

Come See the Paradise (1991). Film about a Japanese/Caucasian liaison during the internment.

Family Gathering: A Search for a Japanese-American Past (1988). Film. A granddaughter searches for facts about her family's internment.

Hamanaka, Sheila. *The Journey: Japanese Americans, Racism, and Renewal* (1990). An illustrated description of Japanese American experiences during World War II.

Hiroshima Maiden (1988). Film. A World War II A-bomb survivor comes to live in the United States.

Hongo, Garrett Kaoru. *Yellow Light* (1982). Poetry.

———. *The River of Heaven* (1988). Poetry about life in Hawaii and mainland experiences.

Houston, Jeanne Wakatsuki, and James D. Houston. *Farewell to Manzanar: A True Story of Japanese American Experience during and after the World War II Internment* (1973).

Inada, Lawson Fusao. *Before the War: Poems as They Happened* (1971).

———. *Legends from the Camp* (1992). Poetry.

Kadohata, Cynthia. *The Floating World* (1989). A young woman's memories of the difficulty Japanese Americans had in finding work after World War II.

———. *In the Heart of the Valley of Love* (1992).

Kaneko, Lonny. "The Shoyu Kid" (1976). Life in America behind barbed wire.

Kashiwagi, Hiroshi. *Laughter and False Teeth* (1975). A play about the bittersweet humor of life for a woman in a concentration camp.

Kawabata, Yasunari. *Snow Country* (1956).

Mirikitani, Janice. *Shedding Silence* (1987). Poetry.

Mishima, Yukio. *The Sound of Waves* (1956). Forbidden love in rural Japan.

Mori, Toshio. *Yokohama, California* (1949). Vignettes of life in San Francisco's East Bay.

Mura, David. *After We Lost Our Way* (1989). Poetry.

———. *Turning Japanese: Memoirs of a Sansei* (1991).

Murayama, Milton. *All I Asking for Is My Body* (1975). Criticism of authoritarianism in the Japanese American community.

Okada, John. *No-No Boy* (1957). A young man is stigmatized after refusing to go to war.

Okimoto, Jean Davies. *Molly by Any Other Name* (1990). A seventeen-year-old adopted girl fights to learn her true identity.

Okita, Dwight. "In Response to Executive Order 9066." Poem in Bruchac's *Breaking Silence*.

Okubo, Mine. *Citizen 13660* (1946).

Saiki, Jessica K. *Once, a Lotus Garden, and Other Stories* (1987). Complexities of ethnic identity.

———. *From the Lanai and Other Hawaii Stories* (1991). Short stories about Japanese Americans in Hawaii before and during World War II.

Shirota, Jon. *Lucky Came Hawaii* (1965).

Sone, Monica. *Nisei Daughter* (1953). Events leading up to and during the internment of a Seattle-born Japanese American.

Takeda, Izumo. *Kanadehen Chushingura.*

Tanizaki, Junichiro. *Some Prefer Nettles* (1955).

Uchida, Yoshiko. *The Dancing Kettle and Other Japanese Folktales* (1949).

———. *Desert Exile: The Uprooting of a Japanese-American Family* (1982).

———. *Picture Bride* (1987). A young girl comes to the United States for an arranged marriage.

Yamada, Mitsuye. *Camp Notes and Other Poems* (1976).

———. *Desert Run: Poems and Stories* (1988).

Yamamoto, Hisaye. *Seventeen Syllables and Other Stories* (1988). Japanese Americans before and after World War II.

Yamasaki, Minoru. *A Life in Architecture* (1979).

Yamauchi, Wakako. *And the Soul Shall Dance: A Play in Two Acts* (1977). An Asian American's search for identity in a racist environment.

Yoshikawa, Eiji. *Miyamoto Musashi* (1953).

Korean

Choi, Sook Nyul. *Year of Impossible Goodbyes* (1991).

Hwang, Sun-won. *Cranes in Flowers of Fire: Twentieth-Century Korean Stories.*

Hyun, Peter. *Man Sei! The Making of a Korean American* (1986).

Kang, Younghill. *The Grass Roof* (1931). A young man's life in Korea before coming to the United States.

———. *East Goes West: The Making of an Oriental Yankee* (1937). A young man in America.

Kim, Richard E. *The Martyred* (1964).

Kim, Ronyoung. *Clay Walls* (1986). Early experiences of Korean immigrants in the United States.

Lew, Walter. "Leaving Seoul: 1953." Poem in Bruchac's *Breaking Silence*.

Song, Cathy. *Picture Bride* (1983). Poetry about Asian American life and immigrant ancestors.

Vietnamese

Alamo Bay (1985). Film about a conflict between Texas fishermen and Vietnamese refugees.

Hayslip, Le Ly. *When Heaven and Earth Changed Places: A Vietnamese Woman's Journey from War to Peace* (1989). Survival during the Vietnam War.

Huynh, Sanh Thong, ed. *The Heritage of Vietnamese Poetry* (1979).

Nguyen Ngoc Ngan. *The Will of Heaven: The Story of One Vietnamese and the End of His World* (1982).

Tran Thi Nga and Wendy Wilder Larsen. *Shallow Graves: Two Women and Vietnam* (1986). Poetry.

Tran Van Dinh. *Blue Dragon, White Tiger: A Tet Story* (1983). Experiences of Vietnamese immigrants.

Truong Nhu Tang. *A Vietcong Memoir* (1985). Former government official tells of war and politics from the Vietnamese point of view.

Vuong, Lynette D. *The Brocaded Slipper and Other Vietnamese Tales* (1982).

Jewish Literature

Beach and Marshall (1991) identify a variety of contemporary Jewish writers, including Saul Bellow, Philip Roth, Bernard Malamud, Norman Mailer, J. D. Salinger, Grace Paley, Arthur Miller, Cynthia Ozick, Isaac Bashevis Singer, Woody Allen, Stanley Elkin, and E. L. Doctorow. Many more can be found in the canon. Included in the list below are a few books that attempt to provide some historical information, books by authors who have already been acknowledged as great artists, and some books by new writers, especially in the area of young adult literature.

Angell, Judie. *One-way to Ansonia* (1985). A young immigrant in the 1890s struggles to keep her dream alive.

Arnold, Caroline, and Herma Silverstein. *Anti-Semitism: A Modern Perspective* (1985). Historical look at anti-Semitism around the world.

Arrick, Fran. *Chernowitz!* (1981). Longtime friends are at odds when an anti-Semitic bully starts trouble.

Asher, Sandy. *Daughters of the Law* (1981). A young girl feels guilty because she is the child of concentration camp survivors.

Asheri, Michael. *Living Jewish: The Lore and Law of Being a Practicing Jew* (1983). Answers questions about Judaism.

Barrie, Barbara. *Lone Star* (1990). A girl whose family has moved from Chicago to Corpus Christi, Texas, tries to adjust, while her family tries to maintain Jewish traditions and cope with the war in Europe.

Baum, Charlotte, and Paula Hyman. *The Jewish Woman in America* (1976). From sweatshop workers to overprotected wives.

Bellow, Saul. *The Adventures of Augie March* (1953). A young man travels all over America in search of American experience.

———, ed. *Great Jewish Short Stories* (1963). Selections from Singer, Paley, the Agada, and more.

Blair, Cynthia. *Crazy in Love* (1988). A girl gives up her chance for romance because the boy is Puerto Rican.

Cohen, Barbara. *People Like Us* (1987). A teenager is caught between following her parents' wishes for her not to date outside her religion and her love for the star quarterback.

Dershowitz, Alan M. *Chutzpah* (1991). Discusses the "otherness" of Jewish Americans, living as guests in one's own home.

Doctorow, E. L. *World's Fair* (1985). Growing up in a lower-middle-class family in the Bronx during the 1930s.

Finkelstein, Norman H. *The Other 1492: Jewish Settlement in the New World* (1989). Account of the persecution of Jews in Europe and of Jewish settlement in the New World.

Girion, Barbara. *A Tangle of Roots* (1979). A family comes to terms with grief over their mother's death.

Gold, Michael. *Jews without Money* (1930). Growing up as a Rumanian immigrant on the Lower East Side of New York at the turn of the century.

Goldreich, Gloria, ed. *A Treasury of Jewish Literature from Biblical Times to Today* (1982). Sampling from the Torah, Talmud, Siddur, and Kabbalah through the literature of contemporary writers like Arthur Miller and Philip Roth. Historical settings and criticism.

Greene, Bette. *Summer of My German Soldier* (1973). A young girl helps a prisoner of war escape and defies the prejudice of an Arkansas town.

Hentoff, Nat. *Boston Boy* (1986). Vignettes about growing up in 1940s Boston, anti-Semitism, and jazz.

Heyman, Anita. *Exit from Home* (1977). A boy breaks free from the yeshiva and political turmoil and makes his way to America.

Hobson, Laura. *Gentleman's Agreement* (1947). A journalist pretends to be Jewish and is shocked by the prejudice he encounters.

Howe, Irving. *World of Our Fathers* (1976). Journey of Eastern European Jews to America and the life they made.

Kemelman, Harry. *Sunday the Rabbi Stayed Home* (1969). Early story in a series of mysteries involving Rabbi David Small.

Kerr, M. E. *If I Love You, Am I Trapped Forever?* (1973). Prejudice in middle-class society.

Konecky, Edith. *Allegra Maud Goldman* (1976). Trials and tribulations of growing up in 1930s Brooklyn.

Lasky, Kathryn. *Pageant* (1986). A young girl grows bored with stuffy friends and strives toward individuality.

Lehrman, Robert. *Juggling* (1982). A cocky soccer player tries to join a team of immigrant Jews and to overcome his shyness with girls.

Levine, Peter. *From Ellis Island to Ebbetts Field: Sport and American Jewish Experience* (1992).

Levitin, Sonia. *The Return* (1987). An Ethiopian Falasha Jew journeys to Israel.

———. *Silver Days* (1989). A family escapes from Nazi Germany and tries to build a life in the United States.

Levoy, Myron. *Alan and Naomi* (1977). Friendship between Alan and Naomi grows as he breaks through her troubled memories of her father's murder by Nazis.

Lewis, Bernard. *Semites and Anti-Semites: An Inquiry into Conflict and Prejudice* (1986).

Malamud, Bernard. *The Natural* (1952). Baseball story.

———. *The Assistant* (1957). Struggle between religious beliefs and adolescence. For older students.

Marzollo, Jean. *Do You Love Me, Harvey Burns?* (1983). Romantic relationship between teens.

Mayer, Egon. *Love and Tradition: Marriage between Jews and Christians* (1985). The ongoing struggle between love and tradition.

Mazer, Harry. *The Last Mission* (1979). A young Jewish boy lies about his age, goes to war, and is taken captive by the Germans.

Mazer, Norma Fox. *After the Rain* (1987). A grandfather's illness and the love of his granddaughter.

Meltzer, Milton, ed. *The Jewish Americans: A History in Their Own Words, 1650–1950* (1982). Personal accounts of Jewish Americans from colonial times to the 1950s.

Miklowitz, Gloria. *Close to the Edge* (1983). A teenager, thinking of suicide, becomes involved with Jewish senior citizens.

Moline, Jack. *Growing Up Jewish; or, Why Is This Book Different from All Other Books?* (1987). A rabbi discusses being Jewish.

Morales, Aurora Levins, and Rosario Morales. *Getting Home Alive* (1986). Also listed in the Puerto Rican and cross-cultural sections.

Moskowitz, Faye. *A Leak in the Heart: Tales from a Woman's Life* (1985). Auto-biographic stories about an immigrant in the 1930s and 1940s.

Olshan, Joseph. *A Warmer Season* (1987). A young man learns about his parents' separation, sex, the aged, and other cultures.

Potok, Chaim. *The Chosen* (1967). Two adolescent boys from the Hassidic and Orthodox traditions have difficulty with expectations.

———. *The Promise* (1969). Sequel to *The Chosen*.

———. *My Name Is Asher Lev* (1972).

———. *Davita's Harp* (1985). A girl is surrounded by the unrest of the Great Depression and of the Spanish Civil War.

Roiphe, Anne. *Lovingkindness* (1987). Radical feminist mother is heartbroken when her daughter joins an Orthodox sect in Jerusalem.

Rosofsky, Iris. *Miriam* (1988). A girl questions life, religion, and faith after the death of her thirteen-year-old brother.

Roth, Henry. *Call It Sleep* (1934). A young boy struggles to assimilate. Roth uses Joyce's stream-of-consciousness to portray the boy's develop-ment in his urban neighborhood.

Roth, Philip. *Goodbye, Columbus* (1959). Struggle between religion and rejection of belief. For older students.

———. *Portnoy's Complaint* (1969). A young man struggles with sex and "the gentile girl."

———. *Our Gang* (1971). Ridicules Nixon's politics.

———. *The Great American Novel* (1973).

Ruby, Lois. *Two Truths in My Pocket* (1982). Six stories about adolescence told through the eyes of teenagers facing the problems of being Jewish today.

Schulberg, Budd. *What Makes Sammy Run?* (1941). The corruption of Holly-wood in its early days.

Schwartz, Howard. *Miriam's Tambourine: Jewish Folktales from around the World* (1986).

Shenker, Israel. *Coat of Many Colors: Pages from Jewish Life* (1985). Essays, stories, and interviews about Jewish culture, from ancient texts to life around the world today.

Simon, Kate. *Bronx Primitive: Portraits in a Childhood* (1982). Biographic account of a Jewish Polish American girl growing up.

———. *A Wider World: Portraits in an Adolescence* (1986). Memoirs of teen life in depression-era New York.

Simon, Neil. *Brighton Beach Memoirs* (1984). Fifteen-year-old Eugene grows up in a lower-middle-class family during the depression.

Singer, Isaac Bashevis. *Yentl, the Yeshiva Boy* (1983). A young woman poses as a boy to continue school.

Tene, Benjamin. *In the Shade of the Chestnut Tree* (1981). Illustrated anecdotes about youth in a Polish Jewish ghetto.

Weidman, Jerome. *Fourth Street East: A Novel of How It Was* (1970). Son of immigrant parents grows up on New York's Lower East Side in the 1920s.

Wiesel, Elie. *Night* (1960). Terrifying account of Wiesel's experience in a Nazi death camp.

———. *Legends of Our Time* (1968). Memories of friends and teachers and the anguished experience of a Holocaust survivor.

Latino Literature

This section includes a variety of Latino works, but it is by no means exhaustive. Latino literature spans races, cultures, and nationalities. *Latino* can, for example, refer to Chicanos, or to Cubans, or to Puerto Ricans, or to Hondurans, or to many, many other nationalities. Thus, the following literature—mostly Chicano, along with some Cuban and Puerto Rican—is a sampling of the literature of only the major populations of "Latinos" in the United States.

General

Bethancourt, T. Ernesto. *New York City, Too Far from Tampa Blues* (1975). A musician adjusts to New York City life.

———. *The Me Inside of Me* (1985). A seventeen-year-old becomes a millionaire and learns that money can't buy everything.

Duran, Daniel Flores. *Latino Materials: A Multimedia Guide for Children and Young Adults* (1979). An annotated list of book titles and films.

El Norte (1984). Film. A sister and brother escape political oppression in Central America only to find misery in the United States.

Garver, Susan, and Paula McGuire. *Coming to North America: From Mexico, Cuba, and Puerto Rico* (1981). The history and lifestyles of three major Latino groups: Mexicans, Cubans, and Puerto Ricans.

Kanellos, Nicolas, and Jorge Huerta, eds. *Nuevos Pasos: Chicano and Puerto Rican Drama* (1979). Anthology.

Rios, Alberto Alvaro. *The Iguana Killer: Twelve Stories of the Heart* (1984). Portraits of young people grappling with questions of sex, friendship, and life.

Schon, Isabel. *A Hispanic Heritage: A Guide to Juvenile Books about Hispanic People and Cultures* (1980). See more recent editions as well.

Vigil, Evangelina, ed. *Woman of Her Word: Hispanic Women Write* (1983). Anthology.

Cuban

Hijuelos, Oscar. *Our House in the Last World* (1983). Influences of the Cuban homeland and life as an immigrant.

———. *The Mambo Kings Play Songs of Love* (1989).

Mexican American

In 1848, with the signing of the Treaty of Guadalupe Hidalgo, much of the northern part of Mexico was ceded to the United States. Mexicans living on that land lost title to their property and many of their civil rights. This marks the beginning of what some call "Mexican American literature," though the literary roots of Mexican American writers go farther back than those of English-speaking writers in the United States.

The following is a sampling of artists who wrote before, during, and after the sixties "revolution" (the Chicano Movement) as well as some nonfiction and young adult fiction. For a more extensive listing, see Marie Stewart Frankson's "Chicano Literature for Young Adults: An Annotated Bibliography" (1990), which includes novels, short stories, poetry, biographies, anthologies, and drama. Charles Tatum's (1990) work has also been very helpful in forming this partial list.

Abelardo. *Chicano: 25 Pieces of a Chicano Mind* (1969).

———. *Here Lies Lalo: 25 Deaths of Abelardo* (1977).

Acosta, Oscar. *The Autobiography of Brown Buffalo* (1972). A young man struggles to find identity within two unaccepting cultures during the civil rights activism of the 1960s.

———. *The Revolt of the Cockroach People* (1973).

Alurista. *Return: Poems Collected and New* (1982). Deals with the poet's role in the Chicano Movement.

Anaya, Rudolfo A. *Bless Me, Ultima* (1972). A young boy's touching relationship with an old curandera, or faith healer, in New Mexico.

———. *Heart of Aztlan* (1979). Illustrated by Morton Levin. A family struggles to hold on to their culture in a new setting.

———. *Tortuga* (1979). The spiritual and physical struggles of a disabled boy in a body cast sent to a Mexican hospital.

———. *The Silence of the Llano: Short Stories* (1982).

———. *The Legend of La Llorona: A Short Novel* (1984). Historic tale of an Indian princess and of Cortez's conquest of the Aztecs.

———. *Lord of the Dawn: The Legend of Quetzalcoatl* (1987). A readable tale about the deity of the Toltecs.

Anaya, Rudolfo A., and Antonio Marquez, eds. *Cuentos Chicanos: A Short Story Anthology* (1980).

Anzaldúa, Gloria. *Borderlands: The New Mestiza* (1987). Poetry and prose about being caught between two cultures.

Arias, Ron. *The Road to Tamazunchale* (1975). An old man dying in the barrio has a wonderful time superimposing fantasy on reality.

Avendano, Fausto. *El Corrido de California: A Three Act Play* (1979). Events surrounding the occupation of California in 1846.

Baca, Jimmy Santiago. *Martin; and, Meditations on the South Valley* (1987). Lyrical narratives about the struggle between middle-class and rural poor life.

The Ballad of Gregorio Cortez (1984). Film. Classic ballad of a Mexican hero running from the Texas Rangers. Based on a popular *corrido*.

Candelaria, Nash. *Memories of the Alhambra* (1977). Hero's search for cultural roots leads him first to Mexico and then to Spain.

———. *Not by the Sword* (1982). Historical sequel goes back to the mid-1850s.

———. *The Inheritance of Strangers* (1985). Historical look at Hispanic New Mexico.

Cervantes, Lorna Dee. *Emplumada* (1981). Limitations of patriarchal society.

Chavez, Denise. *The Last of the Menu Girls* (1986). Seven interrelated stories about Chicanas' everyday experiences.

Cisneros, Sandra. *The House on Mango Street* (1983). Prose poem vignettes about a girl growing up in urban America.

———. *Woman Hollering Creek and Other Stories* (1991).

Corpi, Lucha. *Palabras de Mediodia: Noon Words* (1980).

———. *Delia's Song* (1988). A woman's perspective on life, loyalty, politics, and relationships.

De Casas, Celso A. *Pelon Drops Out* (1979). Satire about a young man who drops out of college to learn about life.

De Hoyos, Angela. *Arise, Chicano! and Other Poems* (1980).

De Leon, Nephtali. *Chicanos: Our Background and Our Pride* (1972).

———. *Chicano Poet: With Images and Visions of the Poet* (1973).

Dwyer, Carlota Cardenas de. *Chicano Voices* (1975). Anthology.

Elizondo, Sergio. *Libro para batos y chavalas Chicanas (A Book for Chicano Guys and Gals)* (1977). Younger teens' relationships with whites.

Fincher, Ernest. *Mexico and the United States: Their Linked Destinies* (1983). Survey of economic, political, and historical interactions between the two countries.

Galarza, Ernesto. *Barrio Boy* (1971). A family migrates from Mexico to Sacramento. Historical information.

Garza, Roberto, ed. *Contemporary Chicano Theatre* (1976). Anthology. Includes several prominent playwrights.

Harth, Dorothy, and Lewis Baldwin, eds. *Voices of Aztlan: Chicano Literature of Today* (1974). Anthology.

Hernandez, Irene Beltran. *Across the Great River* (1989). A family's decision to leave Mexico for a better life in the United States leads to experiences with labor smugglers, a curandera, and the authorities.

Hinojosa-Smith, Rolando. *The Valley* (1983). Multiple views of the Chicano culture of the Rio Grande Valley.

———. *Partners in Crime: A Rafe Buenrostro Mystery* (1985). A murder mystery with a surprise ending.

———. *Klail City* (1987). Sequel to *The Valley.*

Mares, E. A. *I Returned and Saw under the Sun: Padre Martinez of Taos* (1989). Bilingual work of a legendary nineteenth-century New Mexican Catholic priest.

Martinez, Julio, and Francisco Lomelí. *Chicano Literature: A Reader's Encyclopedia* (1985).

Martinez, Max. *Schoolland* (1988). A coming-of-age story about a schoolboy in Texas in the 1950s.

Mora, Pat. *Chants* (1984). A powerful book that intertwines the desert with people's lives, loneliness, love, joy, and despair.

Moraga, Cherríe. *Giving Up the Ghost: Theater in Two Acts* (1986). Chicana lesbian on the oppressive and abusive role of males in her culture.

Morton, Carlos. *The Many Deaths of Danny Rosales and Other Plays* (1983). Satiric collection with social content.

Ortiz y Pino, Jose. *Curandero: A Cuento* (1982). A romantic story about a beautiful girl, a handsome man, an accident, and refound love.

Paredes, Americo, and Raymund Paredes. *Mexican-American Authors* (1972).

Ranck, Katherine Quintana. *Portrait of Doña Elena* (1982). Love and acceptance in an old New Mexican village.

Rebolledo, Diana, Erlinda Gonzales-Berry, and Teresa Márquez, eds. *Las Mujeres Hablan: An Anthology of Nuevo Mexicana Writers* (1988).

Rechy, John. *City of Night* (1963). Beautiful El Paso contrasted with life in the barrio.

Rivera, Tomas. *y no se lo trago la tierra / And the Earth Did Not Part* (1971). Twelve related stories about a boy from a migrant farm family who can call nowhere home.

———. *This Migrant Earth* (1985). Rolando Hinojosa-Smith's translation of *y no se lo trago la tierra.*

Rodriguez, Joe. *The Oddsplayer* (1988). Racism faced by soldiers during the Vietnam War.

Rodriguez, Richard. *Hunger of Memory: The Education of Richard Rodriguez* (1981). Autobiography.

Sanchez, Ricardo. *I Sing about My Liberation* (1971).

————. *Hechizospells* (1976).

————. *Selected Poems* (1985).

Schon, Isabel. *A Bicultural Heritage: Themes for the Exploration of Mexican and Mexican-American Culture in Books for Children and Adolescents* (1978).

Soto, Gary. *The Elements of San Joaquin* (1977). Poetry.

————. *The Tale of Sunlight* (1978). Poetry.

————. *Living up the Street* (1985). Short stories portraying some of the positive experiences of living in the barrio.

————. *Baseball in April and Other Stories* (1990). Eleven short stories about teens in central California, sports, family issues, and the opposite sex.

————. *Who Will Know Us?* (1990). Poetry about boyhood in Fresno.

Sweet 15 (1990). Film. A young girl prepares for a special birthday and learns that her father is an illegal immigrant.

Tatum, Charles, ed. *Mexican American Literature* (1990). Anthology.

Trambley, Estela. *Trini* (1986). A young girl matures through illegal migration and child birth. A haunting story of love and struggle.

Valdez, Luis, and Stan Steiner, eds. *Aztlan: An Anthology of Mexican American Literature* (1972). Historical and contemporary excerpts relevant to modern-day Mexican Americans.

Vasquez, Richard. *Another Land* (1982).

Villanueva, Alma Luz. *The Ultraviolet Sky* (1988). A woman's complex and distressing relationships with her friends, her lover, her son, and others.

Villarreal, Jose Antonio. *Pocho* (1959). A young artist struggles with Mexican and Anglo values, ultimately rejecting both.

Puerto Rican

Algarin, Miguel, and Miguel Pinero, eds. *Nuyorican Poetry: An Anthology of Puerto Rican Words and Feelings* (1975).

Barrio, Raymond. *The Plum Plum Pickers* (1969). A bilingual work about the grim living conditions of migrant workers.

Colon, Jesus. *A Puerto Rican in New York and Other Sketches* (1961). A young man confronts prejudices against his language and race.

Cruz, Victor Hernandez. *Mainland* (1973). Poetry.

————. *Tropicalization* (1976). Poetry.

————. *By Lingual Wholes* (1982). Poetry.

Flores, Juan. *Divided Borders: Essays on Puerto Rican Identity* (1993). Essays on the sociology and culture of Puerto Rico.

Marzan, Julio, ed. *Inventing a Word: An Anthology of Twentieth-Century Puerto Rican Poetry* (1980). Bilingual anthology of twenty-three poets.

Mohr, Eugene. *The Nuyorican Experience: Literature of the Puerto Rican Minority* (1982).

Mohr, Nicholasa. *Nilda* (1973).

———. *El Bronx Remembered: A Novella and Stories* (1975). Twelve stories of survival.

———. *In Nueva York* (1977). Seven interrelated stories of a New York City Puerto Rican barrio.

———. *Rituals of Survival: A Woman's Portfolio* (1985).

Morales, Aurora Levins, and Rosario Morales. *Getting Home Alive* (1986). Also listed in the Jewish and cross-cultural sections.

Ortiz Colfer, Judith. *The Line of the Sun* (1989). Explores contrasts between "the tropical paradise" and the streets of New Jersey.

Rivera, Edward. *Family Installments: Memories of Growing Up Hispanic* (1982).

Thomas, Piri. *Down These Mean Streets* (1967). A boy contrasts his mother's memories of Puerto Rico with his own growing up in East Harlem.

———. *Savior, Savior Hold My Hand* (1972).

———. *Seven Times Long* (1974).

———. *Stories from El Barrio* (1978).

Vega, Bernardo. *Memoirs of Bernardo Vega* (1980). Translated by Juan Flores. Experiences of Puerto Rican workers in a cigar factory in New York City at the turn of the century.

Native American Literature

The Heath Anthology begins the "Colonial Period to 1700" with Native American creation stories, trickster tales, and historical narratives from the Winnebago, Pima, Zuñi, Navajo, Hopi, Iroquois, Tlingit, and Tsimshian traditions. From the earliest of times in colonial history, then, Native Americans have been contributing to the cultural literacy of the United States.

Among the following books are early myths, tales, ceremonial pieces, and other oral lore. A few nonfiction titles are also included. Mostly, however, I've listed some of the contemporary offerings that have exploded onto the literary scene in the last few decades. I would like to especially thank Dr. James Charles of the University of South Carolina at Spartanburg and Alex Kuo of Washington State University for providing me with many of the following titles. The work of the

Native American Authors Distribution Project (1992) has also been extremely helpful in formulating this list. They offer far more titles than I can include in this short space.

Alexie, Sherman [Spokane/Coeur d'Alene]. *The Business of Fancy Dancing* (1992). Stories and poems.

―――. *The Lone Ranger and Tonto Fistfight in Heaven* (1993). Stories and poems.

―――. *Old Shirts and New Skins* (1993). Poetry.

Allen, Paula Gunn [Laguna Pueblo/Lakota]. *Coyote's Daylight Trip* (1978).

―――. *A Cannon between the Knees* (1981). A woman's perspective on urban California and New Mexico.

―――. *Star Child* (1981). Poetry.

―――. *Shadow Country* (1982). Poetry.

―――. *The Woman Who Owned the Shadows* (1983).

―――, ed. *Spider Woman's Granddaughters: Traditional Tales and Contemporary Writing by Native American Women* (1989). Anthology.

Allen, T. D., ed. *Arrows Four: Prose and Poetry by Young American Indians* (1974). Anthology.

Annharte [Anishinabe]. *Being on the Moon*. Poetry.

Apes, William. *A Son of the Forest: The Experience of William Apes, A Native of the Forest* (1829). Autobiography.

Armstrong, Jeanette [Okanagan]. *Breathtracks*. Poetry.

―――. *Enwhisteetkwa: Walk in Water*. Poetry.

―――. *Slash*. Poetry.

Arnett, Carroll/Gogisgi [Cherokee]. *Engine*. Poetry.

―――. *Night Perimeter*. Poetry.

―――. *Rounds*. Poetry.

Ashabranner, Brent [Cheyenne]. *Morning Star, Black Sun: The Northern Cheyenne Indians and America's Energy Crisis* (1982). The Northern Cheyenne struggle to choose between instant wealth and preservation of the land.

Astrov, Margot, ed. *The Winged Serpent: An Anthology of American Indian Prose and Poetry* (1946).

Awiakta, Marilou [Cherokee]. *Abiding Appalachia* (1978). Poetry.

Bataille, Gretchen M., and Kathleen Mullen Sands. *American Indian Women: Telling Their Lives* (1984). Autobiographic accounts.

Beal, Merrill. *"I Will Fight No More Forever": Chief Joseph and the Nez Perce War* (1963).

Bedford, Denton [Delaware]. *Tsali* (1972).

Benai, Edward Benton [Anishinabe]. *Generation to Generation.*

Bierhorst, John, ed. *In the Trail of the Wind: American Indian Poems and Ritual Orations* (1971).

——. *The Sacred Path: Spells, Prayers, and Power Songs of the American Indians* (1983). Chants, prayers, and songs about birth, love, hunting, farming, and death.

Bigjim, Frederick Seagayuk [Inupiaq]. *Letters to Howard: An Interpretation of the Alaska Native Land Claims* (1974).

——. *We Talk, You Yawn: A Discourse on Education in Alaska* (1985).

——. *Sinrock.* Poetry.

——. *Walk the Wind.* Poetry.

Black Bear, Ben, and R. D. Theisz. *Songs and Dances of the Lakota* (1976). Song poems.

Black Elk [Oglala Sioux]. *Black Elk Speaks: Being the Life Story of a Holy Man of the Oglala Sioux* (1932). Autobiography, as told to John Neihardt.

——. *The Sacred Pipe: Black Elk's Account of the Seven Rites of the Oglala Sioux* (1953).

——. *The Sixth Grandfather: Black Elk's Teachings* (1984).

Black Robe (1992). Film. The flip-side of *Dances with Wolves.* Jesuits journey to Quebec and clash with Algonquins.

Blue Cloud, Peter [Mohawk]. *White Corn Sister* (1979). Celebrates the spiritual values of the land through Indian myth.

——. *Sketches in Winter, with Crows* (1984). Poetry.

——. *The Paranoid Foothills.* Poetry.

Boyd, Doug. *Rolling Thunder: A Personal Exploration into the Secret Healing Powers of an American Indian Medicine Man* (1974). Documents a shaman's life.

Brant, Beth [Mohawk]. *Mohawk Trail* (1985).

——. *Food and Spirits* (1991). Short stories.

Brito, Silvester [Comanche/Tarascon]. *Looking through a Squared Off Circle* (1985). Poetry.

——. *Red Cedar Warrior* (1986). Poetry.

Broker, Ignatia [Ojibway]. *Night Flying Woman* (1983). An Ojibway girl moves with her family from the Northeast to the Midwest and is forced to give up living in "the old way."

Brown, Dee. *Bury My Heart at Wounded Knee: An Indian History of the American West* (1971). Chapter after chapter of broken treaties, broken promises.

Brown, Emily Ivanoff [Inuit]. *Tales of Ticasuk: Eskimo Legends and Stories* (1987).

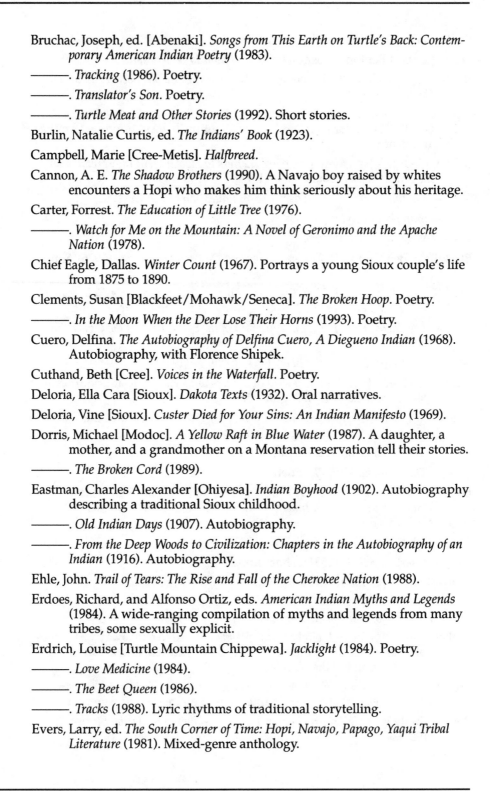

Bruchac, Joseph, ed. [Abenaki]. *Songs from This Earth on Turtle's Back: Contemporary American Indian Poetry* (1983).

——. *Tracking* (1986). Poetry.

——. *Translator's Son.* Poetry.

——. *Turtle Meat and Other Stories* (1992). Short stories.

Burlin, Natalie Curtis, ed. *The Indians' Book* (1923).

Campbell, Marie [Cree-Metis]. *Halfbreed.*

Cannon, A. E. *The Shadow Brothers* (1990). A Navajo boy raised by whites encounters a Hopi who makes him think seriously about his heritage.

Carter, Forrest. *The Education of Little Tree* (1976).

——. *Watch for Me on the Mountain: A Novel of Geronimo and the Apache Nation* (1978).

Chief Eagle, Dallas. *Winter Count* (1967). Portrays a young Sioux couple's life from 1875 to 1890.

Clements, Susan [Blackfeet/Mohawk/Seneca]. *The Broken Hoop.* Poetry.

——. *In the Moon When the Deer Lose Their Horns* (1993). Poetry.

Cuero, Delfina. *The Autobiography of Delfina Cuero, A Diegueno Indian* (1968). Autobiography, with Florence Shipek.

Cuthand, Beth [Cree]. *Voices in the Waterfall.* Poetry.

Deloria, Ella Cara [Sioux]. *Dakota Texts* (1932). Oral narratives.

Deloria, Vine [Sioux]. *Custer Died for Your Sins: An Indian Manifesto* (1969).

Dorris, Michael [Modoc]. *A Yellow Raft in Blue Water* (1987). A daughter, a mother, and a grandmother on a Montana reservation tell their stories.

——. *The Broken Cord* (1989).

Eastman, Charles Alexander [Ohiyesa]. *Indian Boyhood* (1902). Autobiography describing a traditional Sioux childhood.

——. *Old Indian Days* (1907). Autobiography.

——. *From the Deep Woods to Civilization: Chapters in the Autobiography of an Indian* (1916). Autobiography.

Ehle, John. *Trail of Tears: The Rise and Fall of the Cherokee Nation* (1988).

Erdoes, Richard, and Alfonso Ortiz, eds. *American Indian Myths and Legends* (1984). A wide-ranging compilation of myths and legends from many tribes, some sexually explicit.

Erdrich, Louise [Turtle Mountain Chippewa]. *Jacklight* (1984). Poetry.

——. *Love Medicine* (1984).

——. *The Beet Queen* (1986).

——. *Tracks* (1988). Lyric rhythms of traditional storytelling.

Evers, Larry, ed. *The South Corner of Time: Hopi, Navajo, Papago, Yaqui Tribal Literature* (1981). Mixed-genre anthology.

Evers, Larry, and Felipe Molina, eds. *Yaqui Deer Songs/Maso Bwikam* (1987). Song poems. Also on audiotape.

Feldmann, Susan, ed. *The Storytelling Stone: Myths and Tales of the American Indians* (1965). Oral narratives.

Fisher, Dexter, ed. *The Third Woman: Minority Women Writers of the United States* (1980). Includes selections from Mourning Dove, Kaky Bennett, Janet Campbell, Joy Harjo, Nia Francisco, Ramona Wilson, Anna Lee Walters, and Paula Gunn Allen.

Freedman, Russell. *Buffalo Hunt* (1988). Explains the value and relationship of the buffalo to the Native Americans of the Great Plains and compares that to the misuse of this resource by whites.

French, Alice [Inuit]. *The Restless Nomad.*

Geiogamah, Hanay [Kiowa]. *New Native American Drama: Three Plays* (1980).

Glancy, Diane [Cherokee]. *Trigger Dance* (1990). Short stories about Native Americans caught between worlds.

———. *Claiming Breath* (1992). Poetry.

Grinnell, George Bird. *Blackfoot Lodge Tales: The Story of a Prairie People* (1892).

Hale, Janet Campbell [Coeur d'Alene]. *The Owl's Song* (1974).

———. *The Jailing of Cecelia Capture* (1985).

Harjo, Joy [Creek]. *What Moon Drove Me to This?* (1979). Poetry.

———. *She Had Some Horses* (1983). Poetry.

———. *In Mad Love and War* (1990). Poetry.

Henson, Lance [Cheyenne]. *In a Dark Mist*. Poetry.

———. *This Small Sound*. Poetry.

Hinton, Leanne, and Lucille Watahomigie, eds. *Spirit Mountain: An Anthology of Yuman Story and Song* (1984). Mixed-genre anthology.

Hobbs, Will [Ute]. *Bearstand* (1989). A fourteen-year-old whose mother is dead and father kept alive by machines resents his life and feels alienated at school and at work.

Hobson, Geary, ed. [Cherokee/Quapaw/Chickasaw]. *The Remembered Earth: An Anthology of Contemporary Native American Literature* (1979).

Hogan, Linda [Chickasaw]. *Seeing through the Sun* (1985).

———. *Mean Spirit* (1990).

Humphrey, William. *No Resting Place* (1989). Story of the downfall of the Cherokee nation.

James, J. Alison [Anasazi Pueblo]. *Sing for a Gentle Rain* (1990). A high school junior, fascinated by Anasazi dreams, meets a girl from the thirteenth century and falls in love.

Josephy, Alvin. *Biography Series of American Indians.* Biographies of Apache, Iroquois, Cherokee, and other heroes.

Kenny, Maurice [Mohawk]. *Dancing Back.* Poetry.

———. *I Am the Sun.* Poetry.

———. *North: Poems from Home.* Poetry.

———. *Strong the Nation.* Poetry

Lame Deer [Sioux]. *Lame Deer: Seeker of Visions* (1972). Autobiography, with Richard Erdoes.

Lesley, Craig, ed. *Talking Leaves: Contemporary Native American Short Stories* (1991). Winner of the 1992 Northwest Book Award. Louise Erdrich, Elizabeth Woody, Gerald Vizenor, Roger Jack, and Gloria Bird are some of the authors included in the thirty-eight selections.

Marriott, Alice, and Carol Rachlin. *American Indian Mythology* (1968). Oral narratives.

Maxwell, James A., ed. *America's Fascinating Indian Heritage* (1978). Explores eight geographical areas of North America and the diversity of cultures within. Contemporary Native Americans discuss issues.

McCarthy, James. *A Papago Traveler: The Memories of James McCarthy* (1985). Autobiography, with John Westover.

McNickle, D'Arcy [Salish/Kootenai]. *The Surrounded* (1936).

———. *Runner in the Sun: A Story of Indian Maize* (1954).

———. *Wind from an Enemy Sky* (1978).

Milton, John R., ed. *The American Indian Speaks* (1969). Poems and short stories from Simon Ortiz, Norman Russell, Darlene McCarty, Curtis Link, Soge Track, and Janet Campbell.

The Mission (1986). Film about South American Indians and proselytizing eighteenth-century Jesuits in Brazil.

Momaday, N. Scott [Kiowa]. *House Made of Dawn* (1968). A young man struggles to overcome a hostile past. Difficult for secondary students.

———. *The Way to Rainy Mountain* (1969).

———. *The Gourd Dancer* (1976). Poetry.

———. *The Names: A Memoir* (1976).

———, ed. *American Indian Authors* (1971). Anthology features authors such as Chief Dallas Eagle, Thomas S. Whitecloud, Emerson Blackhorse Mitchell, Patty Harjo, Juanita Platero, Mendoza Durango, Grey Cohoe, N. Scott Momaday, James Welch, and Vine Deloria, Jr.

Mourning Dove/Christine Quintasket [Colville]. *Cogewea: The Half Blood* (1927). Problems faced by a mixed-blood girl growing up in the early part of the century.

———. *Coyote Stories* (1933).

Niatum, Duane [Klallam]. *Carriers of the Dream Wheel: Contemporary Native American Poetry* (1975).

Oandasan, William [Yuki]. *Round Valley Songs* (1984). Poetry.

———. *Moving Inland.* Poetry.

Ortiz, Simon [Acoma Pueblo]. *Going for the Rain* (1976).

———. *Fight Back: For the Sake of the People, For the Sake of the Land* (1980).

———. *From Sand Creek* (1981). Poetry.

———. *Fightin': New and Collected Stories* (1983).

———, ed. *Earth Power Coming: Short Fiction in Native American Literature* (1983). Short story anthology.

Peyer, Bernard, ed. *The Singing Spirit: Eight Short Stories by North American Indians* (1989).

Pitts, Paul. *Racing the Sun* (1988). Through his grandfather, a young man learns about the heritage his father rejected.

Reedstrom, E. Lisle. *Apache Wars: An Illustrated Battle History* (1990). Illustrated history of the group that resisted takeover longer than any other western tribe.

Robinson, Margaret [Nootka]. *A Woman of Her Tribe* (1990). Half European American, half Nootka Indian, must a fifteen-year-old choose between cultures?

Rose, Wendy [Hopi/Miwok]. *Long Division: A Tribal History* (1976). Poetry.

———. *Academic Squaw: Reports to the World from the Ivory Tower* (1977).

———. *Lost Copper* (1980). Poetry.

———. *What Happened When the Hopi Hit New York?* (1982). Poetry.

———. *The Halfbreed Chronicles and Other Poems* (1985). Poetry.

Rosen, Kenneth, ed. *Voices of the Rainbow: Contemporary Poetry by American Indians* (1975). Anthology.

Sanchez, Carol Lee. *Conversations from the Nightmare* (1975). Poetry.

———. *Coyote's Journal.*

———. *Morning Prayer.*

Sandoz, Mari. *The Story Catcher* (1963).

Silko, Leslie [Laguna Pueblo]. *Laguna Woman* (1974). Poetry.

———. *Ceremony* (1977). Mixed-blood Laguna returning home must seek healing through ceremony.

———. *Storyteller* (1981).

———. *Almanac of the Dead* (1991).

Stedman, Raymond William. *Shadows of the Indian: Stereotypes in American Culture* (1982). Discusses distorted images and understanding and recognizing the Native American as a vital force in the modern world.

Stensland, Anna Lee. *Literature by and about the American Indian: An Annotated Bibliography* (1979).

Storm, Hyemeyohsts. *Seven Arrows* (1972).

———. *Song of Heyoehkah* (1981).

Tallmountain, Mary [Koyukon]. *Continuum*. Poetry.

Tedlock, Dennis, ed. *Finding the Center: Narrative Poetry of the Zuni Indians* (1972).

Theisz, R. D., ed. *Buckskin Tokens: Contemporary Oral Narratives of the Lakota* (1975).

Tremblay, Gail [Micmac/Onondaga]. *Indian Singing in Twentieth-Century America* (1990). Poetry.

Velie, Alan R., ed. *American Indian Literature* (1979). Anthology. Includes selections from Red Jacket, Lance Henson, and Simon Ortiz.

Vizenor, Gerald [Chippewa]. *Earthdivers: Tribal Narratives on Mixed Descent* (1981).

———. *Touchwood: A Collection of Ojibway Prose* (1987).

———. *The Trickster of Liberty: Tribal Heirs to a Wild Baronage* (1988).

———. *The Heirs of Columbus* (1991).

———. *Dead Voices: Natural Agonies in the New World* (1992).

Wallin, Luke [Creek]. *In the Shadow of the Wind* (1984). Problems arise when two sixteen-year-olds, Pine Basket, a Creek Indian, and Caleb, the son of white settlers, fall in love.

Welch, James [Blackfeet/Gros Ventre]. *Winter in the Blood* (1974).

———. *The Death of Jim Loney* (1979).

———. *Fools Crow* (1986). Historical novel about the massacre of a band of Blackfeet fighting to survive.

———. *The Indian Lawyer* (1990).

Welsch, Roger. *Omaha Tribal Myths and Trickster Tales* (1981). Oral narratives.

Where the Spirit Lives (1989). Film. A Blackfoot Indian girl is taken from home and relocated to a government boarding school.

Whiteman, Roberta Hill [Oneida]. *Star Quilt* (1984). Poetry.

Wiget, Andrew, ed. *Native American Literature* (1985).

Wolfson, Evelyn. *From Abenaki to Zuñi: A Dictionary of Native American Tribes* (1988). Description of sixty-eight Native American tribes, with maps, information about historical and contemporary ways of life, and other information.

Young Bear, Ray [Mesquakie]. *Winter of the Salamander: The Keeper of Importance* (1980). Poetry.

———. *Black Eagle Child: The Facepaint Narratives* (1992).

Yue, Charlotte, and David Yue. *The Igloo* (1988). Illustrated description of the life of Alaskan Natives.

Zepeda, Ofelia, ed. *When It Rains: Papago and Pima Poetry* (1982). Anthology.

Cross-Cultural Literature

Many multiethnic works are about mixed-blood people or individuals who find themselves struggling with dual identities. In "Making a Home of One's Own: The Young in Cross-Cultural Fiction" (1988), George Shannon suggests a number of titles, including:

> Jean Craighead George's *Julie of the Wolves* (1972)
>
> Virginia Hamilton's *Arilla Sun Down* (1976)
>
> Paule Marshall's *Brown Girl, Brownstones* (1959)
>
> Robert Screen's *With My Face to the Rising Sun* (1977)
>
> Laurence Yep's *Child of the Owl* (1977) and *Sea Glass* (1979)

Greene (1988) adds Buchi Emecheta's *Second-Class Citizen* (1974) to the list. Furthermore, in the past few years, there has been an explosion of multicultural readers and anthologies. Several of these publications are discussed in chapter 14. Other titles follow.

Beaty, Jerome, and J. Paul Hunter, eds. *New Worlds of Literature* (1989). A vast resource of culturally diverse literature.

Beilke, Patricia, and Frank Sciara. *Selecting Materials for and about Hispanic and East Asian Children and Young People* (1986).

Blicksilver, Edith. *The Ethnic American Woman: Problems, Protests, Lifestyle* (1978).

Brown, Wesley, and Amy Ling, eds. *Imagining America: Stories from the Promised Land* (1991). Collection of fiction about early immigrants.

Fisher, Dexter. *The Third Woman: Minority Women Writers in the United States* (1980).

Haskins, James. *The Guardian Angels* (1983). True story of a multiethnic group whose volunteers helped to prevent crime in New York City in 1979.

Heath, R. B., ed. *Tradewinds: Poetry in English from Different Cultures—Chinese, Indian, Pakistani, African Caribbean* (1990).

In America. Illustrated series with historical information about more than thirty emerging ethnic groups in America.

Jacobs, William Jay. *Great Lives: Human Rights* (1990). Thirty articles about human rights activists, with special attention paid to women and minority groups.

Moraga, Cherríe, and Gloria Anzaldúa, eds. *This Bridge Called My Back: Writings by Radical Women of Color* (1981). Groundbreaking collection of writings by women of color.

Morales, Aurora Levins, and Rosario Morales. *Getting Home Alive* (1986). Also listed in the Jewish and Puerto Rican sections.

Norwick, Kenneth P., ed. *Lobbying for Freedom in the 1980s: A Grass-Roots Guide to Protecting Your Rights* (1983). A useful handbook for "citizen lobbyists."

Thomas, Joyce Carol, ed. *A Gathering of Flowers: Stories about Being Young in America* (1990). Short stories collected "with the idea that all of us in America are somehow related."

Disabilities

Many classical pieces exist that cast characters with disabilities in a negative light (e.g., *Of Mice and Men, Moby Dick, Richard III, A Christmas Carol, Treasure Island*). Teachers must recognize the effects of this problem and treat such literature with an awareness of and sensitivity to this issue. We should also make an attempt to balance these stereotypic presentations with more positive, well-rounded ones. Reading the biographies of people like Franklin Roosevelt, Beethoven, Stevie Wonder, and Thomas Edison, for instance, can provide students with a better understanding of the accomplishments of people with disabilities. The following are additional titles, mostly for young adults.

Emotional/Mental Disabilities

Bauer, Marion Dane. *Tangled Butterfly* (1980). A seventeen-year-old's mental illness increases as her family denies it.

Cavallaro, Ann. *Blimp* (1983). The story of a relationship between an overweight girl and a boy with emotional problems.

Hautzig, Deborah. *Second Star to the Right* (1981). A fourteen-year-old's obsession with her weight results in anorexia.

Hull, Eleanor. *Alice with Golden Hair* (1981). A girl leaves a special school for the mentally retarded to find work and acceptance at a convalescent home.

Johnson, Julie Tallard. *Understanding Mental Illness: For Teens Who Care about Someone with Mental Illness* (1989). Discusses depression, manic depression, and schizophrenia. Interviews with family members offer solutions to difficult situations.

Klein, Norma. *Learning How to Fall* (1989). A boy recovering in a psychiatric hospital struggles to survive. Mature situations.

MacCracken, Mary. *City Kid* (1981). The story of a teacher who works with emotionally disturbed children.

Mahy, Margaret. *Memory* (1988). A young man's friendship with an Alzheimer's victim helps ease the pain of his sister's death.

McNair, Joseph. *Commander Coatrack Returns* (1989). After becoming deeply involved in the care of her special brother, Lisa is almost taken in by a schoolboy who has difficulty with his own identity.

Neufeld, John. *Lisa, Bright and Dark* (1969). Lisa's family's denial of her mental disturbance forces her friends to take action.

Oneal, Zibby. *The Language of Goldfish* (1980). A thirteen-year-old's sanity is threatened by the difficulty she has handling pressure.

Platt, Kin. *The Ape Inside Me* (1979). A boy has trouble controlling his illness, which gets him into trouble.

Polikoff, Judy (as told to Michele Sherman). *Every Loving Gift: How a Family's Courage Saved a Special Child* (1983). The story of a family's emotional and financial sacrifice to help their brain-damaged son Andy with controversial treatment.

Riley, Jocelyn. *Only My Mouth Is Smiling* (1982). A mother's bizarre behavior forces teenagers to accept her mental illness.

Sachs, Marilyn. *The Fat Girl* (1984). The story of a strange relationship between an overweight girl and her boyfriend.

Slepian, Jan. *Risk 'n' Roses* (1990). New in the Bronx, Skip finds it difficult to be accepted because of her mentally retarded sister.

Smith, Lee. *Black Mountain Breakdown* (1980). A girl suffers a mental breakdown despite apparent popularity, good looks, and academic success.

Snyder, Anne. *Goodbye, Paper Doll* (1980). A seventeen-year-old develops anorexia nervosa and must deal with underlying problems.

Snyder, Anne, and Louis Pelletier. *Nobody's Brother* (1982). A pending divorce threatens to break up stepbrothers and increases Josh's stuttering.

Stren, Patti. *I Was a Fifteen-Year-Old Blimp* (1985). A teenage girl deals with being overweight.

Wolff, Virginia Euwer. *Probably Still Nick Swansen* (1988). A learning disabled student, self-conscious about placement in the resource room, meets a girl who accepts his invitation to the prom.

Physical Disabilities

Anaya, Rudolfo A. *Tortuga* (1979). The spiritual and physical struggles of a disabled boy in a body cast sent to a Mexican hospital.

Eareckson, Joni. *Joni* (1976). A young artist learns to survive after a skiing accident.

Farish, Terry. *Why I'm Already Blue* (1989). Unhappy in his homelife, a thirteen-year-old finds solace in a friendship with the wheelchair-bound boy next door.

Froman, Katherine. *The Chance to Grow* (1983). Informative material about the causes of various disabilities, the purpose of physical therapy, and where to find additional sources.

Girion, Barbara. *A Handful of Stars* (1981). The story of an energetic, active teenager learning to live with epilepsy.

Hall, Lynn. *Halsey's Pride* (1990). After her mother's rejection, a thirteen-year-old learns to live with epilepsy and develops a good relationship with her father and his prized dog.

Hallman, Ruth. *Breakaway* (1981). A hearing-impaired teenager's struggle to cope with a hearing world, his smothering mother, and a determined girlfriend.

Kata, Elizabeth. *A Patch of Blue* (1961). Blinded as a child, a young white woman falls in love with a man who has also suffered the pain of intolerance. Originally published as *Be Ready with Bells and Drums*.

Keller, Helen. *The Story of My Life* (1903). A young girl who can neither hear nor see becomes a productive writer and activist.

Kellogg, Marjorie. *Tell Me That You Love Me, Junie Moon* (1984). Two men, one a paraplegic, the other stricken with a neurological disease, and a woman disfigured by an angry boyfriend find that together they can build relationships.

Klein, Norma. *My Life as a Body* (1987). A high school girl tutors a classmate who is permanently wheelchair-bound. Eventually, they fall in love.

Krementz, Jill. *How It Feels to Fight for Your Life* (1989). Personal accounts of young people who have dealt with serious illness or disability.

Levy, Marilyn. *The Girl in the Plastic Cage* (1982). A teenager stricken with scoliosis must wear a brace, give up gymnastics, face losing her boyfriend, and get along with her family.

Likhanov, Albert (translated by Richard Lourie). *Shadows across the Sun* (1983). A disabled girl in the Soviet Union falls in love with a boy whose father is an alcoholic.

Marsden, John. *So Much to Tell You* (1987). A fourteen-year-old girl, terribly disfigured by an attack, works things out in her class journal.

Perske, Robert. *Show Me No Mercy: A Compelling Story of Remarkable Courage* (1984). A father, paralyzed by an accident that kills his wife and daughter, fights to keep a son with Down's syndrome from institutionalization.

Sallis, Susan. *Only Love* (1980). The story of love between spunky Fran, paralyzed from the waist down, and Lucas, injured in a motorcycle accident.

Savitz, Harriet May. *Run, Don't Walk* (1979). A diving injury leaves a girl in wheelchair, making her an activist for the rights of the disabled.

———. *Come Back, Mr. Magic* (1983). A young man known for his work with disabled people is left in a coma and must rely on the support of others.

Terris, Susan. *Wings and Roots* (1982). The story of a relationship between a 1950s polio victim and a hospital volunteer.

Thiele, Colin. *Jodie's Journey* (1988). A trophy-winning rider shows that her confinement to a wheelchair is not enough to stop her from saving herself and her horse.

Valens, E. G. *The Other Side of the Mountain* (1975, 1978). Two volumes. The true account of a girl permanently paralyzed while training for the Olympic ski team who is determined to lead a meaningful life. Originally *A Long Way Up*.

The Homeless

The number of books about the homeless has increased in recent years as this population continues to grow. Further, the topic is easily combined with many multiethnic titles, since endemic homelessness has existed in many nonmainstream communities long before the problem became a public issue.

Fowler, Tom, Malcolm Garcia, and the staff of the St. Vincent de Paul Ozanam Shelter, eds. *Out of the Rain: An Anthology of Drawings, Writings, and Photography by the Homeless of San Francisco* (1988).

Holman, Felice. *Secret City, U.S.A.* (1990). Several kids from the tenement try to create a place for the homeless in a decaying city.

Hughes, Dean. *Family Pose* (1989). The story of an eleven-year-old living on the streets of Seattle.

Jimenez, Francisco. "The Circuit." Short story in Tatum's *Mexican American Literature*.

Kozol, Jonathan. *Rachel and Her Children: Homeless Families in America* (1988).

Steinbeck, John. *The Grapes of Wrath* (1939).

Szymusiak, Molyda. *The Stones Cry Out: A Cambodian Childhood, 1975–1980* (1986). Dispossessed people in Cambodia.

Torrey, E. Fuller. *Nowhere to Go: The Tragic Odyssey of the Homeless Mentally Ill* (1988). Discusses the policy and practice of deinstitutionalizing the mentally ill.

Homosexuality

A number of titles deal with homosexuality, either directly or indirectly. This literature contributes to the growing acknowledgment of the gay and lesbian presence in our culture. Titles like *Cat on a Hot Tin Roof, Suddenly Last Summer, The Color Purple, Against the Season, The Andrew Is Dead Story*, and many others are currently in our literary canon. The following list, primarily for secondary students, suggests some other titles.

Cohen, Susan, and Daniel Cohen. *When Someone You Know Is Gay* (1989). Teenage homosexuality—its history, scientific information, an AIDS update, and personal commentaries from interviews with gay teens.

Ecker, B. A. *Independence Day* (1983). A sixteen-year-old faces the challenge of declaring his homosexuality.

Garden, Nancy. *Annie on My Mind* (1982). Two high school senior girls fall in love and learn to deal with the consequences of their controversial relationship.

Klein, Norma. *Now That I Know* (1988). An active teenager responds positively to her parents' divorce until she learns a family secret that turns her world upside down.

Koertge, Ron. *The Arizona Kid* (1988). A Missouri boy goes to Arizona with his uncle for the summer and learns about himself, life, kindness to others, romance, and his uncle's gay identity. Includes frank language.

Rench, Janice E. *Understanding Sexual Identity: A Book for Gay Teens and Their Friends* (1990). Dispels myths about gay and lesbian people in an attempt "to work against violence, hatred, and ignorance."

Shannon, George. *Unlived Affections* (1989). A seventeen-year-old discovers some family secrets after the death of the grandmother who raised him.

Older Adults

Arias, Ron. *The Road to Tamazunchale* (1975). An old man dying in the barrio has a wonderful time superimposing fantasy on reality.

Benjamin, Carol Lea. *Nobody's Baby Now* (1984).

Brancato, Robin. *Sweet Bells Jangled Out of Tune* (1982).

Branfield, John. *The Fox in Winter* (1983). Developing a friendship with a ninety-year-old and then coping with his death.

Butterworth, W. E. *Leroy and the Old Man* (1980).

Irwin, Hadley. *What about Grandma?* (1982).

Kerr, M. E. *Gentlehands* (1978). A teenager learns that his beloved grandfather was formerly a Nazi.

Klass, Sheila. *Alive and Starting Over* (1983).

Mahy, Margaret. *Memory* (1988). The story of a young man's friendship with an Alzheimer's victim.

Myers, Walter Dean. *Won't Know Till I Get There* (1982).

Ruby, Lois. *This Old Man* (1984).

Smith, Robert. *The War with Grandpa* (1984).

Wallace-Brodeur, Ruth. *Steps in Time* (1986).

Zindel, Paul. *The Pigman's Legacy* (1980).

Teenage Suicide

This subject is a delicate one, one that teachers should handle carefully. Yet since suicide is one of the leading killers among teenage youth, we must recognize it and learn more about how to deal with it. Although there is much literature in the canon that deals with this issue, little has been recognized as appropriate learning material for young adults. The following list has been developed primarily for the secondary level.

Bennett, James. *I Can Hear the Mourning Dove* (1990). A sixteen-year-old recovers from a suicide attempt and works, along with a friend, to overcome her problems.

Byars, Betsy. *The Burning Questions of Bingo Brown* (1988). A sixth-grader wonders why his teacher had students write on the topic "suicide" and then rides his motorcycle without a helmet and has an accident.

Crutcher, Chris. *Chinese Handcuffs* (1989). The story of a boy confused by his brother's suicide. Mature situations and language.

Gardner, Sandra, and Gary Rosenberg. *Teenage Suicide* (1990). Case studies of teenage suicide along with other information, including prevention suggestions.

Hermes, Patricia. *A Time to Listen: Preventing Youth Suicide* (1987). Open discussion by family and friends of suicide victims as well as by survivors of suicide attempts.

Irwin, Hadley. *So Long at the Fair* (1988). An eighteen-year-old can't accept his girlfriend's suicide and escapes by becoming a drifter.

Klagsbrun, Francine. *Too Young to Die: Youth and Suicide* (1985). Presents the realities of suicide and ways to prevent it.

Mack, John E., and Holly Hickler. *Vivienne: The Life and Suicide of an Adolescent Girl* (1981). Letters and diaries of a suicide victim. Includes both a clinician's and a teacher's view.

McCuaig, Sandra. *Blindfold* (1990). With the help of a psychiatrist, a girl tries to deal with the double suicide of her friends.

Pevsner, Stella. *How Could You Do It, Diane?* (1989). A family copes with a fifteen-year-old girl's suicide.

Pfeffer, Susan Beth. *About David* (1980). A story about the pain felt by survivors after a boy commits murder and suicide.

Radley, Gail. *The World Turned Inside Out* (1982). A fifteen-year-old works through guilt and questions about his brother's suicide.

Vietnam Veterans

The United States is still dealing with the aftermath of the Vietnam War. Much has been written recently on the subject, both fiction and nonfiction. The following is a partial list that may help teachers begin. For an excellent treatment of the subject with extensive annotations, see Larry Johannessen's *Illumination Rounds: Teaching the Literature of the Vietnam War* (1992), which includes numerous references to personal narratives, oral histories, novels, drama, poetry, photography, and films.

Edelman, Bernard, ed. *Dear America: Letters Home from Vietnam* (1985). Letters from soldiers about life on the front lines, injuries, prisoner-of-war camps, and other subjects.

Hoobler, Dorothy, and Thomas Hoobler. *Vietnam: Why We Fought* (1990). The history of the war, the role of the United States, and the change in Americans' views.

MacPherson, Myra. *Long Time Passing: Vietnam and the Haunted Generation* (1984). Five hundred interviews about the human cost of war.

Marshall, Kathryn. *In the Combat Zone: An Oral History of American Women in Vietnam, 1966–1975* (1987). The accounts of twenty women serving in the war.

Palmer, Laura. *Shrapnel in the Heart: Letters and Remembrances from the Vietnam Veterans Memorial* (1987). Interviews with survivors of those commemorated at the Vietnam Veterans Memorial in Washington, D.C.

Rodriguez, Joe. *The Oddsplayer* (1988). Racism faced by soldiers during the Vietnam War.

Terry, Wallace. *Bloods: An Oral History of the Vietnam War by Black Veterans* (1984). Twenty veterans' accounts of heroism, racism, and the horror of war.

9 Educating the Illiterate Intellectual

Ouch! I know I'm getting myself into trouble here because I'm going to talk about *some* teachers and their reluctance to change. Resistance to multicultural education, as I see it, is as much the fault of faculty and administrators as it is the fault of the population at large. If educators do not believe in multiculturalizing the curriculum, and many of them do not, then convincing the community becomes much harder. To avoid this additional burden, those interested in a pluralistic approach to teaching literature must evaluate their own campus climate and plan strategies to promote their goals within their own departments.

While I was teaching "Introduction to Literature" in central Minnesota, my department conducted a survey to determine the level of commitment faculty members had to nontraditional authors. Although the number of professors in favor of expanding their material to include multicultural authors was more than double that of those against, several objected strongly. One commented:

> I am terribly nervous about telling faculty what authors they may or may not teach, and what material they must or must not cover. . . . I teach traditional authors; I would be very angry if forced by the thought police to include nontraditional authors, and I would hence not teach those authors at all well. Leave the choice of this kind of material entirely up to the individual professors.

But leaving the choice up to faculty has perpetuated the status quo. In a moving essay called "The Censorship of Neglect," Rudolfo Anaya (1992) argues that many fine works of literature continue to be excluded simply because our curriculum is

> controlled by groups with a parochial view of what the curriculum should and should not include. . . . These groups have told us . . . what is universal in literature . . . which has kept ethnic literature . . . out of the curriculum. . . . We are tired of being told that we do not understand the needs of our youth because we belong to a particular ethnic group. We are told that because we are Mexican, Native, Black, or Asian American—or women—that somebody else has the right literature and language to describe our reality. (18–19)

Indeed, we are missing some wonderful works because of such exclusion. And that loss is bad enough. But we are also missing the opportunity to provide students with literature that could positively affect their attitudes.

The Naysayers and Miss Bleeding Heart

Of course, there is much speculation about whether or not the implementation of multiethnic literature really does alter attitudes, and this is a fair argument. I do not believe that diverse literature automatically neutralizes mainstream student attitudes. Some studies tell us that reading nonmainstream literature has some effect on reducing racism; other studies show that it has little or no effect; some even show negative effects (see Page 1977; Hogan 1992).

In discussing the merits of teaching multiethnic literature, Page (1977) suggests that

> black literature, as well as Asian American, Chicano, Italian American, Jewish American, Native American, Puerto Rican, and other ethnic literatures, must be incorporated within the fabric of the American literary tradition and read by all students because it is effective, stimulating, and insightful reading. (33)

But he also warns that teaching multiethnic literature will not automatically change the racial and ethnic attitudes of our learners. To determine the effects of African American literature on mainstream students, Page studied three classes. Class 1 read African American literature individually or in small groups. Class 2 read the literature as a class and received "traditional" instruction (i.e., the teacher gave directions, asked questions, led discussion, made assignments, etc.). Class 3 read no African American literature at all. Results of the study showed that reading black literature had either no effect (as measured by the Multifactor Racial Attitude Inventory) or a negative effect on students.

These findings are not surprising for several reasons. "Learning" literature is a difficult business in any case. For instance, a student in one of my own classes—a class that at one point touched on gay and lesbian issues—thought that I had failed miserably in my attempt to make his reading experience successful. That was my mistake. I had not anticipated and planned for the hostility I would face when dealing with these issues. I have tried to do better since. The point is that teachers need to anticipate the problems that some students will encounter when reading diverse literature and be ready to deal with them.

Furthermore, the major literary piece that Page had his test classes read was *Native Son* by Richard Wright. This is a tough novel for anyone. Wright meant to disturb his audience. The main character, Bigger, unintentionally commits murder and then, motivated by fear, saws the victim's head off and forces her body into a furnace! That's pretty upsetting by anyone's standards. Nonetheless, I believe students can benefit greatly from a careful treatment of this book. I have taught *Native Son* in both high school and college settings with positive results. Students are haunted by Bigger's actions and by the message that Wright conveys. The novel can easily provoke discussion about social and political issues or about a young person's inability to escape his or her world. Further, *Native Son* is a beautifully written book that should be "studied" as a masterful "modernist" novel.

Whenever I use this book, students tell me about how it affects them beyond the normal experience. I think that would satisfy Wright. Yet we must be careful as instructors to guide students in their reading; we shouldn't expect them to always "get it" on their own. I suppose I can imagine how some literal-minded reader might be upset with Bigger Thomas and foolishly transfer these negative feelings over to an entire race. But that's where we come in: to guide our students and to help them make distinctions between the literal and the figurative.

Defining Art

By arguing that art has both ethical and aesthetic components, Hogan (1992) harkens back to Horace's description of art, *"dulce et utile,"* sweet and useful, as well as to Sir Philip Sidney's contention that art exists "to teach and delight." Indeed, according to Hogan, "the link between ethics and aesthetics is a nearly constant theme in the Western tradition" and in other traditions as well (186–87). Using these precepts, Hogan justifies the teaching of diverse materials.

I agree. I accept the long tradition of recognizing both the aesthetic and the ethical components of art. And I see no greater ethical imperative in the United States today than the importance of including all of its voices. Discussing the merits of mandatory diversity, Hogan says:

> Thus, the situation is uncertain, but in our present state of knowledge it does appear that mandatory diversity in literary study is quite unlikely to do any harm, and has a reasonable chance of doing some good. Given the urgency of the problems of racism, sexism, and ethnocentrism, the possibility of doing good gives moral import to mandatory diversity. (188)

Diversity in literary study, however, should mean inclusion, not segregation. The students in Page's study suggest "that black literature should be taught in its chronological, historical, literary, and artistic settings within American literature." Of course! In the best of all possible worlds, that's exactly what we should be doing. James Baldwin, for example, should be taught in African American literature courses, in special topics courses where students concentrate on only one author, but most of all in American literature courses.

Still, Hogan notes that, unfortunately, "as nonwhite and women's literatures have entered the curriculum, they have become ghettoized. Of course, if it is a choice between ghettoization and absence, ghettoization is preferable" (189). But we should be moving away from this model as we continue to develop a concept of multiethnicity based on the inclusion of several groups within the same course. The University of California at Berkeley, for example, requires courses in multiethnic education to involve at least three groups, not one. This range provides a much better look at diversity (Takaki 1991).

Developing Materials

One of the problems in teaching or reading multiethnic literature has been, up until very recently, the scarcity and expense of materials. That's why I was so disappointed by Hertzel's review (1992) of *Braided Lives* in the *Minnesota English Journal*. *Braided Lives* is a 1991 attempt by the Minnesota Humanities Commission, working in conjunction with the Minnesota Council of Teachers of English, to put together a collection of multiethnic works by Native American, Latino American, African American, and Asian American artists. When it was published, every English teacher in the state received a copy. I admire the great effort put forth by all those involved in the project. For Minnesota teachers who felt at a loss for materials, *Braided Lives* proved invaluable. In fact, the March 1994 issue of *English Journal* offers a number of interesting articles on strategies for implementing sections of *Braided Lives* into the curriculum.

Hertzel's article, however, presents some troublesome questions. He starts by describing the book as a "splendid selection of writing by American minorities," acknowledging that "the book goes well beyond the usual bland, conservatively safe products of institutional committee compromise" (2). But then he asks the same nagging questions that prevent fellow teachers from using "risky" literature: Is there evidence that multiethnic literature will promote better attitudes? Are teachers trained to teach such literature? Is the purpose of literature to promote cultural awareness and sensitivity?

I believe that the editors of *Braided Lives* intended to make available some excellent literature for the English teachers of Minnesota. And they did. But asking them to offer teaching strategies and historical and sociological backgrounds would be asking for another book, at least. Their intention was to put together an anthology of multiethnic works.

Hertzel is also troubled by the fact that the pieces do not seem to fit into the mainstream of America: "The theme of many of the stories . . . goes directly contrary to principles or beliefs that American schools have traditionally endorsed" (5). But we need to remember that mainstream American optimism often ignores the experiences of nonmainstream Americans. As Juanita Garciagodoy argues in "The Wake-Up Call" (1991) introducing the Latino American section of *Braided Lives:*

> A tragic feature shown in some of these writings is the violence that poverty, racism, and ethnocentrism inflict on the lives of people. Don't recoil from the sorrow in these pages. It is part of this world in which you live, in which you were born and raised and which, if you allow yourselves to be courageously open and free of prejudice and indifference, you can help change in your lifetime. (84)

Should we ignore Garciagodoy's advice and "recoil from the sorrow in these pages" because it somehow goes against traditionally endorsed attitudes? I don't think so. Writers often reflect the environments in which they live, and many racial and ethnic groups in this country face extremely oppressive environments.

Sometimes teachers tell me that their students would "really be upset" by much of the "ethnic literature" that they have read. "It's so violent," they protest. "It's so stereotypic," they complain. But should we shelter our mainstream, middle-class, roof-over-their-heads, full-stomach students? Shouldn't they know that a world other than their own exists? All too often, students live in a vacuum. Hogan laments, for example, that when he teaches *The Merchant of Venice* in his Shakespeare class, "virtually the only students . . . who sympathize with Shylock—at least before we discuss the play—are Jewish" (189).

Of course, not all teachers regard the possibility of teaching multiethnic literature with suspicion. In fact, when Hertzel asked several teachers about the possibility of teaching "minority literature" with "the object of developing appreciation of these cultures," the teachers he spoke to "thought it might work." Asking specifically about James Baldwin's "Sonny's Blues," Hertzel says that the teachers' responses were "interesting because they revealed a kind of innocent anxiousness." Yet still Hertzel warns that "we need to think this thing through" (5).

I think that we can get beyond the hypothetical here. I have taught "Sonny's Blues" (1965) in both high school and college, and, yes, it's a tough story. But it's well worth the effort. The story is about two brothers who have grown up in Harlem. The older brother becomes a math teacher and stays in the neighborhood. The younger brother, a talented musician, gives himself over to drugs and struggles, toward the end, for salvation. Baldwin's description of their physical surroundings is hard to forget:

> We drove along . . . toward the vivid, killing streets of our childhood. These streets hadn't changed, though housing projects jutted up out of them now like rocks in the middle of a boiling sea. . . . Some escaped the trap, most didn't. Those who got out always left something of themselves behind, as some animals amputate a leg and leave it in the trap. . . . It came to me that what we both were seeking . . . was that part of ourselves which had been left behind. It's always at the hour of trouble and confrontation that the missing member aches. (282–83)

Baldwin continues by characterizing Sonny as a young man trapped in his environment, first losing one parent, then another; then his older brother joins the army. Sonny wants to escape. But as an African American teenager living with his brother's in-laws, too young to join the military, with no outside connections, what can he do?

I suppose we can look at this story in two ways. Negatively, it could be seen as a sordid tale of a man growing up in a squalid place, on drugs and in trouble. Not very appealing. On the other hand, "Sonny's Blues" could be seen as a story that presents us with all kinds of ethical questions about growing up, making decisions, and accepting responsibility. In this sense, Sonny's plight is both unique and universal. These human dilemmas are compelling, and students discuss Sonny's predicament passionately. Moreover, many young people know what it feels like to experience alienation, no matter where they grow up. Of course, the most compelling reason to read the story is that it is a superb piece of literature—moving, beautifully crafted, poetic.

Knowing Our Students

To the naysayers who scoff at those who try to bring literature into the classroom to change attitudes, I say you're selling our students short. True, we can't get to them all. I have had some students who resisted everything I ever tried to present. One unpleasant young man—we'll call him Jerry—wouldn't budge on any issue. He described Ida Wells's shocking essay "Lynching at the Curve" as "another essay blaming the white man for everything." I really don't think literature will make much of a difference with readers like Jerry. I guess I'd have to say that I failed with him in many ways. I do believe, however, that Jerry's writing improved in my class. I also think that we changed his manner of expression by the time the semester was over; the disapproving responses he got from his classmates for his outbursts were not what he expected. If we didn't change his thinking, at least we altered his behavior somewhat by demonstrating that his was not the only voice that deserved to be heard.

That's one student. I've had others. I do not know how many "attitude changes" would show up on an assessment test, but I do think that the thinking of many of my students has opened up as a result of their reading. Continuing with "Sonny's Blues" for a moment, I have had many interesting discussions with students about what life must be like in the environment Sonny was raised in. Most students in American schools know that such places exist. Yet they also need to give some thought to what life is like there. And they can do that through the eyes of Sonny and the other characters they read about.

In his July 1992 Democratic Convention speech, Jesse Jackson pointed out that for some youths in this country, going to jail is a step up. They are fed; they are given clothes; they have a place to sleep. My God, think of it! There are actually people in this country whose lives are better in jail than out! Huge numbers of our population live below the poverty level, are abused emotionally or physically, or dwell in unsafe neighborhoods. I think that we should all understand these issues. We should never "protect" our students from the truth. Instead, we must help them find it.

Although there are many Jerrys out there, there is also a large, good-hearted, but naive and uneducated student population that is receptive to new ideas. They are, in short, willing to learn. They may not change overnight, but at least they are willing to look at the lives of others from different perspectives. And it is up to us to expose them to these different voices.

Though I have not yet analyzed quantifiable data related to this issue, I firmly believe from my own experiences in the classroom that students are moved by the literature they read. Recently, a student came to my office to thank me for giving her the opportunity to read Toni Morrison's *Beloved*. "At first," she explained, "I didn't want to read it. I knew it would be oppressive. But once I saw how beautifully it was written, I couldn't put it down. Morrison is a genius. Thank you for choosing this book for the class."

Whose Canon Anyway?

Finally, Hogan (1992) notes that the whole argument about literary choices is ethnocentric, explaining that "our canon" is Eurocentric mainly because of European political and economic domination. "But in fact there is a Chinese canon, a Japanese canon, an Arabic canon, an Indian canon—indeed, canons" (184). Referring to the Indian literary tradition, he notes:

> I know of nothing in Western literature which so movingly represents the separation of loved ones as Act IV of Sakuntala, no literature more powerfully erotic than the lyrics of Bilhana, nothing which so touchingly evokes the love between father and child as some poems from the Tamil anthologies, no genuinely aesthetic use of intellectually stimulating dialectic comparable to passages in Gora, no more profound and no more emotionally devastating exploration of hopelessness and anonymity than *A House for Mr. Biswas.* (188)

We might make similar claims for many of the literatures of the United States. But first we must learn more about them. As Hogan points out, "it is only under racist and ethnocentric assumptions that one might come to believe aesthetic criteria need to be dropped" to include non-Western, nonwhite, nonmale works (187). He argues, and I agree, that people are often attracted to literature that they can understand because of gender, race, nationality, or other means of identification (189). We should keep this in mind as we look at what we have been given to read in the past and consider what we should be presenting to our students in the future. If, as Hogan says, "part of the point of literary study is to help people transcend narcissism, to understand the universal in literature" (189), then we ought to be making some significant changes. But even if we acknowledge the existence of other literatures, we still face profound Western ignorance of non-Western and Western minority traditions (185).

Perhaps it is not our fault that we don't know about all the literatures of the world. Many of us earned our degrees long before the explosion of multicultural awareness. When I was an undergraduate, we had "the dead white men and Emily Dickinson." Yet now we know differently, and we can no longer deprive students—mainstream or nonmainstream—of these other artistic pieces. To do so is unethical.

Finding Support within Schools and Community

My observation and experience tell me that most teachers are receptive to incorporating nonmainstream literatures into their programs. Once they understand the issues and have had some exposure to the excellent literature that's out there, any resistance they formerly had breaks down fairly easily. What most teachers are more concerned about, and rightly so, are the real barriers to making changes in the curriculum: colleagues, background knowledge, and money.

Support from Colleagues

We must depend on each other for support. Although not all teachers are interested in teaching the same literature, they usually support others' right to teach what they want. I suggest that new teachers seek the support of older, more experienced teachers in adapting the curriculum to better suit the needs of students. And I encourage those of you who have been on your campuses for a while to seek out new people and to look at what they're bringing in. Mentor these people and support them even if you do not want to teach some of their choices. Work together as a department to develop a philosophy about the value of teaching nonmainstream literature.

If you are interested in incorporating nonmainstream literature into your curriculum, tell the rest of the faculty and administration about your policies. Encourage them to work with you in an interdisciplinary fashion. Ask your district's curriculum coordinator to meet with you and define your modus operandi. Tell the coordinator that you'd like to make this a district-wide effort. Get district-level input and support. Arm yourself with NCTE data about censorship and recommended books and be aware of the relevant local, regional, and national agencies within NCTE and other organizations.

Incorporating multicultural literature does create a number of problems for teachers. But according to Anaya (1992), if it's not in your canon, you're part of the problem:

> Have we become the problem itself? Have we become the defenders of the status quo? Is it really we who have refused to see the reality of the African American experience, the Chicano world, the Asian American struggle, the woman's search for her own self-representation? Are we free to teach when we fear the social and aesthetic reality of other groups?

Anaya provides a call-to-arms of sorts, a call that I believe all English educators should heed:

> If you are teaching in a Mexican American community, it is your social responsibility to refuse to use the textbook which doesn't contain stories by Mexican American authors. If you teach Asian American children, refuse the textbook which doesn't portray

their history and social reality. This kind of activism will free you to teach. If you don't refuse, you are part of the problem. But you don't have to be teaching in a Mexican American barrio to insist that the stories and social reality of that group be represented in your textbook. You short-change your students and you misrepresent the true nature of their country if you don't introduce them to all the communities who have composed the history of this country. To deny your students a view into these different worlds is to deny them tools for the future. (20)

Professors do not usually have the same problems with censorship that secondary teachers do, but advocating for ethnic literature at the college level can still create serious tenure and promotion issues. According to Hogan (1992):

> Once it has been decided what the legitimate objects of study are and what sorts of knowledge are valuable, those who wish to study other objects (e.g., Third World literature) and those who have other sorts of knowledge (e.g., of Indian literary history) are put at a disadvantage, for their interests and expertise are devalued. Because it is structural, institutional, such discrimination is harder to see. Despite its invisibility, however, it is clearly stronger and more pervasive. (184)

Further, questions of commitment affect scheduling and course loads. When departments discuss incorporating pluralistic literature, responses, as Hogan notes, are often logistic and defensive: Who will do it? Will we have to hire new staff? What graduate courses will be lost? (184). Supportive faculty must work to bring about change on college campuses to ensure that their colleagues are not shortchanged because of their interest in multiculturalism.

Knowledge

If the classical concept of great literature includes both ethical and aesthetic components, and I think it does, then surely we need to expand our canon in a number of directions. As I said earlier, I believe that most teachers would be willing, even eager, if the real barriers were taken away. Thus, once faculty organize their goals and present a united front, they then need to arm themselves with the knowledge and background required to teach new materials.

We all, in one way or another, find ways to learn as we live our lives as English educators. Some of us take classes. Some, because of a new assignment or new program or strong personal commitment, have learned on their own. English teachers are resourceful; they know their way around the library. Indeed, most of us teach literature because we love to read, because we love to talk about what we read, because we love to learn more about what we read. There is no group that can prepare better. Sure, we're loaded down. And it's very difficult to do any research in new areas of literature. I remember semesters where I met with 165 students each day. Where could I have found the time to read and study?

But today, because of the explosion of diverse literature into a much larger geographic market, the focus on multicultural education across the country, and the English teacher's ability and motivation to learn, the news is good. Many resources are available. Lots of new courses and workshops and conferences are being offered. Teachers should seek funding from their departments and districts for release time or lightened teaching loads so that they can attend workshops or inservice meetings on multicultural issues.

Living close to a college campus is a great advantage. English, human relations, American studies, and other departments often invite noted speakers to campus. In the last few years I have heard Maya Angelou, Elaine Kim, Joy Kogawa, Ishmael Reed, Ronald Takaki, Shawn Wong, and several other speakers at various campuses. In 1991, a Ford Foundation grant funded a consortium of several universities in the Minneapolis area to study women of color in the United States. I attended a series of two-day sessions in which noted women scholars and artists from the African American, Asian American, Latino American, and Native American communities spoke and conducted workshops. That same year I attended a MELUS (Multi-Ethnic Literature of the United States) conference where I heard James Banks, Frank Chin, and Paul Lauter speak.

None of us should feel intimidated or embarrassed because we don't have enough information. As English teachers, we may never seem to have the extra time to seek out that information, but it's out there and it's available.

Money

Collegial support and information are important. But even if we all agree, the question of money always comes up. Often it's the biggest problem of all. My discussion of support from colleagues and knowledge probably had little new to say to those who have already been working at expanding the canon. Perhaps it is helpful to say that we should go to conferences and do research. But who's going to pay for all this retooling? Faculties are already stretched farther than they should be, and many school districts are getting more and more into debt. University systems all over the country are reporting cutbacks.

But there is always money, and English educators need to learn how to get it. Many small grants are available from large and small, public and private organizations. Department chairs, deans, development officers, principals, district coordinators, city officials, university grant officers—all have information about funding available for study. Grants can buy teaching time, offer part-time and full-time leave for study, or pay for substitutes, travel, and registration for conferences. When I began teaching, I wasn't aware of any of these wonderful opportunities to "build my knowledge base." About the only thing I knew how to do was read. Of course, that's a great start. But there's so much more that we can do and share with each other.

For high school teachers, the biggest money issue is books. At every high school I've been to and at every conference and workshop I've attended, teachers lament the fact that they are bound to the books in their districts. "Even if we were in agreement about the need for multicultural literature, we would still have trouble getting the materials," they say. I know that this is true. That's why whenever anybody asks me to recommend an anthology for their program, I first ask how much money the district has to spend on books. My next response used to be "No anthology." If a school invested in one of those costly editions, its book budget would almost certainly be depleted.

Recently, however, I have changed my mind. Almost all major and many minor publishers have "become multicultural." At the 1992 NCTE Annual Convention, I passed by many exhibitors' booths noting the diverse faces and figures on the covers. Leafing through the pages, I saw many pieces by women and ethnically diverse authors; some I recognized, some I didn't. Diverse pieces were incorporated into thematic readers for composition courses and into the poetry, short story, and essay sections of literature anthologies. Books representing every level: elementary school, middle school, high school, and college. We can't complain any longer. It's out there. Some volumes are better than others, but at least there are many from which to choose.

If money is available, several very good ethnic collections have been published in the last few years. *Mexican American Literature* (1990), edited by Charles Tatum, is one example. *African American Literature: Voices in a Tradition* (1992), edited by William L. Andrews, is another. The new Heath series for high school, *Making Cultural Connections* (1992), offers an entire four-year program for multicultural work.

Many teachers are aware of and use paperbacks. But they also point out that after two or three readings, these publications fall apart. The bound copies, they explain, "are very expensive and almost defeat the whole purpose." College and university people are lucky in this respect for not having to worry about expense, because our students buy their own books. Although we have to be sensitive to our students' pocketbooks, we can ask them to buy whatever we want them to read. Money just isn't the same barrier.

If teachers are committed to including pluralistic literature in the accepted canon, then mountains can be moved. Through hard work, solicitation, receptive attitudes, and promoting personal opportunity, we can transform ourselves into a truly literate force that can have a tremendous impact on all of our students. But we have to be committed to change. In summarizing the monoethnic nature of the English curriculum, Applebee (1992) warns:

> As long as these texts remain unchanged, "canonicity" is likely to elude non-white authors and women; they will continue to be at the margins of a culture that is legitimized by its place in the school. [We must find] . . . the proper balance among the many traditions, separate and intertwined, that make up the complex fabric of society in the United States. In their instruction, teachers need to find better ways to insure that programs are culturally relevant as well as culturally fair. (32)

10 The Right Rules for the Right Game: Critical Analysis of Multiethnic Literature

One of the problems with expanding our literary canon to include multicultural perspectives is that we must also expand the criteria with which we judge. That is, if we look at a Native American work, we should attempt to understand it from a Native American perspective. If we critique an African American piece, we should try to analyze it from an Afrocentric perspective. Furthermore, we need to be aware that ethnic authors write for different audiences—members of their own culture, mixed populations, the macroculture—and thus their purpose in writing may be other than we ordinarily would expect.

Still, if I was on shaky ground in the last chapters, then the earth has given way on me in this one. I am, as I hope has been made clear by this time, a rank beginner in the search for understanding the diverse literatures in the United States. Thus, for me to attempt an adequate discussion of any of the following literatures may be presumptuous. Yet by the time I become an expert in all of these areas, I will be retired. So I have decided that I must begin somewhere if I am to begin at all. Perhaps what I lack in formal background, I can compensate for somewhat with experience and enthusiasm. After all, isn't that what we English teachers do best?

This section is a response to sporadic but increasing awareness and identification of multicultural issues in a number of professional journals. And though I know that many teachers are not as uninformed as I, I cannot help but think that there are some, through no lack of interest, commitment, or ability, who find themselves lacking solid background in multicultural literature and so hesitate to teach it.

Indeed, although the last few years have seen the burgeoning of ethnic studies and African American specializations at the Ph.D. level, the climate for these areas of investigation hasn't always been so warm. In a provocative discussion of "new Black aesthetic critics and their exclusion from American 'mainstream' criticism," Martin (1988) points out that new black aesthetic criticism is almost absent in readings of standard literary criticism. He also notes the paucity of courses and comprehensive examinations that focus on such criticism in doctoral programs, thus rendering a corpus of literature almost invisible (379). According to Jay (1991), this "socially constructed ignorance of teachers and students will be a hard obstacle to multicultural literacy, for the knowledge it requires has been largely excluded from the mainstream classroom, dissertation, and published critical study" (274).

But we shouldn't chide ourselves too much. Even though multicultural literature has been largely left out of the canon, other disciplines have not done much better. Indeed, the traditional "history of Western civilization" has virtually institutionalized the exclusion of non-Western cultures and left them outside of history altogether. Asante (1987) points out, for example, that we do not teach the Egyptian "The Coming Forth by Day" as the precursor to the Torah, the Koran, and possibly the Bhagavad-Gita. Nor do our history books represent the Egyptian and Nubian civilizations as the progenitors of Greek and Roman thought (166). As I've noted elsewhere, such exclusions reveal a "xenophobic perspective which all but eliminates a multicultural approach to history and literature" (1988, 50).

Nonetheless, if we believe, as Henry Louis Gates, Jr. (1990) does, that the literary canon is "the commonplace book of our shared culture" (58), and if we are, in fact, a multicultural population, then we needn't argue anymore about whether or not to expand the canon to include diverse literature. We simply need to learn more about the literatures of the diverse peoples that make up the population of what we call the *United* States. We can't understand "American" literature without this knowledge. Jay (1991) writes:

> One cannot . . . adequately interpret works . . . without some knowledge of the various cultures surrounding and informing them. Most writing produced here after the eighteenth century, moreover, borrows words, characters, events, forms, ideas, and concepts from the languages of African-, Hispanic-, Jewish-, Native-, and Asian-Americans. (270)

Writers have been "crossing boundaries" for a long time. Looking at Mexican American literature, for instance, we can see that nationality, language, and culture have blended for centuries. Citing *Bless Me, Ultima*, Jay wonders how we can categorize a work "which crosses so many . . . linguistic and cultural divides" (268). Noting the ancient traditions defined in *Black Elk Speaks* or James Welch's *Fools Crow*, he asks, "Can the borders between Native-, Hispanic-, and Anglo-American literature be drawn without blurring historical traditions which placed all but the Anglo outside?" And Elizabeth Meese cites Leslie Silko's "half-breed protagonist," Tayo, and the other multiracial characters in *Ceremony* as an illustration of the "crossing of cultures" by contemporary writers and readers (quoted in Jay 1991).

In fact, notions of "separateness" have recently come under close scrutiny by a number of critics. In *Playing in the Dark: Whiteness and the Literary Imagination* (1992), Toni Morrison points out that the black presence in America has had a profound influence on white writing, despite the fact that this influence has traditionally been ignored or denied, that white literature has traditionally been thought of as "separate" from such issues:

> For some time now I have been thinking about the validity or vulnerability of a certain set of assumptions conventionally accepted among literary historians and critics and circulated as "knowledge." This knowledge holds that traditional, canonical American literature is free of, uninformed, and unshaped by the four-hundred-year-old presence of, first, Africans and then African-Americans in the United States. . . . [Yet] the contemplation of this black presence is central to any understanding of our national literature and should not be permitted to hover at the margins of the literary imagination. (4–5)

The institution of slavery, the Constitution, and the history of our culture, argues Morrison, have had an impact on the thinking of writers, and there has been an unspoken agreement of silence about this. She mentions several works for which much scholarship exists, but for which analysis of African American characters and themes is almost nonexistent: for example, "the black woman who lubricates the turn of the plot and becomes the agency of moral choice and meaning in Henry James's *What Maisie Knew*," the black woman who "holds the center stage in Gertrude Stein's *Three Lives*," or the problem of race in Willa Cather's "Sapphira and the Slave Girl" (13–14).

Shelley Fisher-Fishkin takes the critique of separateness a step further by asserting that Twain based the voice of Huckleberry Finn on a ten-year-old African American slave (cited in Winkler 1992). Although she has met with some criticism for her views, we already know that Twain adopted a number of dialects for his characters. Fisher-Fishkin's provocative notion would make for an interesting class discussion, and the enterprising student could write a stimulating exploratory paper. I look forward to more discussion on this issue by Fisher-Fishkin and others in the field.

The point here is that if we look at literary criticism in this way, the whole notion of separateness may become obsolete. In fact, Gates (1990) sees a new Rainbow Coalition of contemporary critical theory in "the uneasy, shifting set of alliances formed by feminist critics, critics of so-called minority discourse, and Marxist and post-structuralist critics generally," a coalition that "rejects the 'antebellum aesthetic position,' when men were men, and men were white, when scholar-critics were white men, and when women and persons of color were voiceless" (56). Jay (1991) calls for nothing less than the "uprooting of the conceptual model defining the field" of American literature (264).

To look more critically at the literatures of the United States, however, we must broaden our knowledge of characteristics of literary excellence beyond the traditional Eurocentric models that we have been educated with and continue to teach in our classrooms. Traditional elements such as plot development, characterization, use of symbolism, and so forth simply may not be relevant when we study the literature of nonmainstream writers. Thus, we may be undervaluing the aesthetic quality of nonmainstream work simply because we do not know what to look for.

For example, Li (1992), in discussing the "filiative and affiliative textualization" in Marilyn Chin's poetry, claims that this theme is "the sheaf of other Chinese American verse as well" (178). It's used to create "a sense of cohesive kinship" in Mei-mei Berssenbrugge's "Chronicle," as a means of identification in Nellie Wong's "Dreams in Harrison Railroad Park," and to express "intimacy, enhanced by . . . loss" in Cathy Song's "The Youngest Daughter" (178–79). Can we recognize these qualities when we search for a more "traditional" theme?

Or take the idea that storytelling is sacred and can be used for the purpose of healing, a common view in Native American literature. From a Eurocentric perspective, a work of art is typically appreciated for its aesthetic qualities alone. Thus, an uninformed reader might miss the significance of the healing powers of N. Scott Momaday's *House Made of Dawn* or Leslie Silko's *Ceremony*. Furthermore, if we do not understand the importance of the vision quest or the significance of dreams in many Native American novels and poems, we may overlook or be confused by much of the action.

Similarly, the criteria for African American rhetorical excellence are not necessarily the same as the direct, linear model of the European American tradition. According to Cook (1985), the "flourish of words," the creation of "witty turns of phrase," the "plays on words" to alter the length and rhythms of the expected text, the sequence of narratives for building, in a circuitous way, the powerful message of the text are all part of a carefully formatted pattern that an uninformed audience might miss (261–67). These literary elements and many more have been and will continue to be lost to a lot of us if we do not take the time to learn and examine the characteristic qualities of nonmainstream work.

What follows is in no way complete. In fact, I will merely touch on a few major groups about whom I am learning. In this chapter, I look briefly at African American, Chinese American, Japanese American, Mexican American, and Native American literatures, all of which are becoming increasingly accessible to readers. To include more groups would be beyond the scope of this book.

Clearly, I feel more comfortable discussing some areas than I do others because I have been studying them longer. Thus, my commentary will probably seem uneven to those who are well versed in each literature. For those who will say "But she didn't include _____" or "No one ever talks about _____," please understand that my intention was not to purposely exclude anything. I did the best I could with the time and space that I had. I hope that I will hear from those willing to add to this beginning effort.

African American Literature

Molefi Asante (1987) claims that artists from Afrocentric traditions should be judged not by Eurocentric models, but by styles and characteristics that better represent African American works, by a "Black Aesthetic." He argues that Western rationality and objectivity are inadequate for understanding the Afrocentric thinker, for whom, as I've said elsewhere, "the interactive metaphors of discourse" are interrelated differently (1988, 51).

Similarly, in *The Way of the New World: The Black Novel in America*, Addison Gayle talks about "a black way of seeing":

> In more concrete terms, before beauty can be seen, felt, heard, and appreciated by a majority of the earth's people, a new world must be brought into being; the earth must be made habitable and free for all men. This is the core of the Black Aesthetic ideology and forms the major criterion for the evaluation of art: How much better has the work of art made the life of a single human being on this planet, and how functional has been the work of art in moving us toward that moment when an *ars poetica* is possible for all? (quoted in Martin 1988, 377–79)

And in discussing the style and essence of African American writing, Henry Louis Gates, Jr. (1990) relates the result of his discovery of

James Baldwin at age fifteen:

> I wrote and rewrote verbatim his elegantly framed paragraphs,
> full of sentences that were at once somehow Henry Jamesian and
> King Jamesian, yet clothed in the cadences and figures of the spiri-
> tuals. (58)

At the 1991 NCTE Annual Convention in Seattle, I heard Haki R.
Madhubuti relate a similar story. As a young boy he discovered Richard
Wright, and that discovery changed his world. Finally a writer whose
voice he could identify with and be moved by at the same time.

What follows is a discussion of African American literary theory.
It's only an introduction, a beginning, and should not be taken as anything else. But perhaps it gives readers some knowledge of the power
and difference of African American literature.

Separatist or Syncretist?

According to Gates (1990), "the poles of black canon formation, established firmly by 1849," were originally defined by the question "Is 'black'
poetry racial in theme, or is black poetry any sort of poetry written by
black people?" Gates writes, "This question has been at play in the tradition ever since" (62).

Thus, African American literary theory has historically included
both separatist and syncretic points of view. The syncretists hold that
great African American writers follow Eurocentric forms and belong to
a larger mainstream group. Scholars like Houston Baker and Robert
Stepto believe that mainstream criticism can be combined with African
American forms that identify "the quest for freedom and literacy"
(Savery 1991, 191). This group believes that their argument gives the
writer more tools: those of mainstream traditions as well as those of
distinct African American traditions. Since African Americans have had
to "fit into" a larger whole and remain a "subgroup" at the same time,
this group argues, and since they have managed to be successful at it,
why shouldn't they take advantage of both camps (Martin 1990, 728)?

Separatists believe that true African American artists write with a
distinctive identity of their own. This group "shouted down and transformed" the critics of the forties and fifties, insisting that "'uniquely
black' ways of 'seeing' literature" could not be fairly judged by the criteria of oppressors. The "forceful rhetoric and politically timely messages" of the separatist camp continued to dominate until Henry Louis
Gates, Jr.'s work in the syncretic "use of Euro/Anglo-based critical ideas"
changed the focus of analysis. Nevertheless, Gates's work in "Signification" has moved him closer to the earlier separatists.

Responding to Gates's work, Barbara Johnson points out that "we can have it both ways" (quoted in Kirkpatrick 1990, 814). Gates challenges scholars to. Savery (1991) too allows for differences of opinion and the importance of teaching our students that there is no one answer (196). Contemporary African American literary critics, and specifically Henry Louis Gates, Jr., are moving away from the necessity of authenticating black literature through standard models. They are, according to Spurlin (1990), trying to develop "theories of criticism indigenous to black literature rather than simply mastering only the canons of criticism and imitating and applying these to African-American texts" (732).

Nommo and the Lyrical Attitude

The concept of "nommo" figures centrally in African American literature (see Oliver 1988). Forbidden to learn to read or write, the spoken word became the central medium of communication for the slave in America. And "nommo"—in African discourse "the generative and productive power of the spoken word"—established the ancestral oral traditions on American soil. Indeed, Asante argues that an awareness of "nommo" explains the black American experience of spoken interchanges between preachers and congregations and the "long tradition of masterful orators" like Marcus Garvey, Martin Luther King, Jr., and Jesse Jackson (quoted in Coughlin 1987).

As part of this tradition of oral discourse, African American speakers often use "indirection" to arouse curiosity, suspense, or emotion; sometimes it is used to subvert authority. Building "deductively," the orator skillfully "stalks the issues," speaking circuitously, slowly leading up to the statements. Unlike Eurocentric discourse, which values directness and linear argument, the African American tradition values the use of indirection as a test of rhetorical talent.

The structural emphasis on voice, lyrical quality, and indirection leads to an African American approach to language most consistent with narration. Public orators and preachers often employ narrative devices in their speeches to elicit call-response patterns, "talkbacks," and affirmative hand claps. Examples from the oratories of King, Garvey, Jackson, and the like, as well as from characters drawn from the literary works of Baldwin, Wright, and Jones, demonstrate these characteristics. Asante (1987) uses James Weldon Johnson's "The Creation" to illustrate these devices.

In fact, narrative sequencing offers teachers an excellent method for making connections from text to audience, for linking a lecture or a talk or a work of literature to the lives of students. Those of us who believe that we can link up great literary works with our students' prior knowledge can easily capitalize on this technique. In his discussion of the black folk sermon, Cook (1985) suggests a number of good characters to use for this exercise, such as Ellison's Barbee and the protagonist in *Invisible Man*, those from several Baldwin novels, even the Reverend Shegog of *The Sound and the Fury*. Cook writes that "even though he could not rid himself of certain received racial stereotypes," William Faulkner did recognize the black folk sermon "as a distinct and powerfully moving art form" (264).

Oral traditions manifest themselves in African American literature in other ways as well. The vernacular traditions of spirituals, blues, and labor songs have long been part of African American literature. The blues, perhaps the most widely known of these traditions, is described by Martin (1988) as "a uniquely black index for writing and thinking about what is written." Martin notes, "The blues are 'encoded' with messages of Afro-American culture: the sadness, the happiness, how to survive" (378).

Signifyin(g)

In *The Signifying Monkey: A Theory of Afro-American Literary Criticism* (1988), Henry Louis Gates, Jr., introduced a provocative and exciting new trope for literary critics to contemplate: Signifyin(g). Operative in the oral traditions of African American myth and folklore, in slave narratives, in the novels and poems of the Harlem Renaissance, and through to contemporary literature, Signification is, according to Spurlin (1990), a "formal repetition always repeat(ing) with a difference, a black difference that manifests itself in specific language use"; it is "two-tiered or double-voiced and serves as a trope for African American discourse in a relation of difference to English or Western signification"; it is a "talking back and forth between texts" (733). Gates (1988) demarcates African American Signification from other linguistic signification by an alternative spelling: "Signifyin(g)" or "Signification," both with a capital "S" to distinguish it as different.

Once we begin to look for Signifyin(g), we find a number of relationships between texts in the African American tradition. For example, Ellison's title *Invisible Man* is a response to Wright's *Black Boy* and *Native Son*. Savery (1991) notes:

> Hurston revises both specific passages and narrative strategies from Frederick Douglass, W. E. B. Du Bois, and Jean Toomer. Likewise, Ralph Ellison signifies on Richard Wright. Ishmael Reed signifies on Ellison, Wright, and Baldwin. Toni Morrison signifies

on Ellison; and Morrison and Alice Walker signify on Hurston. (191)

Gates's chapter in *The Signifying Monkey* on Ishmael Reed provides a complicated and fascinating treatment of Signifyin(g) in *Mumbo Jumbo*, Reed's dazzling postmodern treatment of the Black Arts Movement, the Harlem Renaissance, and everything else that has happened in art, history, and civilization for the last two thousand years. I used *Mumbo Jumbo* in my class, and students were amazed by the amount of material that could be put into one book. Reed's work is yet another challenging example of Gates's theory of Signification.

The Pathos of Being Black and American and Other Themes

Commenting on African American literature, Martin (1988) points out the "situational emotive construct of the diction and lexicon choices," the "channeled use of emotion" that reflects the pathos, the horror, of being black and American (373). Indeed, developing an awareness of the black aesthetic requires a sensitivity to the cultural character, the rhetoric, the haunting communication styles of "epic memory," and the racial ethos of the oral traditions that have survived through oppression (Asante 1987; Cobb 1985). Thus, if despair over oppression becomes a dominant theme in some of the literature, it should not be criticized as an aesthetic weakness because it contradicts the American ideal of optimism (Turner 1985).

Critics of African American literature talk extensively about uncovering masks of oppression and secrecy. Teachers must remember the frame of reference for the artist: Africans were brought to this country as slaves. They were persecuted, abused, and robbed of their birthrights. Asante remarks, "Our souls have been stolen" (quoted in Coughlin 1987, A7). This tradition is reflected in much of the literature. (Though certainly not all. For a great variety of styles, moods, genres, characterizations, and perspectives, see *Breaking Ice*, a collection of over three dozen African American contemporary writers edited by Terry McMillan.)

Indeed, much of the literature is tough. John Edgar Wideman's *Reuben* is the story of an old man with an orthopedic disability, a young prostitute fighting to keep her son, and a basketball recruiter who has murderous visions as a result of the hideous racism he has suffered. In *Beloved*, Morrison's Sethe commits infanticide rather than condemn her child to a life of slavery. Perhaps this is the kind of literature the separatist critics are talking about when they say that the parlor manners of Eurocentric critical models simply won't do when looking at African American literature.

Musa Moore-Foster (1991) identifies several other prominent African American literary themes, including the image of Africa and its influence in the United States, kinship and the strength of the black family in spite of poverty, hopelessness and duress, the double struggle of being female and black, male/female relationships, and the problems caused by the duality of bondage and democracy that exists even today. Looking more broadly, Moore-Foster writes:

> The African American literary tradition displays a heightened degree of introspection through which readers may perceive a kaleidoscope of Black Selfhood. . . . [These writers] . . . allow us to examine region, class, and gender along with race, all as expressions of African American identity. (144)

Mexican American/Chicano Literature

The mountain of materials I have collected on Mexican American literature intimidates me. Nonetheless, in this short space, I hope to provide a bit of historical background and to mention a few of the characteristics of Chicano literature. For much of the discussion, I call on the works of Carl and Paula Shirley (1988) and Charles Tatum (1990), beginning sources for high school and college classes reading Chicano literature. Bear in mind that this discussion is only a start, nothing more; I invite everyone to continue where I've left off.

Also, please note that I've decided to limit my discussion to Mexican American/Chicano literature. Latino literature comes from a much larger, more general population that includes Puerto Ricans, Cubans, Nicaraguans, and many, many others. Groups under the umbrella term *Latino/a* represent many different people with many different political, philosophic, and religious views. Garciagodoy (1991) writes:

> The problem of how to refer to us is complicated by the fact that we are, in fact, a very heterogeneous group. We are not all immigrants. We are not all *chicanas* and *chicanos*, nor *puertoriqueños* nor *cubanas*. We do not all speak Spanish. (81)

I have chosen to look only at Mexican American/Chicano literature in this section because Mexican Americans are one of the largest groups of Latino/a Americans and because their history in the United States, as Jay (1991) notes, predates that of European Americans:

> Our peoples and writers have been flowing back and forth over the space these boundaries now delineate since before the colonial adventure began. These borders make little sense when one is studying the histories, say, of Native- or Hispanic- or African-American literature. This crossing of boundaries . . . becomes the

paradoxical center of Mexican-American and Chicano literature, for example, which has been violating borders of nationality and of language since the 1500s. (268)

One more note: I have listened to and read about reasons for and against the use of the term *Chicano*. Some say it is very old. Most attach it to the political activity of the sixties. Some like it; some don't. Some find it "too closely linked with a political or social movement with which they do not identify" (Shirley and Shirley 1988, 7). Still, according to Shirley and Shirley (1988):

> It has gained in use and popularity over the last two decades to the point that for many it is a symbol of pride. It is a common term used by most Chicanos when they refer to themselves as a group, and it is the term most frequently used to designate their history, culture, and literature. Most authors and scholars and virtually all reference works employ the word. (7)

I have chosen to follow Shirley and Shirley's example in *Understanding Chicano Literature* and use the terms Chicano and Mexican American synonymously.

The History of Chicano Literature

Any introduction to Chicano literature should start with a history lesson, because many assume that this "genre" began in the sixties. Further, to suggest that "English language dominance defines American literature" is ethnocentric (Candelaria 1990, 1). In fact, the literature of Mexican American people goes back to the sixteenth century. Candelaria (1990) writes:

> U.S. ethnic art and literature are *not* recent, post-1960s phenomena resulting from the counterculture movements of that decade. Rather, they date back to the pre-American past of Native myth and legend, to the *belles lettres* of the Spanish Colonial period, to the *mestizo* balladry of New Spain, to the antebellum African American narratives and song, and on and on. The *roots* of ethnic-identified U.S. American literature are thus ancient in both "old" and "new" world terms. (1)

During the "Spanish Conquest" period, Spanish explorers fought for dominance and brought Mexican Indians under control. Though they caused much suffering, many explorers settled and married, creating "a new race of *mestizos*" (Tatum 1990, 4). Exploration continued until, by the late eighteenth century, Spanish ranchers were settled all over Texas, New Mexico, Arizona, and the southern half of California (to San Francisco).

In the nineteenth century, the *mestizos* fought bitterly and gained their independence from Spain. But during the westward expansion of the United States, "Anglos" poured into the Southwest looking for farmland, ranches, and gold. They were welcomed by some, seen as a threat by others. Eventually, U.S. government encouragement precipitated the Mexican American War, which, by the way, was denounced by Frederick Douglass and Abraham Lincoln, then a congressman from Illinois. No matter. With the Treaty of Guadalupe Hidalgo in 1848, the United States won control over the entire Southwest, as we know it today. Thus, by the middle of the nineteenth century, the United States had engulfed all of Mexico's northern territories (Tatum 1990).

During these years, from the sixteenth century to the mid-nineteenth century, literature flourished in the area now known in the United States as the Southwest. Indeed, Mexican American literature is as old as Spain's presence in the New World, though it has long "been overlooked by non-Chicano 'majority' readers and critics" (Shirley and Shirley 1988, 4). Garcia (1976) tells us that Mexican American folklore fused

> the best tradition of 16th century Spanish genres, antedating the literary genres of the Eastern American colonies by one hundred years . . . with the mysticism of the *indio* (Mexican Indian). Mexican-American folklore brought to American literature one of the first genuine forms of cultural pluralism, the indio-hispanic synthesis. (84)

Like many other folklore traditions, the songs, stories, and poems of the culture were passed orally from one generation to another by storytellers. And, like many other folklore traditions, Mexican American tales feature heroes and heroines who solve riddles and receive a reward, humorous views of human folly, animals that act and speak like people, lessons and morals, fiendish villains who play cruel jokes, magic and enchantment, and ghostly apparitions that frighten wayward people into mending their ways (Tatum 1990, 21).

Four popular folklore characters appear in much of the literature: *La Llorona* (the Weeping Woman), *La Bruja* (the Witch), *La Curandera* (the Healer), and *La Muerte* (the Angel of Death) (Garcia 1976). *La Llorona* was wronged by her husband, drowns her children in revenge, and dies in remorse. (Sound familiar? Wouldn't this folktale make for interesting comparison with *Medea?*) Her restless spirit takes many forms as she interacts with characters in stories. *La Curandera*, the Healer, also plays a prominent role, as evidenced in *Bless Me, Ultima*, Anaya's story of a young boy who learns to love the old woman who comes to help his family.

Because of "a strong oral and written tradition," poetry has always been one of the most prolific genres in Chicano literature (Shirley and Shirley 1988, 11). The *corrido,* or folk ballad, is a running narrative depicting a hero or heroine involved in an adventure, sometimes a misadventure. Dating back to pre-Columbian times, *corridos* tell of "heroic deeds, catastrophes, wars, and everyday events" (Shirley and Shirley 1988, 12). One of the most famous *corridos* is the 1901 tale "The Corrido of Gregorio Cortez."

Most Chicano historians and writers consider the "acquisition" of the Southwest Territory by the United States a disaster for Mexican Americans. Although the Treaty of Guadalupe Hidalgo guaranteed Mexican peoples living in the conquered territory U.S. citizenship, the new "Mexican Americans" suffered greatly. Families that had lived on land for generations were cheated out of their property, and the new Mexican Americans were the victims of extreme racial prejudice (Tatum 1990; Shirley and Shirley 1988). Reaction to the violence and denial of the years following the "treaty" engendered political leaders who became "symbols of resistance against domination." This period also gave rise to cultural heroes about whom *corridos* were composed that remain popular even today.

After the acquisition, numerous Spanish language publications flourished all over the borderland, from Brownsville, Texas, to San Diego, California. Spanish language theaters were present in many midsized towns, though these theaters became "more English" through the thirties (Tatum 1990). Resistance to oppression produced heroic figures, and the struggles of the common people precipitated strikes to improve working conditions for Chicanos. And as reflected in much of the contemporary literature, they are still fighting today.

Contemporary Literature and the Chicano Renaissance

With the sixties came a renaissance in Mexican American literature. According to Shirley and Shirley (1988):

> In many ways, the poetry, novels, plays, short fiction, and other literary works written after 1965 represent a break with the works that preceded them. The chief source of this break lay in the Chicano movement's rejection of the efforts toward assimilation made by Mexican Americans after World War II through the early 1960s. (16)

From the sixties on, Chicano literature focused chiefly on social and political issues. Shirley and Shirley (1988) note:

> In the modern age . . . there are several characteristic themes and subjects expressed by Chicanos writing in all genres. Among these are the themes of social protest and exploitation, the migratory experience, self-exploration or definition (which includes the exploration of myths and legends), and life in the *barrio*. . . . There is also *La Raza*, which has a spiritual connotation that joins all Spanish-speaking peoples of the Americas. (8)

According to Tatum (1990), the harsh realities of prejudice and poverty, loneliness and alienation, best describe contemporary Chicano fiction. In addition, many authors "interweave this stark realism with satire, allegory, fantasy, and myth, creating many multifaceted and highly imaginative works" (287). Tatum compares the magical realism of Ron Arias's *The Road to Tamazunchale* to the writings of Colombian Gabriel García Márquez and Mexican Carlos Fuentes. Magical realism, a "blending of wild fantasy and stubborn reality" (Laskin 1989), is also central in Rudolfo Anaya's *Bless Me, Ultima.*

Shirley and Shirley (1988) describe Rolando Hinojosa-Smith as "the most prolific Chicano novelist." They note that "like many Chicano authors, Hinojosa-Smith presents contrasts and conflicts between Anglo and Chicano people, but he does so through irony, gentleness, and humor." His first novel, they say, is characterized by "fragmented time and space, shifting narration, and a phantasmagoria of characters" (111).

Movement Poetry

Cordelia Candelaria identifies a number of "polar opposites" that define the spirit of "Movement Poetry," the poetry of the sixties revolution: Raza nationalism versus universalism, Mexico and Aztlan versus the United States, equity and justice versus racism, tradition and communalism versus capitalism, holism and pre-Americanism versus the Euro-Western world view (quoted in Shirley and Shirley 1988, 17). The epic poem *Yo Soy Joaquin/I Am Joaquin*, attributed to Rodolfo "Corky" Gonzales, is a well-known example of the mood of Chicano movement poetry. Still, its authorship has recently been called into question by many of the "revolution poets." (See Ricardo Sanchez's parody "I Am Joking" and other related essays.)

Many regard Ricardo Sanchez as one of the strongest poetic voices of the Chicano movement. Sanchez, along with his longtime friend Abelardo "Lalo" Delgado, "cry out against a nation that rejects cultural and ethnic diversity" (Shirley and Shirley 1988, 20). Sanchez's corpus of work was recently archived at Stanford University and is currently the largest collection by a single Chicano poet in existence at a major institution.

Post-Movement Poetry

Although Sanchez insists there is no "post-movement" because the struggle continues, Shirley and Shirley (1988) describe the poetry of the mid-seventies as much less strident than that of earlier years. The poet Alurista, for instance, "draws upon the Amerindian heritage of the Aztec and Mayan world" (30) to represent the concerns of the past and the hope for change in the future. Bernice Zamora gives us a sense of the intertextual links between Anglo and Chicano voices.

Gary Soto, a popular contemporary Chicano poet and fiction writer, appeals to a variety of audiences. His work has won numerous awards and is appreciated by both young and old readers. Many of his themes revolve around young people. According to Shirley and Shirley (1988), Soto's work reflects "a Chicano consciousness of racial identity and the despair that can come from poverty and alienation" (49).

Language: Spanish, Spanglish, English

Introducing the "Hispanic American" section of *Braided Lives*, Juanita Garciagodoy (1991) invites readers "to discover what it means to speak a forbidden language . . . to feel the sense of loss . . . in which mono–lingualism became the rule" (83). Indeed, language seems to be a problem in this country. But I think we've got it backwards. For some reason, many North Americans do not see the value in speaking more than one language. I think it's because most of us don't know how.

But that's changing. In the summer of 1992, I attended a wonderful conference entitled "Crossing Borders: Chicano Realities." Participants were treated to readings from some of the most prominent poets and critics of the last three decades—writers such as "Lalo" Delgado, Felipe Ortega y Gasca, and Ricardo Sanchez—and a variety of other festivities as well, including some wonderfully prepared art exhibits, food, and dancing. I delighted in the facility with which many of the conference participants switched from English, which I understand, to "Spanglish," some of which I understand, to Spanish, almost none of which I understand.

I am envious of people who can speak more than one language and can move from one to the other with ease. Instead of purging our schools of these "foreign" languages, I think we should capitalize on the talent that so many of our students have. In 1989 I heard Samuel

Betances, a noted sociologist and proponent of multicultural education, speak on the issue of nonmainstream students and education. After describing his early childhood experience as a racially mixed English speaker in New York City, he told us of his move to Puerto Rico, where he spoke no English for several years. Upon his return to New York as a teenager, he was told by his teachers that he could no longer speak Spanish. "And there I was," he beamed in his captivating manner, "illiterate in two languages!"

Gloria Anzaldúa (1987) had the same experience. In "How to Tame a Wild Tongue," she says:

> I remember being caught speaking Spanish at recess. . . . That was good for three licks on the knuckles with a sharp ruler. I remember being sent to the corner of the classroom for "talking back" to the Anglo teacher when all I was trying to do was tell her how to pronounce my name. "If you want to be American, speak 'American.' If you don't like it, go back to Mexico where you belong."

Shirley and Shirley (1988), remarking on the "linguistic realism" of Chicano literature, explain that many Chicano writers mix all three languages in their work: English, Spanish, and caló, which mixes the grammar, structure, and vocabulary of each to form a hybrid language. This English/Spanish/caló, code-switching, Spanglish style sometimes confuses non-Spanish-speaking readers who don't want to bother to "figure it out." But such readers are missing out. Professors and teachers of literature must present this linguistic variety as an enrichment, not as a barrier to understanding.

A student of mine once brought up the language issue during a discussion of *Bless Me, Ultima*. She complained that she was not able to "understand it all." "How many others had trouble understanding what was going on?" I asked. Only one hand went up. A young man from Puerto Rico responded, "Too bad she doesn't understand Spanish. She missed all the swearing." Laughter all around.

Gender Issues

Although it is not my purpose here to explore the work of feminist writers specifically, I did note discussions about gender in the work of several scholars (see Candelaria 1990; Garciagodoy 1991; Gómez, Moraga, and Romo-Carmona 1983). And a number of women writers are addressing the issue of gender in their works. In "By Word of Mouth," Gómez, Moraga, and Romo-Carmona (1983) say, "We need *una literatura* that testifies to our lives, provides acknowledgment of who we are: an exiled people, a migrant people, *mujeres en lucha*" (vii). Gloria Anzaldúa

(1987) talks about her discovery of a female voice. Referring to the use of the word *nosotros* for a group that may include women, even for a group made up entirely of women, she notes, "We are robbed of our female being by the masculine plural. Language is a male discourse" (54). And Cordelia Candelaria (1990) talks about changes in society that will affect the lives of Chicano women.

Expanding the Limits of American Literature

In their investigations into Mexican American literature, Charles Tatum (1990) and Carl and Paula Shirley (1988) explore a vast wealth of materials from a number of different genres. They open the way for all of us to investigate this growing corpus of work. As Shirley and Shirley (1988) note:

> Mexican American literature has mushroomed over the last two decades. The sheer volume of high-quality writing . . . is forcing the limits of American literature to expand; as the vitality and excitement of Chicano literature are being increasingly felt, it is taking its rightful place in the field of American letters. (10)

Chinese American and Japanese American Literature

I heard Elaine Kim note several years ago that "much recent literature by Asian Americans deals with establishing identity, with 'fitting into' a country where your family has lived for generations." Indeed, Asian Americans are still often looked upon as foreigners in this country. They are thought to have a suspiciously dual heritage: an American one and an Asian one. Furthermore, according to many observers (Kim 1982; Chan, Chin, Inada, and Wong 1982), the American mainstream has used, confused, and manipulated the Asian image of Chinese and Japanese people throughout the history of their presence in the United States. The "good Asian" and "bad Asian" myths have haunted these groups from the beginning.

Recently, however, attempts have been made to "claim America" for Asian Americans too (Kim 1982, 173). Perhaps we can help by using Asian American literature, both historical nonfiction and fiction, to straighten out some of the misconceptions.

What follows is a brief sketch of some impressions I have gotten from my own reading and from a few of the prominent critics in the area of Asian American literature. Much of the information for this discussion comes from the work of noted critics Elaine Kim (1982), Jeffrey Chan, Frank Chin, Lawson Inada, and Shawn Wong (1974, 1982, 1991), and David Leiwei Li (1992).

One note: When we speak of "Asian Americans," we speak of many racial, ethnic, and cultural groups, recent immigrants and long-time residents, a multitude of literatures. I've thus confined this discussion to Chinese American and Japanese American literature. These two peoples have been in the United States for a long time, seven generations in the case of the Chinese and four generations in the case of the Japanese (Chan, Chin, Inada, and Wong 1982). In fact, their literary traditions are older than some of our European American classics. Only recently, however, have we begun to acknowledge the work of these artists.

Historical Development of the Literature

Jeffery Chan, Frank Chin, Lawson Inada, and Shawn Wong (1974) remind us that Chinese and Japanese immigrants were a literate people (like the Mexican Americans from the Southwest) from literate civilizations, whose "presses, theaters, opera houses, and artistic enterprises rose as quickly as their social and political institutions" (xv). Tracing the early literary traditions of Asian American writers, Chan and his colleagues (1991) describe a struggle for recognition despite exclusionary practices and conscious or unconscious manipulation by a mainstream public and publishers.

Japanese Americans in particular faced the virulent prejudice and internment camps that resulted from the Second World War. Much of the literature of this group was suppressed, emerging only decades later. Nonetheless, according to Chan and his co-authors (1982):

> Japanese America produced writers who came together to form literary-intellectual communities. As early as the twenties, Japanese American writers were rejecting the concept of the dual identity and assuring a Nisei [second generation] identity that was neither Japanese nor white European American. (214)

John Okada's *No-No Boy* (1957) was the first novel by a Japanese American (and the second book by a Nisei writer from Seattle; the first was Monica Sone's *Nisei Daughter*). Like many other nonmainstream works that do not fit the standard criteria of modern fiction, *No-No Boy* was considered a novel of social history rather than a piece of good literature. But as its critics suggest, it was so much more. In fact, it defined itself. According to Chan and colleagues (1982):

> There is no reference, no standard of measure, no criterion. So, by its own terms, Okada's novel invented Japanese-American fiction, full-blown, self-begotten, arrogantly inventing its own criteria. (215)

Many critics failed to appreciate Okada's style because they did not understand the Japanese American idiom. Again, Chan and his colleagues (1982) write:

> John Okada writes from an oral tradition he hears all the time, and talks his writing onto the page. . . . [His] work is new only because whites aren't literate in the Japanese-American experience, not because Okada has been up late nights inventing Japanese-American culture in his dark laboratory. (218)

Okada's hero rejects the dual identity foisted on Japanese Americans. The title is a double rejection: "no" to being Japanese, "no" to being American. His family has spent two years in an internment camp, and he thus refuses to fight for "his country." Because of this, he is rejected by everybody. In my classes, I discuss *No-No Boy* in conjunction with the theme of war and identity and use it alongside Crane's *The Red Badge of Courage*, Silko's *Ceremony*, and Williams's *Captain Blackman*.

Also worthy of note are the several Japanese American works that surfaced after the infamous internment days of American history. Mine Okubo's *Citizen 13660*, an autobiographical account of relocation and camp experience, was printed in 1946, during an extremely anti-Japanese period in our history. Toshio Mori's *Yokohama, California*, often compared to Sherwood Anderson's *Winesburg, Ohio*, was published in 1949. It was written in 1941, but such a work would have found no welcome among the American public at the time.

One final reference: Any discussion of the history of Japanese American literature should include the work of Hisaye Yamamoto, who wrote the only pre-war rural Japanese American literature available (Chan et al. 1991, 339).

Barriers to Inclusion

Critics point to a number of reasons for why many Chinese American and Japanese American works were not accepted by the American mainstream: they weren't easy to understand, they weren't of interest, they didn't "fit in" with popular stereotypes of the Asian in America. Or, perhaps they made the general readership uncomfortable by reminding it of the less-than-hospitable reception Asians have traditionally received in this country. Frank Chin has said that his play *The Chickencoop Chinaman* was difficult to get published because it was "too ethnic," and "the ethnicity of yellow writing embarrasses white publishers" (quoted in Kim 1982, 174).

Aside from the denial of the existence of credible Asian American literature until very recently, literature *about* Asians has done much to damage both the public image and the self-image of Asian Americans. In the beginning chapters of her book *Asian American Literature: An Introduction to the Writings and Their Social Context* (1982), Elaine Kim presents an informative account of the misperceptions and stereotypes that face Asians, from the "good" Chinaman, Charlie Chan, to the "bad" Chinaman, Fu Manchu, from the exotic seductress to the scheming dragon lady.

I heard Professor Kim speak a few years ago. She brought with her a series of videos to demonstrate the "whitening" of Asian women so that they would be acceptable to an American audience. She ended with a shot of the beautiful Eurasian in one of the Rambo movies (I get them mixed up), pointing out that it must have been difficult for Rambo to find a woman with such Caucasian features in the middle of the Vietnamese jungle.

To counter continued ignorance and misperception, Jeffrey Chan, Frank Chin, Lawson Inada, Shawn Wong, and others formed a group called the Combined Asian Resources Project, or CARP, a tough fish which in Japanese tradition symbolizes strength. CARP's mission is to collect and disseminate authentic Asian American literature and to observe the conflicts and struggles among Asian Americans regarding their art. Because of the group's efforts, the landmark publications *Aiiieeeee! An Anthology of Asian American Writers* (1974) and then *The Big Aiiieeeee! An Anthology of Chinese American and Japanese American Literature* (1991) are now on the market. Besides presenting a wide variety of literary works, the *Aiiieeeee!* editors provide excellent background for beginning readers. As a result of collections like these, the corpus of Asian American literature has gained much wider attention.

Popularity versus Authenticity

One of the nagging issues for some Asian American literary critics is the difference between what they view as authentic artistic work and pieces that have received commercial success because they have appealed to what the American mainstream expects to see as "Asian." In examining the works of Chinese American and Japanese American writers, then, we must be aware of the discrepancies between those who write for white audiences and those who, at least for some Asian American critics, write with integrity, not pandering to Anglo audiences and feeding their stereotypes.

A critical point for the *Aiiieeeee!* editors is whether or not Asian American writers abandon their own heritage to be accepted into the mainstream. Chin (1991) argues that they do not have to. He contends that Chinese and Japanese immigrants and their children have preserved the myths, folklore, and traditions of their heritage. The literary legacies of China and Japan were well known to those who emigrated to this country. Chin criticizes some of the more popular Asian American writers who have adapted their heritage to fit a Western mold, using, for example, the autobiographical model, which is a Western form. Instead, Chin believes that true Asian American writers have preserved the traditional forms. These classic tales were well understood by immigrants and their children:

> The Chinese people . . . have already set the canon, kept it, taught it, and used it. . . . No matter how dangerous it was to tell these stories, [they] made sure their children heard the three classics of the heroic tradition: The Romance of the Three Kingdoms, The Water Margin (Outlaws of the Marsh), Journey to the West (Monkey). . . . Likewise, the Issei—Japanese first-generation—[knew these classics] along with their own evolution of the forms of the heroic tradition, Momotaro (Peach Boy) and Chushingura (The Loyal Forty-Seven Ronin). (34)

The *Aiiieeeee!* editors identify Louis Chu's *Eat a Bowl of Tea* (1961) as the first Chinese American novel set in America. Retaining the traditional forms, Chu's novel is a version of the *Three Kingdoms* tale. I found this book to be fascinating because it reveals the effects of exclusion on Chinese American men who came to this country without their families. They performed various services, earned their wages, and dreamed of their return to China someday. In fact, to compensate for this empty life, fraternal societies were created in large cities like New York and San Francisco. According to Chan and his colleagues (1982), Chinese America was

> basically a bachelor society, replete with prostitutes and gambling, existing as a foreign enclave where the white world stands at an officially prescribed distance, where Chinatown and its inhabitants are tributaries to a faceless and apathetic authority. (212)

Still, for me, *Eat a Bowl of Tea* is basically the story of a father and son in New York's Chinatown, an arranged marriage, a young woman's dilemma, a disgracing of the family name, and a journey to a better life. I missed Chu's adaptation of the traditional *Three Kingdoms* and *Water Margin* tales of "exile, warlike loneliness, promises made and promises broken, marriage and betrayal, a hero running away from home to the original stronghold and to new promise and a new life" (Chin 1991, 50). As an uneducated Western reader, I did not understand the true significance of the story. I must read it again.

Chu's style is also worthy of note for the way in which it portrays exquisitely the Chinatown life of the time. According to Chan and his co-authors (1982):

> The manner and ritual of address and repartee is authentic Chinatown. Chu translates idioms from the Sze Yup dialect, and the effect of such expressions on his Chinese-American readers is delight and recognition. . . . He knows Chinatown people, their foibles and anxieties, and at once can capture their insularity as well as their humanity. (212).

In distinguishing between "the real and the fake," Chin and the *Aiiieeeee!* editors (1991) identify "real" Asian American literature by its use of Asian fairy tales and the Confucian heroic tradition as a source and by the ability of the writers to be understood on their own terms. Yet my colleagues Alex Kuo, Rory Ong, and Marian Schiachitano remind me that not all critics of Asian American literature agree with Chin and his associates. Recently taken up by a number of scholars (see Kim 1990; Kondo 1990; Lowe 1991), the question of "authenticity" remains a matter of debate.

Filiative and Affiliative Textualization

In tracing the dual movement of "filiative" and "affiliative" elements in the work of numerous Chinese American poets and novelists, Li (1992) builds a strong case for looking at the "gestures of family devotion" in Chinese American literature. "Filiative" elements involve a tribute to ancestors; "affiliative" elements involve efforts to build a community. Together, the two elements work to give Chinese Americans both historical anchorage and present legitimacy as an ethnic entity (198).

In his article, Li traces the filiative "adherence to descent" in the works of several poets. He notes, for example, Marilyn Chin's reference to "The Parent Node" in her poem "The End of a Beginning." Li asserts that this ancestral connection exists in the work of many other poets too, that it is "the sheaf of other Chinese American verse" (178). He cites, for example, Mei-mei Berssenbrugge's "Chronicle," Nellie Wong's "Dreams in Harrison Railroad Park," and Cathy Song's "Youngest Daughter."

To look at affiliated efforts to embrace a communal awareness of the past and the need for identification in the present, Li uses Laurence Yep's novel *Dragonwings.* Yep uses his understanding of his ancestral traditions (e.g., of the folk epic *Romance of the Three Kingdoms*) to connect early traditions to a fantasy world. Steeped in the traditions of Chinese mythology and with a flair for science fiction, Yep delights his young readers with a tale of mystery, fantasy, and fascination. (In much of his popular young adult literature, Yep also deals with the difficult problems of growing up, including the additional challenges faced by cross-cultural and Chinese American children in a white world.)

Li cites Shawn Wong's *Homebase* as another example of Chinese American literature "authenticating the ethnic self in significant traditions." In this novel of self-discovery, Rainsford, the main character, comes to see a centrally symbolic tree as his "homebase" and as the basis for, as he says, "the stories of four generations of my own life" (182–83).

Citing other examples, Li notes that Maxine Hong Kingston represents "a sibling product, a sister's voice and a daughter's song" in her novel *China Men*, which again exhibits the quest for filiative and affiliative wholeness. Li concludes his discussion with examples from the work of David Henry Hwang, Frank Chin, and Amy Tan. In each case, he illustrates the presence of devotion to family, community, and tradition.

Common Themes

The struggle for identity and manhood is prevalent in much of the writing of Asian Americans. This is a particularly troubling issue because it relates to stereotypic and racist beliefs about "the good Asian," the emasculated Asian. A number of books deal with father-son relationships, which, due to the history of Chinese American and Japanese American males and limited family life, has created problems. Chu's *Eat a Bowl of Tea*, for instance, portrays a strained relationship between father and son. The same is true in *No-No Boy*, where the main character sees his father as weak, as someone who has given up. In Shawn Wong's *Homebase*, another very good novel for young adults, the main character's father is dead. But that doesn't keep him from struggling with memories of him, his grandfather, and his great-grandfather in his search for identity. Less optimistic is Chin's *The Chickencoop Chinaman*, which portrays Chinatown in decay. In Chin's story, the characters must leave Chinatown to become men; in the dying, restrictive, unpleasant environment of Chinatown, their manhood is denied.

Some historical symbols remain as well. Chinese American writers continue to use trains and journeys to symbolize their often tragic railroad heritage, and Japanese American writers use recurring images of the desert as a reminder of the internment days, which have not been forgotten. Yet many Asian American writers have made a deliberate effort to make Asian American literature "more accessible" to mainstream readers (Kim 1982, 214). Further, much of the new literature is characterized by "new styles and fresh language as well as new combinations of genres and forms" (Kim 1982, 217). Milton Murayama's *All I Asking for Is My Body*, for example, uses four dialects to portray reality. Sansei (third generation) poet Ron Tanaka uses "simple Japanese words and phrases, especially as spoken by Issei personae . . . linguistically [mixing] the world of the American-born Japanese" (Kim 1982, 218).

Asian Americans have also continued their affinity with African American writers, "because the Asian American experience has been shaped in large part by poverty and discrimination" (Kim 1982, 237). In fact, African American presses were some of the first to recognize, acknowledge, and publish Asian American writers.

Contemporary Asian American writers have worked aggressively to overcome harmful stereotypes and assert their own identity. Maxine Hong Kingston believes that all Asian Americans must "recognize themselves as warriors instead of victims" (quoted in Kim 1982, 253). Janice Mirikitani says that "although she might be 'angry,' she is not bitter" (quoted in Kim 1982, 253). The *Aiiieeeee!* editors (1982) write:

> Asian-American writers are elegant or repulsive, angry and bitter, militantly antiwhite or not, not out of any sense of perversity or revenge but out of honesty. America's dishonesty—its white supremacy passed off as love and acceptance—has kept seven generations of Asian-American voices off the air, off the streets and praised us for being Asiatically no-show. A lot is lost forever. But from the few decades of writing we have recovered from seven generations, it is clear that we have a lot of elegant, angry, and bitter life to show. (204)

These themes, existing throughout the works of Asian American authors and poets, would be interesting ideas to bring to students. As Kim (1982) writes:

> Contemporary Asian American writers are in the process of challenging old myths and stereotypes by defining Asian American humanity as part of the composite identity of the American people, which like the Asian American identity, is still being shaped and defined. (279)

Native American Literature

I would like to quote my friend flo wiger's introductory remarks (1989) as she addressed an audience of Minnesota educators interested in working with Native American students:

> Before I begin, I want you to be very clear about who I am. I am a
> Lakota person. I have one voice. I do not speak for all the Lakota
> people much less for all Indian people. I will share with you my
> thoughts, my knowledge, and my ideas. But I do not represent
> "the Indian perspective" any more than I would expect any other
> Lakota to speak for me. In my culture, everyone has the right to
> think and speak as he or she sees fit.

Similarly, to attempt to monolithically define the literatures of Native
American peoples in a few pages would be as difficult and as unfair as
trying to describe all of European literature—perhaps even more so,
because we are talking about more than five hundred nations separately
and officially recognized by the United States government.

My intention in this section is thus more modest. First, I would
like to point out some of the misunderstandings we have of Native
American literature, a consequence of both the unreliable accounts we
have depended on for so long and a failure to take into account a world
view very different from our own. Then I will describe a few of the
elements of Native American literature that teachers might begin to use
in the classroom.

A History of Literature

Perhaps the most insulting premise that can be made about literature in
America is that it began with Columbus. We have already established
that the "New World" was inhabited tens of thousands of years before
the arrival of Europeans. Dreaming of his tribal ancestors, Black Elk, the
Lakota holy man, says that perhaps they were "older than men can ever
be—old like hills, like stars" (Lincoln 1982, 80). And "voluminous" traditional literature existed. According to Chapman (1975), "the bits and
pieces . . . that have been put in written form and published add up to
many thousands of volumes" (3). Lincoln (1982) notes:

> Each tribe . . . can be traditionally defined through a native lan-
> guage, an inherited place, and a set of traditions (speech, folk-
> lore, ceremony, and religion), a heritage passed from generation
> to generation in songs, legends, jokes, morality plays, healing ritu-
> als, event histories, social protocol, spiritual rites of passage, and
> vision journeys to the sacred world. (80)

Similarly, Diane Glancy (1991), who identifies Native Americans as
"those-who-were-here-when-the-others-came," writes:

> In the old days, literature was the oral tradition and the teepee-
> lining painted with exploits of the individual and the tribe. Even
> the name of the person, the clothing and marks of body-paint,
> told a story.

Thus, before Europeans ever arrived, the oral traditions of storytelling and ceremony were integral to the lives of Native American people (Stensland 1979, 3).

Yet this tradition of literature has long been ignored and misunderstood by Western observers. Wiget and Mulford (1990) note that because of the literature's dramatic nature, the written word really isn't sufficient to convey its correct meaning. Perhaps it is this element that has made Native American work so difficult for outsiders to understand.

Conversely, the Western concept of literature was altogether strange for the Native American. What value did something written have? Native Americans called the white man's writing "talking leaves." They saw it as magic, as a trick, as something not quite straightforward. It seemed to hold no religious, spiritual, or medicinal value. The suspicion seems warranted when we consider that the United States government broke 389 of the written treaties it made with the various Native American nations (Lincoln 1982, 84).

The Meaning of Tales

Carol Miller begins her article "Tellers in the Circle" (1989) with a quotation from Leslie Silko's *Ceremony:*

> I will tell you something about stories,
> (he said)
> They aren't just entertainment.
> Don't be fooled.
> They are all we have to fight off
> illness and death.

One basic difference between Native American literature and Western literature is purpose. That is, Native Americans do not typically compose literature for the sole purpose of self-expression or emotion. As Paula Gunn Allen (1975) writes, to do so would be "arrogant, presumptuous, and gratuitous. . . . The tribes seek, through song, ceremony, legend . . . to . . . share reality, to bring the isolated private self into harmony and balance" (113). Tales thus serve to transmit values, messages for good. Literature is ceremonial, created to bring about harmony through song, legend, stories, and myths. The language of stories is tied to all other elements of life. Lives are bound through oral traditions to the earth, to other living beings, to each other. Literature is part of the whole, part of the circle of life (Lincoln 1982).

The European American tradition typically separates literature into genres: poetry, short stories, novels, and so on. Native Americans, however, do not always make such distinctions. Many forms can exist in the same piece. The purpose and desired effect is more important than the mode. For instance, though it might appear to be a traditional novel, Silko's *Ceremony* actually incorporates many forms.

Using Western criteria to analyze and evaluate Native American literature, then, is incorrect and unfair. Recognition of Native American literature has suffered greatly as a result of this practice. According to Lincoln (1982), Native American literature has often been considered "barbaric, heathen, pagan" (85). To be accepted as "good" in the American mainstream, Native American writers have had to abandon their own forms and "imitate" European ones. The earlier writings of James Eastland, for instance, reflect this "adjustment," though his later writings show a return to and embracing of Native American traditions and styles.

The Word as Sacred Tool

Lincoln (1982) writes that in Native American literature:

> Words are penetrant as arrows; the craft, ceremony, power, and defense of the tribal family depend on them. A well-chosen word, like a well-made arrow, pierces to the heart. (93)

In fact, he goes on to say that, for Native Americans, "a thought is a spiritual act; a word has the magical power to actualize spirits" (100). So it is that N. Scott Momaday (1975), discussing his own spiritual interaction with words while writing *The Way to Rainy Mountain*, can write:

> Then it was that that ancient, one-eyed woman Ko-sahn stepped out of the language and stood before me on the page. I was amazed. Yet it seemed to me entirely appropriate that this should happen. (98)

In addressing the First Convocation of American Indian Scholars in 1970, Momaday described the significance of language and its relationship to the Native American:

> It seems to me that in a certain sense we are all made of words; that our most essential being consists in language. . . . In one of the discussions yesterday the question "What is an American Indian?" was raised. The answer of course is that an Indian is an idea which a given man has of himself. And it is a moral idea, for it accounts for the way in which he reacts to other men and to the world in general. And that idea, in order to be realized completely, has to be expressed. (Momaday 1975, 96–97)

For Native Americans, this expression took the form of an oral tradition, which, according to Momaday, is a "process by which the myths, legends, tales, and lore of a people are formulated, communicated, and preserved in language by word of mouth . . . a combination of art and reality, the realization of the imaginative experience." Later, when defining the relationship between humanity and language, Momaday says:

> Generally speaking, man has consummate being in language, and there only. The state of human being is an idea, an idea which man has of himself. Only when he is embodied in an idea, and the idea is realized in language, can man take possession of himself. (104)

World View

Major nineteenth-century writers like Emerson, Whitman, Melville, and Thoreau recognized the difference and importance of the Native American world view (Chapman 1975, 20–21). But the typical Western view of nature and culture is in opposition to Native American conceptions, wherein nature and culture are inseparable, even identical (Miller 1989, 4). As Paula Gunn Allen (1975) writes, the "basic assumptions about the universe and, therefore, the basic reality experienced by tribal peoples and westerners are not the same" (112). And this difference has led to misunderstanding.

Miller (1989) explains that the central representational image within Native American societies has been, and remains, the circle, "the sacred hoop." This image accounts for the Native American perception of life, time, nature, everything (12). Black Elk notes, for instance, that "everything does try to be round." Thus, in contrast to our linear Western existence, life for Native Americans is an integrated whole, a complete circle. Stensland (1979) writes, "Religion, food gathering, songs, poetry, ceremony—all are one. All Indians are poets and singers" (5).

Consider time. Miller (1989) explains, "Among Western peoples, for example, time is linear; for Native Americans, time is circular, without divisions, uninterruptedly continuous" (13). Thus, time in much of the literature of Native American peoples does not follow the linear development typical of many Western works. Momaday's *House Made of Dawn* is a good example. Students sometimes have trouble with certain sequences in the book and need some preparation for this difference. Indeed, I heard once Roberta Hill Whiteman speak on Native American literature, and she made a similar suggestion (Native American Women's Institute 1989).

Further, because Native Americans see everything as an integrated whole, the Native American, Lincoln (1982) writes, "assumes a place in creation that is dynamic, creative, and responsive, and he allows his brothers, the rocks, the trees, the corn, and the nonhuman animals . . . the same and even greater privilege" (114). There is no hierarchical chain of being, no Judeo-Christian sense of superiority over the rest of the animate and inanimate world.

Miller (1989) also attributes the traditional Native American culture's ability to avoid a patriarchal social system to this concept of the integrated circle (13). In many of the sacred stories of Native American peoples, female and male deities share equal and almost always complementary presence, function, and significance. In the Pueblo sacred story, for example, Thought Woman or Grandmother Spider personifies the Creator. In Ojibway myth, Gitchie Manito may personify the Great Mystery, but the Earth has a feminine identity and precedes man in being (13).

Finally, Native Americans draw no hard and fast distinction between the spirit world and the natural world. Lincoln (1982) says that the spirit world and the natural world often intermingle through dreams, "most intense in the traditional vision quest" (100). In this vein, the film *Black Robe* (1992) includes an interesting portrayal of dreams as actions. The hero in the film *Thunderheart* (1992), a contemporary murder mystery, also experiences a vision, a vision that his Oglala Sioux companion identifies for him. And Tayo, the main character of Silko's *Ceremony*, incorporates visions like these into his healing process.

The Trickster

The Trickster figure, who sometimes goes by the name "Imitator," is a popular figure in much of the tales and folklore that have come down through the generations. According to Lincoln (1982):

> Trickster teaches comically, by negative example, that this shifting world bears careful study, that the behavior of things is often other than it appears, that masking and duplicity remain basic to nature, and that all survive despite this trickery, perhaps even learning from it. (127)

The Native American Trickster, unlike the tricksters of the Western tradition, such as Odysseus, isn't necessarily a heroic character. Miller (1989) writes, "Coyote, Rabbit, and Nanabozho are as frequently comedic as heroic, as often foolish as doughty, for it is their foolishness that by contrast illuminates correct conduct" (13). According to Ballinger (1991–92), the difference between the European/American picaro and the Native American Trickster is that the Native American character is open to the "multiplicity" of life, unlike the European trickster, whose birthright or circumstances dictate his situation. The Native American Trickster "is on or beyond the margin because of his character alone." This fellow is "lascivious, gluttonous, arrogant, disobedient, greedy, cruel, reckless, lazy." Still, we recognize his traits in all of us. He is the "all person," and while we laugh at him, we laugh at ourselves too, because he represents us all (21–25).

Teaching Contemporary Native American Literature

Those of us who are just beginning to introduce Native American litera-ture into the mainstream of our curriculum must anticipate the responses we are likely to encounter from our students. Some will have difficulty looking beyond the literal meanings of characters and their actions. They may, for example, view Tayo, Silko's hero in *Ceremony*, or Momaday's Abel in *House Made of Dawn*, or even Welch's Jim Loney in *The Death of Jim Loney* as ne'er-do-wells without considering context at all. They might miss entirely the significance of the literature's healing powers, its cer-emonial characteristics, its reference points; they might misunderstand the problems of disenfranchisement, oppression, and a host of other stressful conditions under which Native Americans live. As Stensland (1979) tells us, the familiar themes of Native American literature reflect the tragic results of whites' betrayal and violence (3). Glancy (1991), for instance, tells us of "stories of resilience, defiance, power, vision, tough-ness, pain, loss, anger, sarcasm, a humiliation built on welfare, a humor built on irony" (14).

So what are we to do with literature that we fear students will misunderstand, literature that might inadvertently end up reinforcing negative stereotypes? Do we avoid teaching it? Do we submit to the "censorship of avoidance"? When introducing Native American litera-ture, my colleague Alex Kuo approaches these issues by foregrounding the literature with relevant themes. He characterizes Native Americans for his students as a population living under "house arrest," an apt metaphor when examining more carefully the conditions under which many are forced to live. He explains economic pressures, fetal alcohol syndrome, repatriation, sovereignty, conflicts between traditional and activist groups, rural and urban living, mixed bloods and their relation-ships, and more. Once students understand and appreciate the contexts from which the authors draw their stories, they are better able to learn from their reading and to appreciate the literature as art. Kuo cautions, however, against the easy temptation to read these stories and poems only within the constraints of these social and political issues; good lit-erature always stretches and blurs the boundaries.

Allen (1975) also warns educators to be careful of using "really sacred materials" in the classroom for study, since educators may not be prepared to teach them. Teaching ceremonial materials without the proper background and knowledge could cause resentment or confusion; teachers even risk using taboo or culturally inappropriate material (132).

There are many excellent writers from which to choose when we and our students are ready to tackle specific literature. Prominent among new writers is Louise Erdrich, whose *Love Medicine, Jacklight* (a collection of poetry), *Tracks,* and *The Beet Queen* have received wide attention and many awards. Erdrich's husband Michael Dorris is author of *Yellow Raft on Blue Water,* a book popular among young adult readers. The couple's *The Crown of Columbus* offers a fictional treatment of the search for the real Columbus story. Leslie Marmon Silko's *Ceremony,* a haunting novel about a returning serviceman coming to grips with his past, has won great popular acclaim. And the works of James Welch, N. Scott Momaday, Paula Gunn Allen, and many more have exploded over the last few decades into a huge corpus of work that offers exciting prospects for interested readers.

Miller (1989) describes Allen, Erdrich, and Silko as storytellers in the traditional sense. But, she adds, they have been able to translate oral traditions into talking leaves, preserving the healing powers and identity of Native American tribal life while telling new stories—realities of what was and what is. The healing power of storytelling is an important element in each of these contemporary women's works.

Momaday and Vizenor see their role as that of "tricksters," "word warriors," "arrowmakers" (where arrowmaking is synonymous with wordmaking). Silko, Allen, and Erdrich "have literally and figuratively assumed their roles as tellers of stories created, as in the old way, out of a primal bonding of memory and imagination" (Miller 1989, 6). From these two traditions and purposes, we get some of our finest contemporary writing.

The literatures that have been described in this chapter come from traditions very different from the Eurocentric one to which we have become so accustomed. As teachers of multicultural literature, we must recognize and appreciate the multitude of perspectives from which the literatures of our culture come. Though few of us can claim to be experts in any of these areas, we must at least try to learn, seeking the assistance of our friends and colleagues and encouraging others to join us. What I have attempted here is a beginning.

11 What the Canon Did Not Teach Us about Learning Styles

A lthough many of us have made great strides in expanding our awareness of diverse literature, the way we teach it often remains the same. The mismatch between how we teach and who we teach is an increasing problem in this country, particularly as changing demographics move us closer to the "majority minority" population that is predicted by the year 2000 (Henry 1990). The situation is exacerbated by the relative lack of nonmainstream teachers, and projections for the future predict almost no gains in recruiting people of color into the field (Zeichner 1992). The result is that mainstream teachers must continue to adapt a hitherto monocultural approach to accommodate a multicultural student body.

Current research suggests that perhaps monoethnic teaching and dropout rates are related (Bennett 1990) and that, as a result, we ought to increase our understanding and implementation of other methods of instruction. Becoming aware of other world views, implementing less culture-bound strategies, adapting our questioning techniques, encouraging cooperative and collaborative learning activities, and expanding reader-response programs to validate and empower students might help to stem the tide of ever-increasing high school and college attrition rates among students of color. Indeed, if we attempt to define literature from authentic points of view, then we must also look at the variety of ways in which people learn.

The following discussion adequately covers neither the broad area of learning styles nor the relationship between learning preference and cultural, ethnic, and racial diversity. For more complete discussions in these areas, teachers should examine the extensive work of James Anderson, Lisa Delpit, Signithia Fordham, and others in this field.

There Must Be Something to This Learning Style Thing

In *Marching to Different Drummers* (1985), Guild and Garger differentiate among learning styles. They begin by asking why some people balance their checkbooks down to the penny—like my sister Liane—while others do not bother to do it at all—like me. I thought I knew the answer: Liane, an accountant, knows how to do those things. I find such precision and order unappealing. Is Liane smarter than I am? Guild and Garger assure us that such "talents" are not indicative of one's intelligence. What they are indicative of is one's learning preference. The concept intrigued me enough to take David Kolb's "learning preference" assessment (1986) and apply Bernice McCarthy's 4MAT system (1980) to discover my own perceiving preferences and processing tendencies. I discovered that my learning preference is divergent: I ask *why* more often than *if, how,* or *what.* I am a diverger.

This made sense to me. As a result, I now value some of the habits that I had previously thought marked me as rather disorganized. I see now why I need to "take in" a lot of information, mull it over, observe others, go off in a corner, sleep, eat, generally "absorb reality," before coming forward with a plan, before sitting down and "pouring it all out" at the computer. I finally understand why I must keep little piles of papers and books around me while I work, even though it would take only moments to put them away. There is method to this madness.

But it is the "assimilator," says Kolb, who likes traditional classrooms. Wait a minute! So do I. I am also skillful at making linear outlines for term papers, which I used to require of my students because I found them so workable for my own writing (perhaps because my own teachers insisted on them). Kolb tells us that though individuals have a general learning preference, they have the ability to operate in other areas as well. Thus, while my preference is to "diverge," I can also "accommodate," "assimilate," and "converge" (Kolb's three other learning style categories).

There are other ways to identify learning styles. Some of us learn better visually (seeing); some auditorially (hearing); some kinesthetically (through activity, such as writing). I think that I use all of these modes. And because I am not sure how each of my students learns best, I try to give information using all three of these methods. I certainly do not want to leave anyone out.

The Impact of Culture on Learning Style

If learning styles vary from person to person, do they perhaps vary from culture to culture in any distinctive way? Research tells us that certain cultural factors do have an impact on learning preference. A study by K. M. Evenson Worthley (cited in Bennett 1990) identifies five major areas:

1. Socialization process—the more control over child rearing, the more "field dependent"

2. Sociocultural tightness—the more pressure for conformity, the more "field dependent"

3. Ecological adaptation—the more dependent on environment, the more highly developed perceptual skills (e.g., the Native Alaskan's sophisticated reliance on weather or the African American's adaptation in a hostile community)

4. Biological effect—nutrition and physical development

5. Language—emphasis on written (field independent) or oral (field dependent) language

Other studies have found that African American and Latino students tend to be field dependent, that they respond to others' feelings and opinions, welcome opportunities to ask questions seeking guidance and affirmation, and personalize activities. Mainstream students, on the other hand, tend to be field independent. That is, they tend to be more analytical, more focused on impersonal or abstract aspects of the environment, more task-oriented; they tend to work independently and to enjoy individual recognition (Dunn and Dunn, Bennett, Banks and Banks, Ramirez and Castaneda, and Gollnick and Chinn, cited in Whetten 1991, 17–19).

If students from different cultures tend to have different learning styles, then it stands to reason that teachers from different cultures tend to have different teaching styles as well. Bennett (1990) points out that learning styles and teaching styles are closely related, that we tend to teach using the same styles that we prefer to use when we learn. The problem with this is that our learning and teaching preferences are not always the same as those of our students, especially if those students are from nonmainstream groups. Indeed, since the majority of teachers are from the mainstream, teachers have tended toward a monoethnic teaching style that doesn't accommodate all learners.

As our schools become more diverse, we must become more knowledgeable about different options in instruction. If African American and Latino students tend to be more field dependent, then it behooves teachers of these students to offer appropriate learning strategies to accommodate them, strategies such as group work, noncompetitive opportunities for oral discourse, and so forth. Indeed, as Shirley Brice Heath comments in discussing the importance of training educators to use this wider repertoire of teaching strategies:

> One of our best hopes for increasing and enhancing the opportunity for children of subordinated cultures and languages is to have

more and more people in colleges who have the sensibility and the teaching experience necessary to understand minority children. They also must be people who are willing to take the relevant social science and linguistic and historical knowledge and bring that to bear on thinking about how institutions and policy work. (quoted in Goldberg 1992)

Conflicting World Views

Bennett (1990) describes the term *world view* as the way in which "a cultural group perceives people and events" (47–48). Individuals within groups develop similar styles of cognition—similar processes for perceiving, recognizing, conceiving, judging, and reasoning—and similar values, assumptions, ideas, beliefs, and modes of thought. Since the "world view" of this country's macroculture is primarily British and Western European, those who do not come from this cultural background often operate from a totally different frame of reference. And those in the majority misunderstand.

For example, in contrasting "the Navajo way" with the Western world view, Bennett (1990) finds fundamental differences between each view's conception of time, the future, patience, age and old age, family, wealth, and nature (49). And in comparing the Western world view with the African world view, Linda James Meyers claims that the difference is "at the heart of present cultural differences" between European American and African American culture:

> The Western world view is segmented; the African world view is holistic.... Western culture tends to compartmentalize reality and focus on the parts. The African cultural focus is on the whole, and the tendency is to integrate all perceived existence into the total reality.... Western culture assumes a reality that is materialist and limited to comprehension via the five senses.... African culture assumes a reality that is both material *and* spiritual viewed as one and the same. This view allows for a reality that goes beyond the comprehension of the five senses and is known in an extrasensory fashion. (quoted in Bennett 1986, 20)

The question for educators is this: How will these differences manifest themselves in the classroom?

The "culture" of the classroom presents a number of conflicts for nonmainstream students. In her booklet *Culturally Responsive Teaching*, Ana Maria Villegas (1991) explains that for mainstream students, school is an extension of the home and community culture. Yet for many minority children, the classroom culture often clashes with home and community expectations. According to Anderson (1988), mainstream children go through school and into their jobs in consonance with the learning patterns that are provided for them. They develop following a

> linear, self-reinforcing course. Never are they asked to be bicultural, bidialectic, or bicognitive. On the other hand, for children of color, biculturality is not a free choice, but a prerequisite for successful participation and eventual success. . . . They are castigated whenever they attempt to express and validate their indigenous cultural and cognitive styles. Under such conditions cognitive conflict becomes the norm rather than the exception.

This conflict manifests itself in unexpected behaviors, such as silence, lack of participation, and failure to be competitive, behaviors often misinterpreted by teachers to mean that nonmainstream students are less academically capable. A look at the lower tracks in most schools reveals the tremendous overrepresentation of students from culturally or linguistically nonmainstream backgrounds. And all of us who have taught in this system know about the self-fulfilling prophecy that is created by the system's lowered expectations for so-called "lower ability" students. We also know that once a student is put into a lower-level class, his or her chances of getting out are limited.

Language development is of primary concern here, because facility for language is where racial majority children excel. For them, school culture reinforces home and community culture. Villegas (1991) writes that, in contrast,

> minority children frequently experience discontinuity in the use of language at home and in school. They are often misunderstood when applying prior knowledge to classroom tasks. How can they use their own experience if their established ways of using language and making sense of the world are deemed unacceptable or prohibited in the classroom? (7)

Since language is a part of culture, taking someone's language away is a denial of that culture's validity. Unfortunately, this happens all the time. Author and poet Gloria Anzaldúa (1987) was punished for trying to tell her teacher the correct pronunciation of her name. Sociologist Samuel Betances (1989) suffered as a child for using Spanish, his primary language, in class. One Anishanabe woman was even paddled in elementary school because she was caught speaking her own language (Native American Women's Institute 1989).

We must understand that languaging patterns are different for different cultural, ethnic, and socioeconomic groups, even if they speak the dominant language. Shirley Brice Heath's work in Trackton with African American students revealed that the differences among European American family questioning and African American family questioning presented problems in the classroom for African American students. At home questions were "real" inquiries demanding answers unknown to the questioner, whereas in the classroom teachers asked rhetorical questions for which they already knew the answers. This seemed strange to the African American students (cited in Villegas 1991, 7–8).

In a similar study, Sarah Michaels looked at the very different narrative styles of black and white children in the first grade. The stories told by the black children were often "a series of implicitly associated anecdotes." The white children's stories were more topic-centered. Since the latter group's products were more closely related to the teacher's expectations, greater value was assigned to them by the teacher (cited in Villegas 1991, 8).

Ramirez and Price-Williams compared stories told by Mexican American and Anglo-American children. They found that the products of the Mexican American group "were lengthier, indicative of greater verbal productivity, and included more characters" than those of their Anglo-American counterparts. Yet the Mexican American children were criticized by their teachers for being too "flowery, too excessive" in their descriptions (cited in Anderson 1988, 4–9).

Trying to determine why Warm Springs Indian Reservation children were silent in class, Susan Phillips observed that these same children "were used to a high degree of self-determination, that they learned by watching adults, and that they were often taken care of by siblings whom they turned to for help." Rather than being "slow" or "shy," these children were uncomfortable with the classroom's method of learning (cited in Villegas 1991, 4).

Consider one final example. Up until very recently, most academic activities have been directed, competitive, individual. Testing and assessment have almost always been thought of as a singular event. Yet this puts many of our students at a disadvantage. Describing inner-city African American youth, Geneva Gay and Roger Abrahams define learning preferences that are almost the opposite of those of mainstream students. For the African Americans in the study, competition and individual excellence were valued in play, but cooperation was valued in work situations:

> Because so much of the transmission of knowledge and the customs of street culture take place within peer groups, the black student is prone to seek the aid and assistance of his classmates at least as frequently as he does the teacher's. What is nearly always interpreted by teachers as cheating, copying, or frivolous

socializing may in fact be the child's natural inclination to seek help from a peer. (quoted in Bennett 1990, 69).

Acute differences such as these are stinging reminders of the mismatch between the strategies we use to teach and the ways in which many of our students learn. Fortunately, the current emphasis on collaborative learning, whole language learning, reader response to literature, and other educational strategies will be a great advantage for many nonmainstream students—and all others whose learning styles have not been well accommodated in the past.

Warning: Avoid Stereotypes

While we need to know more about ethnic and racial minority learning style characteristics, we must also be careful when generalizing about groups of people. Consider the Chinese American whose family has resided in California for seven generations. Compare that student with the Cambodian refugee who has been in the United States only since last year. Or compare the Latina whose family came to New York from Puerto Rico fifty years ago with the Honduran recently granted asylum in this country.

We can make terrible mistakes if we group people together just because of race or ethnicity. One year I participated in a mentoring program where I was "assigned" a Laotian student. Since I was supposed to give advice and help him with his socialization, I contacted him and invited him for a visit. After my little speech about how I was "there for him," assuring him that he could discuss all of his troubles with me, he informed me that he was an honors student, had been in this country for several years, and wasn't sure what I wanted from him. Was I embarrassed! His name had been "kicked out" of the computer and given to me with no other preparation or thought to this placement.

Over the years, I've noticed that some strategies and materials work for some students; other techniques and materials work for other students. Like many teachers, I have come to understand and believe a variety of things about the classroom through observation—before I learned the theory behind my conclusions. In fact, teachers' observations over time are, for me anyway, some of the most valuable data we have regarding student success. We should use these perceptions to enhance the learning experiences of all of our students.

If we apply what we know about field sensitivity, learning styles, cultural considerations, the young and not-so-young learner, and motivation, then our observations make sense. Literature instructors can make more use of this information and apply it to the material they offer students. We can motivate students to read if they can identify with the characters or if they can vicariously relate the story to their experiences. Recall the young African American student who spoke to my class in Minnesota who hadn't read anything in school yet zipped through *The Autobiography of Malcolm X* and *Invisible Man.* Maya Angelou, Richard Wright, Gloria Anzaldúa, Haki R. Madhubuti, Henry Louis Gates, Jr.—all self-actualized through the beauty and closeness of literature they could identify with. I once had a student who "hated to read" but carried *Popular Mechanics* (absolutely impossible for me to understand) with him at all times. And what about the multitude of students who "hate poetry" while making millionaires out of numerous musical groups?

In her piece "I Know They Can Learn Because I've Taught Them," Hodges (1987) tells us that she taught "in every ghetto of New York City" for fourteen years. She describes her abandonment during that time of the "analytical, lecture-and-recitation" approach in favor of "global, tactual-kinesthetic experiences: high interest activities that seem real, require movement, and involved working with others." In a short time, she raised her students' low scores on New York proficiency exams dramatically. She notes:

> Millions of young people are "at risk" because . . . they need an education. It is simply not true that we don't know what to do about it. We do. We must teach them in accord with the way they learn. (3)

What Can We Do?

The most obvious strategy is for teachers to learn about their students and their communities and to apply this information to their classrooms and develop personal bonds. Further, we must have high expectations, provide a framework that includes culturally relevant elements in the classroom, expand our teaching strategies, include contributions by different groups in our curriculum, develop a collaborative environment in which cooperative grouping and peer tutoring takes place, facilitate interaction among individuals from different groups, develop a better means of assessment, and encourage parental involvement.

Since, as Zeichner (1992) points out, the teaching force will, in most instances, continue to be "white, Anglo, monolingual, and mostly female" for a long time, we had better improve our abilities to work toward intercultural communication in the classroom. Yet such improvement seems a low priority in teacher education reform. Methods of instruction privilege mainstream learning styles, and both student teaching programs and prospective teachers tend to avoid inner-city situations. Zeichner argues that if we were preparing "teachers for diversity, we would not have today such a massive reluctance by beginning teachers to work in urban schools and in other schools serving the poor and ethnic and linguistic minority students." In fact, though, less than five percent of the 45,000 or so education faculty in the United States have taught for even a year in the classrooms of one of our large urban school districts (Haberman 1987).

Applying Knowledge of Learning Styles to the Multiethnic Classroom: A Summary

Again, a caveat. There is so much to know. This overview only hits the surface. We need to keep abreast of all of the new research on student learning styles. For now, though, here's a quick, general description of what learning styles are, how they differ among groups, and how, in general, we should apply this knowledge to the classroom.

Learning style is the preferred—though not the only— manner in which a person approaches an educational experience or task (Bennett 1990, 142–57). One learning style is no better than another. The problem arises when teachers make no accommodations for the variety of learning styles among their students. Teachers should present all information in a variety of ways to accommodate all students. Too often, teachers teach in a way that privileges the students who have learning preferences similar to their own.

Since we have substantial evidence that nonmainstream children possess learning styles that differ from those of mainstream students, the teacher's presentation of information often inadvertently puts nonmainstream students at a disadvantage. African American children whose experiences are outside the mainstream, for example, might tend to process information differently, viewing things more in their entirety than in isolation. They might prefer intuitive reasoning to deductive or inductive reasoning; personal stimuli to nonsocial, objective stimuli; and approximate concepts of space, numbers, and time. They might rely on nonverbal as well as verbal communication.

African American students, as well as other nonmainstream students, tend to be field sensitive rather than field independent. This means that they like to work with and assist others and value other people's opinions. They tend to seek guidance and rewards from teachers. By contrast, field-independent learners prefer to work alone, to gain individual recognition, and to compete. They are task-oriented and inattentive to social environment, and they maintain more formal relationships with the teacher. Field-sensitive students do better when objectives and global aspects of the lesson are explained, when concepts are presented in a humanistic way, and when these concepts are relevant to their lives and experiences. To work most positively with students who are field sensitive, teachers need to express approval and warmth and confidence in the students' ability. They need to hold informal discussions, emphasize the global aspects of the lesson, and help students apply concepts to their personal experiences.

To accommodate the cultural mismatch, we do not have to imitate the learning styles of all groups. Instead, Courtney Cazden and Hugh Mehan suggest that we need a "mutual accommodation in which both teachers and students adjust their actions with regard to the common goal of academic success through cultural respect" (quoted in Villegas 1991, 7).

The Kamehameha Early Education Project (KEEP) in Hawaii is one example of how we can apply what we know to improve the quality of education for our students. Some of KEEP's Polynesian students were getting poor reading scores and were unresponsive in school. At home, however, "they were clearly adept learners." Researchers noticed that the older siblings were responsible for a great deal of the younger ones' learning. KEEP then modeled peer tutoring after what they witnessed in the homes and brought the "talk story," a Hawaiian tradition, into the classroom. These two changes substantially improved the reading scores of the students (Villegas 1991).

Villegas suggests we work to bring about more changes like the one mentioned in the KEEP program. She also calls for teachers to be aware of and respect cultural differences, to investigate the resources available to us in our communities, to use cultural knowledge to meet instructional needs, and to be aware of the misperceptions that cultural misunderstanding can cause.

Earlier in this book I suggested that some of the great minds in our culture are going to waste because students are not getting enough food, are languishing in classrooms where nothing is going on, or are afraid of their school environment. In addition, our knowledge of learning styles should tell us that many of our students are able to take less advantage of the education they do receive because they are never given a chance to learn in the way they most prefer. If we can become more sensitive to the variety of learning styles our students bring to the classroom, we *can* make a difference.

III Teaching Strategies for Multicultural Literature

12 Approaches to Teaching Multicultural Literature

While reading a selection from Living Tapestries: Folk Tales of the Hmong, *I looked up to see a twenty-eight-year-old Hmong woman with tears streaming down her face. I thought I had insulted her by reading this tale aloud. After class she came to my office to thank me. "No one has ever read literature from my people in any of my classes," she told me. This is a perfect example of why we need multicultural literature in the classroom.*

Chris Gordon, St. Cloud State University

There are no set rules for teaching literature. Instructional approaches depend on a number of variables: student needs, teacher background, available material, curricular requirements, community influence, class size, time of day, and many other factors. Most teachers have a fairly comfortable repertoire based on what has worked for them in the past. In fact, much of what we teach is dictated by what we already know and what we are pretty sure will be acceptable. Let's be honest. No one welcomes a fight, whether it comes from students, colleagues, administrators, or parents. We typically self-censor our materials, sometimes consciously, sometimes unconsciously. Who can blame us? One "roasting" over "unacceptable literature" is enough to send any sensible teacher back to that twenty-year-old anthology.

On the other hand, if we continue to take the safe road, we'll never get past the "white men and Emily" syndrome that we've been suffering from all these years. Those of us who have been around a long time must lead the way, and we must give our support to teachers new in the field.

Recently, my teaching methods class read and discussed Cormier's *The Chocolate War.* Though the students were moved by it, many said they would be hesitant to teach it for fear that their communities would disapprove. They were right to have misgivings. But what I found disturbing was the advice that many of my students received during their field experiences from teachers who definitely said that though they liked the book, it would be too controversial to teach. If this is the attitude that educators have about teaching nontraditional literature, then literature written by culturally diverse authors doesn't stand much of a chance of even entering the classroom, let alone the canon.

Teachers give a variety of reasons for not wanting to teach multicultural literature:

> "I'd like to, but I hardly have time to teach what I already do."
>
> "I'd like to, but I'm required to teach other materials."
>
> "I'd like to, but I'm not familiar with any good titles."
>
> "I'd like to, but I'm teaching the advanced placement [or college-bound or regular or basic] group and it's not relevant."
>
> "I'd like to, but I have a heterogeneous group and could never teach those topics."

Nonsense to all of this! Still, I've used some of the same excuses myself. Many times I've been overwhelmed with papers to grade, reports to get out, and committees to meet. The thought of developing a new course or modifying an existing one made me dizzy.

In this chapter, I will offer my suggestions for teaching pluralistic literature and for curricular reform. I'll begin with suggestions for using a chronological approach to teach American literature, because that's as traditional as it gets. Then I'll discuss a variety of thematic treatments for literature and touch briefly on the genre approach, which still sees frequent use, particularly in introductory college literature courses.

What Should We Do When We Multiculturalize?

Those of us who are new at this must be careful not to end up with nothing more than what James Banks (1988) calls a "heroes and holidays" approach to becoming multicultural. That is, if we want to truly pluralize our curriculum, we must do more than march out our "ethnic display" for African American History Month or Viva la Raza Week. Not that we should do away with these additions to our calendars. Certainly a Native American literature course or a "gender-fair" museum exhibit are steps in the right direction. But we should not be satisfied with such a minimal effort. We need to work to integrate diverse literature into the mainstream of our curriculum.

In defining "levels of integration of ethnic content," Banks sees a "heroes and holidays," or "contributions," approach as only the first level of curricular reform. Adding a book or an ethnic unit to a course is limited, he claims, because the ethnic content is still viewed "from the perspectives of mainstream . . . writers" (2). In defining more advanced levels, the "transformation and decision-making and social action approaches," Banks suggests that

> the key curriculum issue . . . is not the addition of a long list . . .
> but the infusion of various perspectives, frames of reference, and
> content from various groups that will extend students' under-
> standings of the nature, development, and complexity of U.S.
> society. (2)

Thus, a teaching unit called "The Westward Movement" might become "The Invasion from the East" when a Lakota perspective is introduced. Or perhaps it becomes "Two Cultures Meet in the Americas" (Banks 1988, 1–2).

According to Ronald Takaki (1991), the multicultural course required at the University of California at Berkeley must consist of comparative minority studies. The class might, for example, study Latino, African American, Asian American, and European immigrants and investigate concepts of class and gender. Such a policy is far ahead of that of those institutions which simply require students to pick *a* "multicultural course" from a list of many. Students might choose a course in Native American studies *or* a course in African American studies *or* a course in women's studies. Thus, even though students are exposed to one group, all other groups are excluded. This "minority of choice" approach may be a start, but it's nowhere near perfect. We need to take note of the creative strategies for multicultural education that are being developed at a number of institutions nationwide.

A Chronological Approach to Teaching American Literature

This is the approach that I always took, starting with the colonial period and going forward. Yet up until the last decade or so, my curriculum included white male writers almost exclusively, with a few women thrown in here and there depending upon what was offered in the latest anthology. I started with the typical Puritan beginnings, with a nod to Anne Bradstreet and Sarah Kemble Knight, followed with the Revolutionary pieces, and moved up through the early-nineteenth-century fellows and the Transcendentalist gentlemen. I "did" Hawthorne, Melville, Longfellow, and Whitman, and, of course, Emily Dickinson, our nineteenth-century woman of choice. Marching along through my anthology and selected novels, the only women I included were Willa Cather, Edna St. Vincent Millay, Lillian Hellman, and Eudora Welty. I did include some diversity when I got to contemporary writers: Richard Wright, Ralph Ellison, James Baldwin, and Lorraine Hansberry. Still, nonmainstream did not "happen" in my class until the middle of the twentieth century. I knew vaguely that something was missing, but my access was limited and my commitment was weak.

Today, much more is already included; instructors shouldn't have to go any further than the text. I inventoried the table of contents of my *Heath Anthology of American Literature* (1990) to see what I could recognize from "the old days" and what was "new." It appears that there is a lot more to American literature than "the canon" my former students and I had the opportunity to read. For example, *The Heath Anthology's* "Colonial Period to 1700" collection includes Native American "origin and emergence stories," historical narratives, and trickster tales from the Winnebago, Pima, Zuñi, Navajo, and other nations. "The Literature of Discovery and Exploration" section begins with Columbus, de Vaca, Casteneda, and other writers of the Spanish period of dominance over the so-called "New World." Subsequent sections include "Poetry of the Revolution: A Collection of Poetry by Women" and "Emerging Voices of a National Literature: African, Native American, Spanish, Mexican." The "Early Nineteenth Century: 1800–1865" compiles "Tales from the Hispanic Southwest," while "Explorations of the 'American Self'" has selections from Frederick Douglass and Harriet Ann Jacobs. "Issues and Visions in Pre–Civil War America" includes the "Indian Voices" of William Apes, Chief Seattle, and others. And "The Emergence of American Poetic Voices" presents Native American oral poetry and slave poetry.

In addition to works from our long-accepted traditional canon, the second volume of *The Heath Anthology* features "The Development of Women's Narratives," "African American Folktales," and "Issues and Visions in Post–Civil War America." Authors include Standing Bear, Charles Eastman, and W. E. B. Du Bois. Also included are ghost dance songs and several famous *corridos*. "New Explorations of an 'American' Self" includes Booker T. Washington, Abraham Cahan, Sui-sin Far, and others. "The Modern Period: 1910–1945" features a large section on the Harlem Renaissance and a section of poetry by early Chinese immigrants called "Carved on the Walls." The "Contemporary Period" is filled with the literature of nonmainstream writers. Major figures like Tillie Olsen, Ralph Ellison, Saul Bellow, and James Baldwin are acknowledged, but so are newly acclaimed artists like Nicholasa Mohr, Maxine Hong Kingston, Leslie Silko, Louise Erdrich, Mari Evans, Sonia Sanchez, Amiri Baraka (LeRoi Jones), Audre Lorde, Ishmael Reed, Bernice Zamora, Janice Mirikitani, Pedro Pietri, Roberta Hill Whiteman, and a host of others.

The preceding list is an example of how one very excellent anthology successfully handles the issue of multiculturalism while maintaining the traditional chronological survey approach. There are, increasingly, many other such anthologies on the market. Today, most of the large and small book companies have begun to publish multiethnic authors in their mainstream anthologies. The Norton anthology *New Worlds of Literature*, for example, is another excellent collection that includes a variety of wonderful pieces that have only recently come to proper public attention. Although many secondary school districts cannot afford these expensive new anthologies, they can at least begin to consider them, and teachers can prepare to negotiate with each other, administrators, and school boards for these much needed volumes.

Thematic Approaches to Teaching Literature

In developing ideas for a thematic approach to literature, I created a "wish list" for an imaginary—though certainly feasible—multicultural U.S. literature course. Actually, it was fun. I encourage everyone to try it. I'm calling my course "Diversity and the American Dream: Literature of the United States." Arranged thematically, readings for this course might look like this:

Unit One—We the Americans: Beginnings

Authors with origins all over the world describe their homelands and trace their circumstances of migration. Excerpts from:

Alex Haley's *Roots*

Maureen Crane Wartski's *A Boat to Nowhere*

Gregory Orfalea's *Before the Flames*

Rose Cohen's *Out of the Shadow*

Gro Svendsen's *Frontier Mother*

Marie Hall Ets's *Rosa*

Ignatia Broker's *Night Flying Woman*

Ole Rolvaag's *Giants in the Earth*

E. L. Doctorow's *World's Fair*

Isaac Bashevis Singer's "Tanhum"

El Norte (film)

Unit Two—A Cross-Cultural Look at Who We Are

The fabric of American life as told by diverse voices. Excerpts from:

Willa Cather's *My Antonia*
Richard Wright's *Black Boy*
Amy Tan's *The Joy Luck Club*
Rudolfo Anaya's *Bless Me, Ultima*
Charles Eastman's *Indian Boyhood*
Yoshiko Uchida's *Journey to Topaz*

Unit Three—Tales and Folklore from Our Past

A gathering of tales and folklore from many traditions.

John Steptoe's *Mufaro's Beautiful Daughters*
Tales of La Llorona (many versions)
Romance of the Three Kingdoms
Ai-ling Louie's *Yeh Shen*
Joseph Jacobs's *Tattercoats*
Robert San Souci's *The Talking Eggs*
Charlotte Huck's *Princess Furball*

Unit Four—On the Margins

Perspectives of life outside the mainstream. Excerpts from:

Joy Kogawa's *Obasan*
Ralph Ellison's *Invisible Man*
Alan Dershowitz's *Chutzpah*
Helen Keller's *The Story of My Life*
Gus Lee's *China Boy*
Michael Olivas's "History Class"
Tran Thi Nga's "Letter to My Mother"
Brent Staples's "Night Walker"
Pat Mora's "1910"
Studs Terkel's "Stephen Cruz"
Janice Mirikitani's "We, the Dangerous"

A look at the problem of homelessness. Excerpts from:

Lorna Dee Cervantes's "Freeway 280"
Francisco Jimenez's "The Circuit"
Jonathan Kozol's *Rachel and Her Children*
John Steinbeck's *The Grapes of Wrath*
Mike Rose's *Lives on the Boundary*

Unit Five—Who Are Our Heroes?

Uncovering history through fiction and nonfiction, myths are dispelled and true heroes emerge. Excerpts from:

> Michael Dorris and Louise Erdrich's *The Crown of Columbus*
>
> Fred Ross's *Conquering Goliath: Caesar Chavez at the Beginning*
>
> *The Autobiography of Malcolm X*
>
> Helen Keller's *The Story of My Life*
>
> Other biographies and autobiographies of students' choice

Unit Six—What Is Family?

A look at diverse views of family relationships. Excerpts from:

> Zora Neale Hurston's *Their Eyes Were Watching God*
>
> Louise Erdrich's *The Beet Queen*
>
> Maya Angelou's *I Know Why the Caged Bird Sings*
>
> Amy Tan's *The Joy Luck Club*
>
> Chaim Potok's *The Chosen*
>
> Toni Cade Bambara's "My Man Bovanne"
>
> Mordecai Richler's "The Summer My Grandmother Was Supposed to Die"
>
> William Faulkner's "Barn Burning"
>
> Richard Goldstein's "The Gay Family"

Unit Seven—Growing Up in a Changing World

Excerpts from:

> Nancy Garden's *Annie on My Mind*
>
> Annie Dillard's *An American Childhood*
>
> Chaim Potok's *The Chosen*
>
> Marion Dane Bauer's *Tangled Butterfly*
>
> Katherine Mansfield's "Her First Ball"
>
> Waring Cuney's "No Images"
>
> Countee Cullen's "Incident"
>
> Gary Soto's "Jacket"
>
> Mourning Dove's *Cogewea*
>
> James Baldwin's "Sonny's Blues"
>
> Norma Klein's *Learning How to Fall*

Unit Eight—A Study of Values

Excerpts from:

Harper Lee's *To Kill a Mockingbird*

Elie Wiesel's *Night*

Rudolfo Anaya's *Bless Me, Ultima*

Marilyn Levy's *The Girl in the Plastic Cage*

Joni Eareckson's *Joni*

Frank Chin's *Donald Duk*

Sandra Cisneros's *The House on Mango Street*

Henry David Thoreau's "Civil Disobedience"

Mark Twain's *Huckleberry Finn*

Bharati Mukherjee's *Jasmine*

George Shannon's *Unlived Affections*

Walt Whitman's "I Hear America Singing"

Langston Hughes's "I, Too, Sing America" and "Let America Be America Again"

Angelina Grimke's "Appeal"

Martin Luther King, Jr.'s "Letter from Birmingham Jail"

Unit Nine—Gender, Race, and Power; or, All (Wo)men Are Created Equal and Some Are More Equal Than Others

Excerpts from:

Richard Wright's *Native Son*

James Welch's *The Death of Jim Loney*

Leslie Silko's *Ceremony*

Maxine Hong Kingston's *The Woman Warrior*

Zora Neale Hurston's *Their Eyes Were Watching God*

You don't have to envision an entire course to use diverse literature thematically, though. Many ideas for thematically pairing or grouping diverse literature with frequently used works have recently been discussed and implemented. The following suggestions come from a variety of public figures, personal colleagues, students, and friends:

Twain's *Huckleberry Finn* with *Our Nig; or, Sketches from the Life of a Free Black* by Harriet Wilson

Austin's *Pride and Prejudice* with Hurston's *Their Eyes Were Watching God*, with marriage as the theme

Ignatia Broker's *Night Flying Woman* with "Sand Creek Survivors" from Gerald Vizenor's *Earthdivers*

Annie Dillard's *An American Childhood* with Maxine Hong Kingston's *The Woman Warrior: Memoirs of a Girlhood among Ghosts*, the story of a Japanese Canadian whose family loses everything during the war (Bischoff 1989)

To portray relationships in Jewish American families, Chaim Potok's *The Chosen* with "The Summer My Grandmother Was Supposed to Die" by Mordecai Richler

Struggles for survival among the homeless using Steinbeck's *The Grapes of Wrath* together with Jonathan Kozol's *Rachel and Her Children*, Raymond Barrio's *The Plum Plum Pickers*, and *Out of the Rain*, an anthology of drawing, writing, and photographs by the homeless of San Francisco

To explore the theme of older adults, Dylan Thomas's "Do Not Go Gentle into That Good Night," Pat Mora's "1910," Richler's short story "The Summer My Grandmother Was Supposed to Die," and excerpts from Louise Erdrich's *Love Medicine*

To explore the theme of "belonging," Dickens's *Great Expectations* with Louise Erdrich's *The Beet Queen*, Shawn Wong's *Homebase*, Richard Rodriguez's *Hunger of Memory*, Richard Wright's *Black Boy*, Tran Thi Nga's "Letter to My Mother," Michael Dorris's "For the Indians, No Thanksgiving," Brent Staples's "Night Walker," Marcel Christine Lucero-Trujillo's "Roseville, Minn., U.S.A.," Lorna Dee Cervantes's "Heritage," and "We, the Dangerous" by Janice Mirikitani

For echoes of family expectations for adulthood and marriage, Hisaye Yamamoto's "Epithalamium" (college level), Amy Tan's *The Joy Luck Club*, *Guess Who's Coming to Dinner*, *Fiddler on the Roof*, *West Side Story*, and *Romeo and Juliet*

Professor Ronald Takaki (1991) suggests using Carlos Bulosan's *America Is in the Heart*, the story of a Filipino immigrant, with Fitzgerald's *The Great Gatsby* to study the immigrant experience for different peoples of the United States. Whereas Jay Gatsby attempts to Anglicize himself to rise in class and win Daisy, Bulosan's hero has no expectations for such mobility. Steinbeck's *East of Eden* could work, too, as would *Homebase*, by Shawn Wong, or *Chutzpah*, Alan Dershowitz's treatise on being Jewish in America.

Beach and Marshall (1991) suggest using the theme of the difficulty of growing up and defining one's identity as an ethnic minority using *Invisible Man*, *I Know Why the Caged Bird Sings*, *Ceremony*, *The Woman Warrior*, *No-No Boy*, *Down These Mean Streets*, and *Bless Me, Ultima*. After reading, they suggest that students "compare these protagonists' experiences . . . [as] they confront certain barriers to their development" (466).

Mark Tonyan, a former student now teaching in central Minnesota, combined *Dances with Wolves* and "POWOW" by Gogisgi/Carroll Arnett (in *The Remembered Earth*) with Thoreau's *Walden*. His students, European Americans, acknowledged that at first it was difficult for them to understand Native American culture. But after the material was presented, their attitudes changed. Tonyan explains:

> If you sat any of my students down to explain the culture of native peoples before it was spoiled by invading Europeans, they would reject your point of view outright. However, as we read issues in *Walden* and related them to *Dances with Wolves*, they became much more willing to grasp some of the ideas and understanding I was trying to bring out for them.

Another former student, Susan Henkemeyer, did a terrific unit entitled "Passages to Freedom: The Underground Railroad, the Ocean, and the River" to which we could add many more pieces. She divided her unit into three parts:

I. The Underground Railroad: The Black Experience

    A. *The Underground Railroad* by Charles Blockson

    B. *A Woman Called Moses* by Marcy Moran Heidish

    C. Videotape of King's "I Have a Dream" speech

    D. Selected poetry

        1. "Theme for English B" by Langston Hughes

        2. "Young Gal's Blues" by Langston Hughes

II. The Ocean: The Immigrant Experience

    A. Documentary video *The Boat People*

    B. *A Boat to Nowhere* by Maureen Crane Wartski

    C. "Neighbor Rosicky" by Willa Cather

III. The River: The Individual's Experience

    A. *The Adventures of Huckleberry Finn* by Mark Twain

    B. Poetry selections

        1. "The River" by Hart Crane

        2. "Two Rivers" by Ralph Waldo Emerson

        3. "The Negro Speaks of Rivers" by Langston Hughes

Other units might focus on the sixties or on the Vietnam War. I have received recently two volumes that contain a wealth of ideas and information for use in the classroom. Brooke Workman's *Teaching the Sixties* (1992) is really a lesson plan for secondary teachers. And for a great source of information, titles, and teaching suggestions, read Larry Johannessen's *Teaching the Literature of the Vietnam War* (1992).

The possibilities here are endless. In my African American literature class, a student who was majoring in music did a fantastic paper on the influence of African American literary and musical traditions, including that of "Signifyin(g)" jazz on the development of contemporary rap music.

For interesting historical information and a wealth of multiethnic literature, Ishmael Reed, Kathryn Trueblood, and Shawn Wong's *The Before Columbus Foundation Fiction Anthology* (1992) is a must-buy. So is their poetry anthology. Both include a variety of great literary pieces as well as commentary. *Understanding Others: Cultural and Cross-Cultural Studies and the Teaching of Literature* (1992) is an excellent collection of literary analyses of multiethnic work. And *MELUS*, the journal of the Society for the Study of the Multi-Ethnic Literature of the United States, is yet another wonderful source of information. The 1991–1992 editions featured topics such as "Native American Fiction: Myth and Criticism," "Before the Centennial," and "Varieties of Ethnic Criticism." The editors are also pleased to provide an index of all of their past publications for first-time subscribers.

The Genre Approach

Drama

The traditions of theater in Chicano, Chinese, Japanese, and Native American culture are older than most of the dramatic literature we consider American. Moreover, there are so many multicultural plays already in the new anthologies that we can no longer excuse ourselves for not using them in our classes. I'll mention a few that have been used successfully by me or someone I know:

> *A Soldier's Play* by Charles Fuller was very popular with my classes. It's a psychological story about the effects of racism on African Americans in the military.
>
> Hansberry's *A Raisin in the Sun* is an old favorite and has been used successfully by many of us.
>
> Wakako Yamauchi's *And the Soul Shall Dance* is a very interesting look at the mystery of Japanese immigrants from the perspective of an American-born Japanese girl. Hiroshi Kashiwagi's *Laughter and False Teeth* portrays with bittersweet humor the betrayal of

the internment camp. Both of these short plays are in *The Big Aiiieeeee!* collection.

Tatum's anthology contains Luis Valdez's *The Buck Private*, a play about a young man who proudly goes to war, never to return.

The Berkeley Repertory Theatre recently put on Zora Neale Hurston's play *Spunk: Three Tales* to a very enthusiastic audience.

African American women playwrights, beginning with one-act plays like Alice Dunbar-Nelson's *Mine Eyes Have Seen* and *They That Sit in Darkness* by Mary Burrill, have a long history of success on the stage.

Larry Johannessen lists a number of titles in his book about the Vietnam War, *Illumination Rounds*, including Oliver Stone's *Platoon* and *Salvador*, Tom Cole's *Medal of Honor Rag*, and the collection *Coming to Terms: American Plays and the Vietnam War*, which includes Stephen Metcalfe's *Strange Snow*.

Nonfiction

Any number of titles and topics are possible here. Most of the readers we now use for college composition courses contain a number of essays by nonmainstream authors. I would particularly recommend Colombo, Cullen, and Lisle's *Rereading America* (1989), which I have used for several courses.

Donna Mahar, a former student and now an outstanding middle school teacher in Camillus, New York, notes that students enjoy reading about real persons with whom they can make a personal connection. In this regard, she recommends essays by James Baldwin, Maya Angelou's *I Know Why the Caged Bird Sings*, and Eloise Greenfield's "Langston Terrace," "Mama Sewing," "Banker Maggie Walker," and "Autobiography of Geronimo." Nonfiction accounts of African American cowboys turned into a great term paper for another student of mine. Researching the Japanese internment period and eventual reparation litigation would also make for fascinating and illuminating study.

Speeches make an excellent area of study as well. I have used King's "I Have a Dream" speech as an example of persuasive discourse in the classical tradition. Other sources include speeches by Barbara Jordan, Caesar Chavez, Chief Joseph, and Chief Seattle.

Short Stories

This genre is perhaps at once the most popular and the most attainable. Since many diverse authors are already in the anthologies, teachers can rediscover and use them without having to spend a lot of money ordering new material. High schools often have a variety of short story collections that can be used easily and without much expense. If not, librarians are usually quite willing to develop a list of suggestions for students searching for literary pieces from multiethnic sources.

With her middle school class, Donna Mahar uses short stories like "The Circuit" by Francisco Jimenez, "Zlateh the Goat" and "Shrewd Toadie and Lizer the Miser" by Isaac Bashevis Singer, "Home" by Gwendolyn Brooks, and "Those Saturday Afternoons" by James Baldwin. She too points out the wealth of choices available in this genre.

Poetry

The work of dozens of nonmainstream poets has been collected into numerous anthologies. One of the poems that I have seen my own students use successfully is "1910" from *Chants* by Pat Mora. Langston Hughes's "I, Too, Sing America" makes for interesting comparison with Whitman's "I Hear America Singing"; I think I'd add Claude McKay's "America" as well.

A former student, Mary Atkinson, introduces a unit on African American poetry by beginning with Run DMC's "It's Tricky," "You Be Illin,'" and "Proud To Be Black," along with DJ Jazzy Jeff and the Fresh Prince's "Parents Just Don't Understand" (I love this one; my kids used to play and sing it for me all the time). She continues with Hughes's "I, Too, Sing America," Nikki Giovanni's "Housecleaning," and Etheridge Knight's "For Black Poets Who Think of Suicide." To bring in Malcolm X, she includes Ted Joans's "My Ace of Spades," Larry Neal's "Malcolm X: An Autobiography," "Malcolm" by Sonia Sanchez, and "A Poem for Black Hearts" by Amiri Baraka (LeRoi Jones). To study the contributions of Martin Luther King, Jr., students read "Martin Luther King, Jr." by Gwendolyn Brooks, Haki Madhubuti's (Don L. Lee) "Assassination," and Nikki Giovanni's "The Funeral of Martin Luther King, Jr." She adds Jean Toomer's "Blood-Burning Moon," Baldwin's essay "If Black English Isn't a Language, Then Tell Me, What Is?" and Alice Walker's "Beauty: When the Other Dancer Is the Self."

Young Adult Literature

An excellent example of work that incorporates "classic," young adult, and multiethnic elements is the work of Virginia Hamilton. In a very interesting discussion, Moss (1992) shows the influence of the gothic conventions of Faulkner and Edgar Allen Poe on Hamilton's work. Seeing similarities of style between the "gothic and grotesque effects of these writers," Moss portrays Hamilton's *The House of Dies Drear* and *The Mystery of Drear House* as extensions of this earlier literary form. A similar approach to other popular contemporary writers would make a great unit of study for junior and senior high school students.

Shannon (1988), concerned about children "caught between two mirrors—two ways of seeing—each presenting a different image of the self" (14), recommends several interesting cross-cultural, multiethnic, young adult novels, including *Arilla Sun Down*, a "biomythography" of belonging by Virginia Hamilton; Laurence Yep's *Child of the Owl* and *Sea Glass*, both stories about Chinese-Anglo children who struggle with their identity; and *Annie on My Mind* by Nancy Garden, the story of two girls who discover their attraction for each other. Shannon further suggests Richter's *The Light in the Forest*, a story about a white boy raised by Lenni Lenape Indians, and its sequel, *A Country of Strangers*; Clark's *Santiago*, the story of a Native American child raised as a Spanish don; Screen's *With My Face to the Rising Sun*, "a psychological rite of passage"; Jean Craighead George's *Julie of the Wolves*; poems by Langston Hughes, including "Cross"; and Adoff's *All the Colors of the Race*. Greene (1988) adds to this theme with Marshall's *Brown Girl, Brownstones*, a story about a girl whose family has immigrated from Barbados, and Buchi Emecheta's story of a young Nigerian woman who moves to London, *Second-Class Citizen*.

Finally, I asked Donna Mahar to share her thoughts on teaching multicultural literature in a middle school in an almost totally European American suburb in New York. She responded:

> One thing I would like to share with other teachers is the power that students gain through a multicultural approach. They really respect the strength of words and realize that it is important to take risks. I credit multicultural readings with the great success my students have had in publishing their work in *Stone Soup*, the local paper, *Merlyn's Pen*, and *Creative Kids*. By having strong, diverse models to work from, their writing, and, in turn, their self-esteem, flourished.

Teaching Strategies: Whole Class, Small Groups, Pairs, Individuals

Laura, a student in my special topics seminar, once referred to the nineties as "the era of small groups." Indeed, we've learned a lot about the importance of grouping, nondirected teaching, and "hands-on" instruction; we've embraced this strategy and made it ours. But I don't buy this completely, and neither does Laura. Students may tire of the lecture approach, but they also get tired of anything that is overdone. And I don't blame them.

I just returned from a three-day workshop in an area only tangentially related to my field. (I will not be more specific because I don't want to hurt the feelings of those who directed the project.) The trainers had great energy, were very well organized, and were firmly committed to their work. But for three days participants were placed in one group after another. Each group was slightly different, and I appreciate the modeling the facilitators tried to provide, but enough is enough. Brainstorming in areas where one knows very little becomes frustrating after a while. Sometimes I just want to listen to someone who knows more than I do.

Don't get me wrong. I strongly recommend grouping for a number of reasons. I like workshops, individual projects, jigsaw groups (where everyone in the group becomes an expert in a certain area and then teaches everyone else), partners, and so forth. And after speaking so highly of group interaction for field-dependent students, I certainly am not condemning this strategy now. It's just that I think we can overdo anything. I try in my classes to model what I think all teachers at all levels should do: vary activities. We should never do the same thing all the time.

Thus, I recommend whole class, small group, pairs, and individual assignments; I recommend them all. The literature we have been talking about can be used in many different ways. Sometimes we want to do a close reading of a particular piece. For example, I believe Richard Wright's *Native Son* needs thoughtful discussion. I might start out in groups providing questions for students to consider. But then I'd have the class reconvene so that we could all talk about some of the important issues. (Beginning teachers who are not always successful with a whole class discussion should not be discouraged. This teaching strategy, in my opinion, is the most difficult of all.) When I taught Ishmael Reed's *Mumbo Jumbo,* a fabulous postmodern novel, my class went through a very literal interpretation of what, for most students, was so abstract that they could not understand it without a great deal of guidance. And that's okay; it's my job to observe and accommodate the needs of my students.

Many times we weave together several pieces that different students have been reading under one theme. That works well too. Sometimes students lead discussions. Other times they work in groups and talk about common readings. At the same time they might do a few readings on their own because they are interested in other titles. They then tell the rest of the class what they've done. I also lecture. Sometimes I think that I know more than my students and have more background information, which I then share with them while they take notes. I think that's okay too.

I have taught a lot of the literature that I have mentioned in this book, both in high school and in college, to "honors" students and to "average" students and to some who might be considered "below average." Most of the literature I've talked about can be taught in a number of ways. It's up to the instructor to decide the focus of the class, the amount of material that needs to be covered, and all of the other curricular variables that figure into our plans.

Idea the Last

I'll end this chapter by creating another multicultural American literature course that I would love to teach. The theme I would choose is "war." Not that I like war. On the contrary, I find the topic very disturbing, especially since over the years I've had a number of students go off to war and never come back. But I think this topic fascinates young people, and it's pretty common in the literature.

Take, for instance, Stephen Crane's *The Red Badge of Courage*, a novel typically read in American literature courses. How can this story be "multiculturalized"? Along with *Red Badge*, we might offer Dalton Trumbo's *Johnny Got His Gun*, a horrifying story about a young soldier who wakes up in a hospital and can neither see, nor hear, nor taste, because his face has been shot off. He has no appendages. About the only thing he has left is his mind, which is perfectly intact. I both hate and love this story and have used it like Listerine. I do think that it gives more "hawkish" students something to think about.

But these novels are still pretty traditional. So let's add Leslie Silko's masterfully crafted *Ceremony*, a story about a young mixed-blood Laguna Indian who goes to war, fights for his country, and returns only to be mistreated by everyone. His sickness is in his soul, and his story is a quest—through ceremony—for healing. This book gives an interesting slant to the typical courage theme.

Next I would add John Okada's *No-No Boy*, which tells the story of a Japanese American who, after his family spends two years in an internment camp, refuses to join the army. He is then rejected by everyone, raising questions not usually addressed. To show the terrible effects the war had on Japanese Canadians, I could use Joy Kogawa's *Obasan*. I would also add the film *Glory*, a wonderful movie about a courageous African American regiment that fought in the Civil War and earned the dubious privilege of becoming cannon fodder.

To address Vietnam, I'd use *Born on the Fourth of July*, Ron Kovic's autobiographical description of a young soldier who goes off to fight for his country and returns to suffer indignities as a paraplegic (also an Oliver Stone film). I'd add Bobbie Ann Mason's *In Country*, a story about a young girl trying to establish an identity based on her father's tragic death in Vietnam. Students could also share readings from Wallace Terry's *Bloods: An Oral History of the Vietnam War*, accounts of war as told by African American soldiers, and Kathryn Marshall's *In the Combat Zone: An Oral History of American Women in Vietnam, 1966–1975*. I would also present John Williams's *Captain Blackman*, a fascinating story of a military history buff wounded in Vietnam. The hero's hallucinations take him back to the Revolutionary War, proceeding forward with each war the United States has been involved in and focusing on the treatment of black soldiers throughout.

The more I think about this proposed course, the better I like it. I know it would be great! And if I've talked anybody into teaching it, I hope you'll let me know how it goes. I think students in high school and college would find this literature informative, exciting, and very worthwhile reading.

There are a number of ways to structure a literature class. Even when professors and teachers feel they must cover works that have long been in the curriculum, many ways exist to incorporate multicultural works into the mainstream. Quite simply, multicultural literature can be implemented into any curriculum if we are committed to expanding our programs and to becoming truly multicultural.

13 Composition Pedagogy in a Multicultural Setting

For students, writing is empowerment. In most disciplines, the ability to express oneself well through writing almost guarantees academic success. But more than that, good composing skills enhance learning and critical thinking, encourage both free and focused data gathering, establish rhetorical environments in which students create their own ideas, and develop within students the confidence that will increase their chances for success, not only in school, but in the workplace as well. According to Haki Madhubuti (1985), "The language is the tool, the weapon, and writers must train themselves to use it as a carpenter trains to use wood and nails, or as a farmer trains to use earth" (169).

The result of all this is that students who are poorly prepared for college writing often do not get to college. Those who do get there often struggle, from their entry-level composition course until they either complete their degrees or drop out. In fact, in "Killing Them Softly: Why Willie Can't Write," Janis Epps (1985) argues that "composition is the gatekeeper of the inequalities perpetuated in the American system," that, in effect, unequal writing instruction is "one of the most effective instruments in perpetuating an oppressed and impoverished status in society" (154–56).

Nowhere is the division between the "haves" and the "have nots" in composition instruction viewed with greater alarm than by educators concerned with the status of the nonmainstream student in higher education. Although the number of African American students who graduate from high school has increased in the last decades, their enrollment in higher education has declined (Rice and Alford 1989, 68). The same is true for Latino students (Fields 1988). Although nine percent more Native American students are graduating from high school now than in 1970, their enrollment in higher education has stabilized since 1976. And a growing number of students of color attending community colleges and vocational schools terminate their educational

Portions of this chapter first appeared in "Successful Writing Programs and Methods of Assessment for Non-mainstream Students" in the *Arizona English Bulletin* 34 (Spring 1992): 15–20. Reprinted with the permission of the *Arizona English Bulletin*.

careers at the end of two years (Applegate and Henniger 1989). The attrition rate for nonwhite students in four-year programs also gives educators cause for serious concern (Nickolai-Mays and Kammer 1987).

We can blame the disappointing results of the last two decades of effort on lack of funding, extreme budget cuts, biased assessments, the little contact students of color have with nonmainstream faculty and professional staff, absence of multicultural curricula, strained relations with white students, poor tutoring programs, and more. But we must also acknowledge that prominent among these issues is the poor academic preparation that many nonmainstream students receive in courses that should provide them with the composing skills necessary to meet the demands of college writing. Although many entering mainstream students suffer from similar writing deficiencies, insufficient preparation (Nickolai-Mays and Kammer 1987), little opportunity and experience in composing, bicultural ambivalence (Dean 1989), and cultural differences (Harris 1986) often put nonmainstream students at a greater disadvantage.

In a compelling argument for positive reinforcement, Glenda Gill (1992) discusses the many difficulties that African American students face in mainstream colleges. Gill cites the case of a "well-bred, calm, quiet African American male" who came to her office and told her "he was not sure he would survive in college." One of four children in a single-parent home, he not only felt the burden of succeeding in school for himself, but also for his mother, who had pinned so much of her hope for his future to his success in college. Besides working full-time at a local fast food place to supplement his mother's meager income, the young man felt other pressures as well: the sea of white faces he encountered each day, his longing for a girlfriend and the social life that so many of his classmates seemed to have, the discomfort of having to share "chunks" of his papers in front of a class that seemed so alien.

Crediting Cleo Martin's method of positive feedback, Gill offers several suggestions for helping such students, including reader response sheets and open assignment topics. She points to the reinforcement Maya Angelou received from mentors like John Oliver Killens and James Baldwin of the Harlem Writers' Guild and underscores the positive effects of encouragement and interest on those students who sincerely make the effort. She writes, "Many serious, hard-working African Americans are being relegated to the ash-heap, and teachers can help by providing them with positive reinforcement" (226).

Gill also cites an African American admissions officer at a major university, who makes an important observation: "We must keep black male students in the most rigorous courses . . . because there is extreme pressure on the black male child to be anti-intellectual—an athlete, an entertainer, or a criminal" (228). Gill continues by saying that in her own twenty-nine years of teaching, she has come to see that many white and black teachers are afraid of African American males. While she admits that perhaps some black males do not want to study—note that the same can be said of many racial majority students as well—"the vast majority do. One of the hindrances to their success is teachers who are afraid to challenge them" (228–29).

I agree with Gill and her admissions officer colleague. In the twenty-five years I have been teaching, I have noticed the same thing. Teachers and administrators sometimes want to be "right on." Instead, they are "right off." They handle "their blacks" and other "minorities" with kid gloves, and their students see right through it.

Judging from conversations with my friends and former colleagues still teaching in the San Francisco bay area, in Texas, and in central New York, it sounds like this form of discrimination continues. Some teachers are wary of nonmainstream students because they think that they pose a threat to the equilibrium of the class. They are different. Their needs are different. Their composing skills are so varied that it is difficult to "teach" writing at all.

How do teachers manage such diversity in experiences, skills, culture, and exposure to writing practices? Many do what they have been doing all along: they "manage" their classrooms. They anchor their students to their desks, giving them skills sheets or workbooks or anything else that will get them through the period without too much fuss. Those who behave get good grades. Those who don't get into trouble. Those who show any promise or potential, or those who might like to improve their composing skills, often get left behind. And when we factor in the issue of multicultural literature, we get into the same problems of time limitations and self-censorship that I've been talking about for the last dozen chapters.

Recently I visited some classrooms taught by a friend, who was at the time teaching predominantly Filipino students. I collected some writing samples as part of a study I was conducting on the influence of writing prompts. Later, when analyzing my data, I found that many of the essays written by these students received high scores from raters. Puzzled, I asked my friend why her students had done so well when they were, after all, ESL students who, according to my expectations, should have fallen far short of such writing quality. Fran then gave me a lesson in composition pedagogy. She told me that if ESL students could just "hang on" and comprehend what the rest of the class was reading, she never put them into lower-level ESL classes. In her class these students had the opportunity to write constantly, the opportunity to improve their composing skills and become good writers.

We do not need to elaborate on the variety of reasons—none of which have anything to do with intelligence or writing potential—that many students of color are put into remedial classes early on, with little hope of getting out. What is important for us to focus on is that the poor self-esteem and academic underpreparedness that results (Fields 1988) marks these students for almost certain failure in college unless intervention is immediate and intense.

Characterizing the teaching of composition in this country, Foster (1983) makes a distinction between what he calls "closed" and "open" capacities. He then describes the "closed" capacities of the skills-oriented classroom, where the pedagogical emphasis is on "correct," surface-level writing. Yet while the composing process does involve many of these conventions, real writing, and the teaching of real writing, depends on the "open" capacities of imagination, inventiveness, and reasoning power, which, for a variety of reasons, many of our nation's nonmainstream students do not have the opportunity to experience. Even if we put aside the drug, economic, and morale problems of many inner-city communities, where minority populations often predominate, the overcrowded, less-than-optimal conditions of these neighborhood schools pretty well preclude teaching composition as it should be taught.

According to a 1974 National Council of Teachers of English position statement on teaching composition, "Learning to write requires writing; writing practice should be a major emphasis of the course. Workbook exercises, drill on usage, and analysis of existing prose are not adequate substitutes for writing." Yet such activities continue to be common in many of our nation's classrooms. Misunderstanding the nature of writing instruction, teachers force students into completing endless exercises in "getting rid of errors" and word attack skills. Such students are not composing. They are, instead, being "managed" in overcrowded classrooms, perhaps to the satisfaction of administrators who know little about teaching composition.

What happens to students who receive such substandard opportunities to compose? The sad fact is that they not only learn inadequate writing skills, but they also develop a negative concept of themselves as writers and, thus, as academic achievers. Our literature is replete with examples of nonmainstream students who have been thwarted in their attempts to express themselves. Given only the most mundane writing tasks, they are seldom challenged to think, to posit, to learn.

Youdelman (1978) cites the example of a professor who refused to use such topics as racism, housing discrimination, and the Vietnam War, opting instead for topics like "describe your favorite room," because he felt that his students couldn't "handle abstraction." When the students of such professors actually have the chance to write in other classes for more enlightened instructors, they often "interrupt themselves . . . and ask 'Is this right?' in a purely mechanical way." Accustomed to intellectual oppression, these students suspect all teachers. Youdelman points out the danger and damage to people living under this kind of intellectual oppression, who seek "to buttress themselves against it, [but] find that they have internalized all the limitations which the system itself preaches" (566).

Underprepared nonmainstream students have long been ignored. When they write, we do not listen to what they have to say. Smitherman (1972) cites the example of a position paper written by an African American college freshman responding to the then-current Vietnam War:

> I think the war in Viet Nam bad. Because we don't have no business over there. My brother friend been in war, and he say it's hard and mean. I do not like war because it's bad. And so I don't think we have no business there. The reason the way in China is bad is that American boys is dying over there. (65)

The instructor returned this paper to the student with only one comment: "Correct your grammar and resubmit." Two decades later this pedagogy still persists in many places.

The problem for many of us is that we "get stuck"; we attach ourselves to dialectal features and then don't address the more important issues. In doing so, we fool ourselves and our students into thinking that we are tackling the "true grit" of composition. The irony is that we never come close.

I once conducted a writing workshop where several teachers insisted that they must teach skills before composition. Fixated on the issue of dialect, they could not get past sentence-level errors, which, according to them, had to be "taken care of" before they could "do anything with the writing." I showed them a passage from Mina Shaughnessy's germinal work *Errors and Expectations* (1977). In the passage, Shaughnessy discusses the impact of open enrollment on the New York city college system in the early 1970s. Any student, no matter what his or her skills, could enter freshman English. Shaughnessy used the following example to show us that there is a big difference between a student who "cannot write" and a student who has had no opportunity to experience writing:

Passage written early in semester

Yesterday I saw something horrible. As I was walking down the street. I saw a man and his dog. Though this was a average man and his dog. This was a man beating his dog to death. Which made me sick. I scream for him to stop. Though I didnt get any answer from the man.

Passage written one month later

I am the smartest girl in this class. This isn't a conceited statement, but a true one.

I started this class February 4, 1974. I didn't know anything about English, till I got myself interested in this class. This was a very great step for me. For the reason that I'm learning extremely fast.

The first assignment we had was a writing assignment. I made so many mistakes that it was truly ridiculous. The teacher returned my paper for me to correct it. The teacher helped me correct it and find the reasons why I made the mistakes.

The second writing assignment we had was a little more difficult. I had my heart in this assignment not to make any mistakes, but I was wrong. I made fewer mistakes but they were there. This time I had to find them myself and understand why I made them. I found most of them but I really couldn't understand how I made such idiotic mistakes. This is where proof reading comes in. If I had proof read my papers there wouldn't have been that many mistakes.

The third writing assignment was a great challenge for me but I was determined to get it right. I wrote with all my new technique and I did really great. My teacher thinks it's a great improvement. Now you know I'm the smartest girl in this class. (277)

For me, this example says it all. Many students simply lack the opportunity to write. Once we get the juices flowing, then we can begin to worry about product. Within one month, this student's ability to generate prose increased tremendously, just because she had been given the chance.

Many of my own students—soon to be teachers—ask me why we still teach grammar if we have known for at least three decades that the formal teaching of grammar has nothing to do with writing improvement. After lengthy discussions, we come to the following conclusions about teaching grammar:

1. It is "clean," easy to teach and to correct, and acceptable to the public.

2. It is much easier and faster to grade than compositions, reader responses to literature, oral presentations, and the like.

3. We should not mislead students or parents or administrators by allowing them to believe that a steady diet of formally taught grammar will improve composing skills.

4. It makes teachers look smart and students look uneducated; it drives a wedge between students and their teachers, especially language minority students and those who speak a dialect different from the "language of empowerment."

On the other hand, we decide the following about teaching language skills:

1. Our language, the history of language development, and sociolinguistics are interesting areas of study, and students should be given the opportunity to take these courses if they wish.

2. Language skills should be taught on the basis of usage, often individually, to improve personal and public writing, to enhance style, and to increase students' ability to follow "accepted forms."

3. Students should have an opportunity to become exposed to an alternative dialect, one we call the "language of empowerment," which has become, as a result of historical coincidence, a dialect commonly accepted by people in economically advantaged positions.

Assessment

Assessment through essay testing is another important area of college writing in which nonmainstream students often do not fare well. According to Applebee, Langer, and Mullis (1989), topic differences "not only produce different estimates of overall writing performance, but also may have different effects on the performance of subgroups . . . [which] may serve to exaggerate or minimize differences in levels of performance" (24–25). Commenting on a recent writing assessment in South Carolina, they note that different writing prompts generated uneven responses from African American and European American students, illustrating that writing quality is influenced by cultural as well as other recognized considerations.

Analyzing essays from the National Assessment of Education Progress, Geneva Smitherman and Sandra Wright found significant correlation between the frequency of Black English and lower ratings. Though raters were told to consider other rhetorical features, they focused primarily on dialectal errors. Thus, essays the researchers considered "devoid of content, meaning, and message" were rated higher if they showed less evidence of dialectal difference (Smitherman-Donaldson 1987).

The sociopolitical dimension of writing competence and multiethnic students is an important issue. If the "mainstream perspective" in composition pedagogy and assessment of writing quality were expanded to include non-value-laden differences, then, according to Wagner and Coe (1982), "basic writers, 'dialectal' writers, or poorly prepared writers would not be held back by the boundaries of their so-called remedial or non-traditional characteristics." Wagner and Coe further state:

> If we do not develop abilities to perceive reality from multicultural perspectives in writing classes, we reinforce class-bias and sexism as well as racism by reinforcing the values and concepts of the dominant minority only. . . . It is one of the functions of English teachers to make certain their students have access to ["Standard English"]. But [they] must also make clear to their students that "Standard English" is in no sense superior to other dialects. (18)

Successful Models

Fortunately, the news is not all bad. A number of programs around the country have identified the connection between writing ability and college achievement and are doing something about it. The excellent work that the National Writing Project, originally the Bay Area Writing Project, has done in the last twenty years is one example. The project reaches out to provide research, enrichment, and writing experiences for teachers from kindergarten through college, who, in turn, bring their expertise back to their schools and into their classrooms. The Puente Project, a particularly exciting extension of the Bay Area Writing Project, has turned a fifty to sixty percent first-year dropout rate in fifteen California community colleges into a seventy to eighty percent retention rate (Dean 1989).

Many states are improving strategies for increasing and retaining students who transfer from community colleges to four-year programs (Cage 1989). A study of special English writing courses in a sample of California community colleges showed positive effects on student participants, including improved writing proficiency, more positive attitudes, and higher enrollment the following semester (Slark et al. 1987). In one California State University study, subscores on writing ability were highly related to persistence until the end of the freshman year (Stock et al. 1986). Students who showed "high potential" at St. Mary's

University in San Antonio completed a five-week summer program with an English composition component. These students, sixty percent of whom were Mexican American, had a much higher retention rate than similar students who did not go through the program (Trevino and Wise 1980).

Letting Basic Writers Write

In an attempt to concentrate on the real problems of novice writers, Paul Ramsey (1977) once taught a course on "teaching teachers to teach Black dialect students to write." According to Ramsey, though, "Our discussions of 'the teaching of writing to dialect speakers' always ended up on 'the teaching of writing' " (198). Ramsey reports:

> What I learned from our inability to stay on the topic of the course was that maybe we did not really need the course. The real problem was not how to teach Black dialect speakers to write, but how to teach any student to write. The basics of writing—how to organize, how to develop a paragraph, how to write with specificity rather than in generalities—are aracial. (198–99)

Yet because he is his department's one African American professor, Ramsey's colleagues often assume that he must "know something about . . . dialect problems." Ramsey points out, however, that the papers he is asked to look at as a result of this belief usually contain few real language errors. Though he agrees that the papers are usually poorly written, the issue was that the students really did not understand how to write. They didn't understand

> that a paper is about one thing which we call a "thesis" and . . . is constructed in paragraph units . . . about one . . . topic. I suspect that if a white student had come with a similar paper, my colleague might have thrown up his hands in dismay . . . but at least . . . would have been able to see the student's paper and not just the student's pigmentation. (200)

Our approach to composition pedagogy and its specific application to "at-risk" nonmainstream students should be clear. We know that all novice writers share certain characteristics. Royster (1985) points out that African American students are not "special problem-ridden writers." Looking at national trends in writing achievement, she notes that students in general are "at risk" and that African American students are no exception. The exceptional writing quality of many nonmainstream students involved in good writing programs speaks for itself, and the dire need of many mainstream students for adequate writing instruction is equally obvious.

In discussing the special problems that some basic writers do encounter, Mina Shaughnessy (1977) comments that dialectal errors in language use are compounded by the fact that, unlike students who learn English as a second language, "native" nonstandard English speakers have had no success with written language. Further, they have not identified any real or valid reasons for their failure in the classroom. Still, Shaughnessy reminds us that while errors count, they don't count for nearly as much as most English teachers think. Teachers should keep in mind the cost to themselves and to their students of mastering certain forms and be ready to cut their losses when the investment seems no longer commensurate with the return (120–22).

For instance, in a study analyzing the composing processes of three African American adolescents with low, moderate, and high use of nonstandard dialect, Fowler (1979) found that the high dialect user had the most frequent pauses and transfers and took the most time composing. Fowler thus makes a number of suggestions for making the high dialect user more comfortable and thus more efficient in a writing program. Instructors need to provide such students with more time for nonstop writing, more time for sentence-combining exercises, role playing, and the like, and more encouragement to develop tone, style, and a sense of audience. Instructors should also give students more opportunity to develop through groups and better revision opportunities. These instructional strategies impact positively on the writing performance of nonmainstream, indeed all, students.

Defining "basic writers" as beginners who must learn by making mistakes, Shaughnessy (1977) explains that the major problem basic writers have is that they have not written enough:

> Compared with the 1000 words a week that a British student or even the 350 words a week that an American student in a middle-class high school is likely to have written, the basic writing student is more likely to have written 350 words a semester. It would not be unusual for him [or her] to have written nothing at all. (14)

Even when these students are asked to compose, the assignments they are given are often artificial, strained, and unnatural. Thus, Farr and Daniels (1986) suggest that teachers develop student fluency through writing, that they understand and appreciate student writing competence, have positive expectations, and create writing activities for real reasons and wider audiences. They also suggest that teachers maintain appropriate readings, encourage collaboration and conferencing, provide less grammar instruction, teach mechanics in content, and offer cumulative evaluation.

This point is so obvious that it should no longer have to be said. What Shaughnessy and so many others are encouraging is that students need to write in order to improve their writing. They must establish their own voices, develop the confidence to express their ideas and opinions, and be able to organize their thoughts in a meaningful way. They must be motivated by and feel engaged in the writing they do.

Further, students of color with good potential yet less than adequate academic preparation have special needs that can be accommodated by recognizing them as positive additions to the college community. Royster (1985) points to the "unnegotiated mandate of the Black college," which succeeds in making such students competitive and competent in school and in the work force rather than labeling them as "remedial" or "nontraditional." Indeed, college composition classes do not always take into account individual and culturally sensitive learning styles or the impact of differing world views (Bennett 1990). Discussing the effects of the monocultural teacher in the multicultural classroom, Terry Dean (1989) explains that many minority and international students feel a bicultural ambivalence in the English class, suggesting that their difficulty in composing is often due to their lack of awareness about or interest in commonly assigned topics.

Incorporating Multiethnic Literature into the Composition Class

According to Ely (1980), redesigning college composition and humanities programs to include African, Asian, and other literatures improves the academic success and self-esteem of minority students. Similarly, Taylor and Bradford (1985) note that incorporating oral histories into freshman writing courses, using a variety of folk and rhetorical traditions, and including nonmainstream literatures and other worthwhile artistic models lessens the alienation that many nonmainstream students experience.

Observing that "many 1990s youth come from families seldom reflected in works of the Western literary canon," Athanases, Christiano, and Drexler (1992) illustrate an impressive model for promoting good writing through the study of multicultural literature. Their article, "Family Gumbo: Urban Students Respond to Contemporary Poets of Color," describes a course called "Interlinks," which "integrates U.S. literature and history around key social issues." Here's a sampling of issues and works from the course:

American slavery: *Narrative of the Life of Frederick Douglass*

Manifest destiny and westward expansion: *Dances with Wolves; The Jungle* (Sinclair)

The Great Depression: *The Grapes of Wrath* (Steinbeck)

Impact of industrialization: *Hard Times* (Terkel)

Chinese immigrants: *The Kitchen God's Wife* (Tan); *Strangers from a Different Shore* (Takaki)

Struggle for racial equality: *The Autobiography of Malcolm X* (with Alex Haley); *Before the Mayflower* (Bennett)

Mexican Americans: *The House on Mango Street* (Cisneros); "The Ballad of Gregorio Cortez" (Paredes and Paredes)

Using Nancie Atwell's (1987) strategies for "borrowing mode, topic/theme, and technique," "Interlinks" students borrow from the poets they read. Tensions between old ways and new ways, memories of the old country and its traditions, and conflict in the mainstream are all themes with which immigrant students can identify. Athanases, Christiano, and Drexler's article contains a number of lovely poetic pieces produced by students who, without a course like "Interlinks," would very likely have dropped out of school. Writing enhances writing! Indeed, besides helping them write their own poetry, exposure to poets

> helped make students' later work on autobiographical essays and college application essays richer and more genuine than the more predictable fare we have all received for such assignments. The emphasis on elaboration with concrete detail also served the students well in later writing. (53)

In "Developing Student Voices with Multicultural Literature," Linda Blair (1991) notes that today's classes contain an increasing number of language minority students. The challenge, she tells us, is to find material appropriate both to these students and to native speakers of English. Thus, drawing from Christopher Sten's model course on the immigrant experience, Blair has students read autobiographical narratives in a unit called "Voices in American Literature." Centered on the themes of alienation, assimilation, and acculturation, the unit includes works like Rudolfo Anaya's *Bless Me, Ultima*, Willa Cather's *My Antonia*, Maxine Hong Kingston's *Woman Warrior*, Richard Rodriguez's *Hunger of Memory*, Ole Rolvaag's *Giants in the Earth*, John Edgar Wideman's *Brothers and Keepers*, and Richard Wright's *Black Boy* (24).

Using these multiethnic works as models, students create their own "strong honest voices" through narratives based on their own experiences. Integrating their writing with literature, small-group discussion, presentations, and panels, students achieve real success with their projects. Blair writes, "I ask students to write about what they know best—themselves—using models of writing which underscore the 'public' voices which speak 'private' thoughts" (25). Using multicultural literature as a writing prompt thus becomes a valuable strategy for improving students' composing skills.

Greenberg (1982) also mentions the successful use of small groups. In discussing dialect differences between students in her college freshman composition class, she notes that small groups can make "optimal use of heterogeneity . . . to create opportunities" for students to benefit from each other's strengths. This technique, she reports, fosters "language experimentation" by allowing students to interact with each other using "mutually acceptable forms in speaking and writing." Helping each other "extend the range of their . . . discourse . . . they provide each other with immediate feedback about the ways in which their errors impede the reader's understanding of their meanings" (106–7).

Kaleidoscope

Students of color on white campuses need reinforcement and recognition. One of the most successful projects I have witnessed is *Kaleidoscope*, a multicultural magazine sponsored by Dr. Judy Kilborn, director of The Write Place at St. Cloud State University in Minnesota. I am proud to have been associated with this magazine, both as one of its original reviewers and as a moral supporter.

A collection of student poetry, short stories, essays, artwork, and photography, *Kaleidoscope* celebrates the multicultural experiences of African American, Native American, Latino, French, Japanese, Pakistani, Chinese, Indonesian, Palestinian, and South Korean students struggling in an almost totally "Anglo" world. Judy Kilborn encouraged students from all over the campus to participate, enlisted the help of many of her tutors in The Write Place for editing, typing, and other chores, and secured grant money from the university's Diversity Fund to produce the publication.

The results of her efforts are impressive. This excellent literary magazine has become an annual publication and has an increasingly enthusiastic audience. When I last spoke to Judy, she was arranging the magazine's annual awards reception for exceptional work. Through her planning and some great writing, many students of color have crossed into the mainstream of campus life.

Challenging Painful Memories: Writings from Victims of Abuse

Reader response, journaling, free association, and other writing-to-learn techniques allow us to know our students better as they continue to improve their composing skills. Indeed, when people write in a safe environment, they often use this medium to work through personal problems. Although a discussion of the therapeutic qualities of composing would be beyond the scope of this chapter, I would like to at least touch on a few examples of what is possible for students who, for some painful reason, feel like they are on the margins of their groups.

One nontraditional student—she was over thirty years of age—challenged my interpretation of Sylvia Plath's haunting poem "Daddy." For this student, the poem was about child abuse. "Not exactly," I corrected her, as if only I knew the right answer. She insisted, telling me that she had been an abused child and the "boot in the face" and smothering images of the poem represented her own horrible childhood. Her understanding was different from mine, not incorrect. She told me later that reading the poem had had a lasting and positive effect on her, that while it had brought back a lot of unpleasant memories, having to write about it had helped her acknowledge some hidden feelings about her father, feelings she had carried around since her youth.

Another student wrote a compelling piece about the physical abuse she had received from her husband. After a lot of encouragement from me and the entire class, she revised the essay, and it is now part of the literature available at a local women's shelter.

One student told me through his writing that he had been molested as a child and that, after many years, he had told his mother, who in turn told his father. He was ignored by both. After a lot of discussion, I convinced him that he needed more counseling support. He finally agreed to go.

One young woman in my class struggled with a persuasive piece about day camp, counseling, and child abuse. A usually straightforward, no-nonsense kind of writer, Cherry had unusual difficulty with this piece. After several more revisions than I would ordinarily recommend, she worked through her composing troubles, which turned out really to be the problem she was having coming to grips with what she was writing about: her experiences with a sexually abusive parent who ran a scout camp. Her final essay was a masterpiece. But what Cherry gained from writing it was even more important.

After a discussion on child abuse and the use of related multiethnic literature in classrooms, one teacher of Scandinavian heritage whom I would consider mainstream in every way told me that she had always felt marginalized, that she did not "fit in." She presented me with a moving poem about childhood abuse, which, she said, "might give comfort to someone else who has gone through similar experiences." I have shared this poem with two subsequent students—one male, one female. They have both been impacted by it. Although I cannot thank its author publicly, she should know how important her words have been to at least two others.

In 1974, the Conference on College Composition and Communication passed a policy resolution called "The Students' Right to Their Own Language." In challenging English teachers to carry on the "unfinished business of the resolution," Geneva Smitherman-Donaldson (1987) reminds us that we must

> reinforce the need for and teaching of the language of wider communication . . . and reinforce and reaffirm the legitimacy of nonmainstream languages and dialects and promote mother tongue instruction as co-equal language of instruction along with the language of wider communication.

If English/language arts educators are interested in the retention and success of minority students, then they must be committed to providing adequate preparation and strong, effective composition instruction at all levels. If writing instruction is, indeed, the gatekeeper of inequality preventing students' access to academic and lifelong success, then it is incumbent upon us to open the gate and let everyone in.

14 Interdisciplinary Connections in Teaching Multicultural Literature

Years ago, while teaching American literature, I asked the members of our history department if they wanted to join forces. Most of the teachers weren't interested. One was, though, and we developed a cooperative program for readings, papers, and debates. The program, while not exactly a team course (the two classes were offered at different times), was a successful joint effort between two departments and two disciplines. It was also an opportunity to bring nonfiction into the English classroom.

Today, this team approach is old hat. But it's a smart-looking old hat nonetheless. I still like the concept, as do many other educators. I have visited many institutions that have incorporated this interdisciplinary approach into the curricular mainstream. The English-history connection is particularly popular because the two areas are easily related, but literature also is complemented by—and complements—the study of art, music, science, philosophy, politics, and other disciplines. If we want to understand the Romantic poets, then perhaps we should listen to the Romantic composers. If we want to learn more about modern novels, then perhaps we should look at the philosophy or art or political climate of the first half of the twentieth century.

Interdisciplinary approaches to learning are also popular with students, and many successful programs have been developed over the years using this approach. While supervising in Texas, I observed student teachers who were involved in an environmental unit that took the form of a three-day camping trip. In preparation for this activity, students read Thoreau's *Walden*. During the trip, they kept journals, conducted research on ecological issues for science, and learned about the historical significance of the national forest they were in. Those taking art classes had an art project to complete, while music students were to develop instruments and provide accompaniment for various activities. The physical education people had a number of options from which students could choose to fulfill their requirements. Both the preservice teachers and their students came away from this experience feeling connected to surroundings that had previously seemed irrelevant to their lives.

So, if interdisciplinary programs have been so successful, why can't we expand this idea to include intercultural connections as well? Not only are there connections among disciplines, but also among groups and peoples and cultures. My purpose in this last chapter, then, is to develop a multicultural approach to interdisciplinary learning. As in the "writing across the curriculum" movement that is now well ensconced in campuses nationwide, we must work with our colleagues in other disciplines to pluralize curricula to provide a more realistic approach to our view of the world. Literature should not be taught in a vacuum. Linking multiethnic literature, both fiction and nonfiction, to other disciplines validates the contributions of diverse groups and gives students a better picture of what the world is really like.

Bringing in the Community's Culture

In October 1992, I attended the inauguration of my friend Dr. Josephine Dunbar Davis as the third president of York College in Jamaica, New York. As part of the celebration, President Davis participated in an enstoolment, a West African ceremony signifying the selection of an important leader. The festivities were attended by a number of people from the community who look to York College and its president as shining lights in an otherwise oppressive environment. I asked Dr. Davis about the enstoolment, and she responded by telling me that the ceremony was part of the culture of a number of people in the South Queens area who probably never would have had the opportunity to view it for themselves. She wanted to bring it to them. The enstoolment was an extravaganza, as anyone who knows Josephine would expect. There were elders leading the procession of dignitaries, ceremonial prayers, exquisite African robes, and music and drum orchestras the likes of which I had never heard before.

But my favorite part was the participation of local students. The violin club from Lyndon B. Johnson P.S. 223Q performed. So did the gospel choir. Next came P.S. 123's Dance Presentation Project with "I Am Somebody." The students of Huntington Prep P.S. 40, Youth of the African Diaspora, did "A Recitation and Tribute." The Martin Players of August Martin High School followed with a dramatic presentation. Next the Devore Dancers performed. All told, the entertainment ranged from African drum ensembles and African dancing to theatrical pieces and lip-sync routines. Young children and adolescents from all over South Queens gathered to share their exceptional talents on this exciting day.

Countless opportunities like this one exist for making the culture or cultures of a particular community the focus of an interdisciplinary unit. For example, I recently participated in a workshop at an Ojibway reservation in the Midwest. Our task was to come up with an interdisciplinary curriculum that would both appeal to and motivate the reservation school's students while covering a number of academic subjects. Since ricing is an important activity for the Ojibway people of this region—economically, socially, and aesthetically—our group decided to use it as the centerpiece of our unit. Employing an interdisciplinary model and a few tribal council publications (see Thomas Vennum, Jr.'s *Wild Rice and the Ojibway People*, St. Paul, MN: Historical Society Press, 1988), we came up with the following study plan:

Ricing: An Interdisciplinary Approach

English: read Gerald Vizenor's "Ricing Again"; tell a favorite story or create a poem about a ricing experience; dramatize an experience; describe the meaning of ricing in family lore or personal experience

Ojibway language: select terms/vocabulary for ricing (gather from the class, books, or someone on the reservation); learn or create a written or oral story or song in Ojibway

Science: study the effects of pollution on ricing or the relationship between water levels and ricing conditions

Social science: describe the social scene of the harvest; explain the laws of the ricing industry and their effect on local bands

Math: study the economic benefits of ricing for traders and harvesters; evaluate exchange rates for rice and rum; answer questions such as how did the credit system work? what percent of income came from wild rice? what percent of the work cycle did wild rice account for?

Music: gather some of the songs and music of ricing season and perform them

Art: collect photos or illustrations created for the season; create personal sketches, paintings, and the like

Physical education: re-create a "ricing" sport and play it; create one of your own and play it

Curricula like this creatively showcase the culture and talents of our students and help them realize the valuable contributions that they can make.

Teaching Literature through Music

As part of a final seminar project, two of my students, Melissa Dunkel and Annette Wells, presented our class with an array of music written as an extension of classical literature (which they recorded for those of us who brought blank tapes). Their selections ran the gamut from classical music to multiethnic pieces to contemporary songs. Of course, there were the more obvious selections, such as Felix Mendelssohn's "You Spotted Snakes" from *A Midsummer Night's Dream*. But they also included selections like "Brave Ulysses" from *Disraeli Gears* by Cream *(The Odyssey)*, "Rock Steady" from *Nothing Like the Sun* by Sting (the Bible/Noah), "Calypso" by Suzanne Vega (*The Odyssey* again), and a host of others. What impressed me most was the variety of multiethnic music they provided. A partial list of their selections follows:

> *African American:* "Bourgeois Blues" by Ledbelly (Huddie Ledbetter), an African American blues and folk singer of the 1920s and 1930s. This song deals with the racism African Americans face. "I Don't Dig You Jack" by Blue Lou Barker, from *Mean Mothers*. Barker talks about the Jack who takes her body and her money. She tells him to leave. Alice Walker says, "When I started working on *The Color Purple*, I was listening to a lot of Bessie Smith, Ma Rainey, and the women on the *Mean Mothers* album. I loved the way they dealt with sexuality, with relationships with men" (quoted in Samuel G. Freedman, "Black Writers and Black Music," *New York Times*, 14 October 1984). Also "Murder's Home" and "Tangle Eye Blues," both prison songs recorded in the 1980s at the Mississippi State Penitentiary. Melissa and Annette also included a number of jazz selections, the only indigenous American art form in music—and one created by African Americans. All three of the following selections come from the 1960s, when African American jazz artists were using their music as an expression of art and as a symbol of the then-rising Black Nationalistic (or "Black Power") Movement: "Flamenco Sketches" by the Miles Davis Sextet, "Solar" by Bill Evans, and "The Promise" by the John Coltrane Quartet.

> *Greek:* "Mistokrasi mou" ("In My Wine"), from *Bouzoukee: The Music of Greece*. Bouzoukee music is about old folk themes and became popular after World War II. This is a dance that originated as an ancient ritual honoring the moon goddess and Mother Earth. The woman dances for the man, illustrating her charms with slow movements, while the man dances quickly and awkwardly. "Nisiotikos Choros" ("Island Dance"), from *Syrtos*. Based on an ancient inscription from about the time of Caligula (37–41 A.D.) found in a temple dedicated to Apollo.

> *Indian:* "Kafi-Holi" ("Spring Festival of Colors"). Sophisticated rhythms. Ravi Shankar, sitar.

Japanese: "Echigojishi," from *Koto Music of Japan*. An eighteenth-century folk song based on the ancient Lion Dance performed in the festivals of Echigo in the eastern part of Japan. "Shin-Takasago," also from *Koto Music of Japan*. A nineteenth-century song based on *Takasago*, a famous Noh drama. (Takasago is a seaside town near Kobe that is frequently cited in Japanese literature for its scenic beauty. *Takasago* describes happiness and joy.)

Jewish American: "Jewish Dance" by the Andy Statman Klezmer Orchestra. Klezmer music is the product of Jews who migrated before and around the time of World War II. The music is both happy and mournful and is used for dancing at marriages and other celebrations.

Latino: "Tinku," a love song from Bolivia. "Vientos del Pueblo" ("Winds of the People") by Inti-Illimani of Chile.

Native American: "Smoke Song" and "Stop Song," a war dance recorded in 1972 by Nez Perce Native Americans Oscar Broncheau, Cyrus Red Elk, and Jim Morris, three drummers remaining from a group of over two dozen in the mid-1920s.

South African: "Buya Uz'ekhya" by Ladysmith Black Mambazo, a South African a cappella group.

West African: "Hunter's Dance," from the album *Musique d'Afrique Occidentale*. Composer, performer, and recording date unknown.

Melissa and Annette offered even more music to encourage discussion in the classroom: Sting's "They Dance Alone," a song about political prisoners recorded during his Amnesty Tour of 1986; Tracy Chapman's "Why?" a statement on love, hate, and hunger; Stevie Wonder's "Black Man"; Bob Marley's "War" and "Redemption Song." And at the end of their presentation, Annette and Melissa expressed the same thought that many educators have when they make decisions about curriculum and materials: "There's so much more." Thus the now familiar caveat: this is just a beginning.

Diverse Curricula and Materials for General Education Courses

In a recent conversation with Richard Law, director of the general education program at Washington State University, I learned of the Association of American Colleges Engaging Cultural Legacies Project. Washington State University is one of eleven "resource" or mentor institutions for this project. So, a few years ago, WSU began an initiative to revise its general education program. What Dr. Law and his associates initially discovered was "an obvious Western bias" in the courses students were required to take. "This tradition," Dick told me, "was in direct conflict with the group's identified efforts to internationalize curriculum." (Remembering the required "History of Western Civilization" from my own undergraduate days, I concurred.)

Dick told me, "It became clear to us that we needed to counteract this well-established concept in our liberal arts education. We wanted students to learn that much of the development of world civilization is non-Western—and that was not the impression they were getting given the information they were receiving in their classes." Thus, a "World Civilizations" course was developed by twenty professors from history, literature, philosophy, anthropology, and foreign languages. The course traced "the emergence of an interdependent world community" and was "global, comparative, [and] interdisciplinary in content and methodology" (*Washington Center Newsletter* 1992). All students are now required to take this course.

The result of these changes is that Washington State University's "humanities core curriculum and integrated general education program embodies many of the best components of new core programs nationally" (*Washington Center Newsletter* 1992). What is even more remarkable, though, is that World Civilizations is linked to the English department's entry-level composition course, English 101, through the development of a curriculum "designed to further students' cultural literacy, foster a global perspective, and develop a sense of enduring issues in civilization and culture" (*Washington Center Newsletter* 1992).

Anchoring this curriculum is *Writing about the World*, a text prepared by Susan McLeod and some of her graduate students for use by all English 101 instructors at WSU. Describing this volume, Dr. McLeod points out in her introduction that

> we set out to find readings that . . . help students learn academic reading and writing strategies, but that also raised issues of cultural diversity and of gender. Our work is, therefore, in line with the resolution passed at the 1989 Conference on College Composition and Communication: "Resolved, that CCCC adopt a curriculum policy that represents the inclusion of women and people of color in the curriculum on all levels." (iii)

The text is divided into four sections, "organized according to some of the ways cultures organize themselves": Science and Technology, Government and Politics, Art and Literature, and Religion and Philosophy. Selections come from around the world. Students thus have the opportunity to explore the complexity and diversity of many world views.

Indeed, *Writing about the World* takes a look at some challenging multicultural perspectives. In a review of current multicultural texts for composition classes, Shapiro (1991) points out that most are developed for one of two different audiences: mainstream students or marginalized students. She cites *Writing about the World* as a text for students "already able to handle college-level work." I agree. The challenging selections in this work are definitely designed for students academically prepared for the university (although Sue McLeod tells me that a number of community colleges have begun to use this text in their composition courses).

Nonetheless, *Writing about the World* is only one of a growing number of multicultural texts that could be used in interdisciplinary composition or general education courses. What follows is an incomplete listing of some of the excellent materials now available.

Another volume that Shapiro reviews is Marilyn Smith Layton's *Intercultural Journeys through Reading and Writing.* She describes its selections as geared toward mainstream students who have had little interaction with diversity. In her preface, Layton emphasizes that "students, like teachers, can't know who they are or what they might become . . . unless they encounter ideas and truths that help them to see themselves in an expanding world." She has thus made her selections to represent "the full range of voices in an intercultural conversation" (xix). The selections include essays, short fiction, and plays arranged in sections that center around "The Challenges of Intercultural Experience" and American cultural values, particularly as defined in work, love, family, and self. Each is well worth inclusion.

Shapiro also cites Barbara Roche Rico and Sandra Mano's *American Mosaic: Multicultural Readings in Context,* which focuses on seven ethnic groups and gives a variety of selections to illustrate the inherent multiculturalism of the United States. I have used *American Mosaic* and can personally attest to its success in the classroom. Starting with a section on early immigrants, Rico and Mano divide their work into sections on Chinese immigrants, the African American migration north, the Harlem Renaissance and the civil rights struggles of this century, the history of Puerto Rico and its relationship with the United States, the Japanese American internment experience, the economic and cultural boundaries of Mexican Americans, and the pride and cultural heritage of Native Americans. I was surprised to see how much of this information was new to—or had been forgotten by—so many of my students. They certainly gained a much better understanding of what it means to be out of the mainstream. One caveat, though: instructors must understand that *American Mosaic* is a multiethnic work and should be studied in its entirety; it should not be compartmentalized.

If put to good use, *American Mosaic* can be a rich resource for students beginning to conduct research on their own. For instance, a few years ago, a controversy over Native American spearfishing erupted while I was teaching a class using this text. Many class members were fishers and had, in my opinion, great misconceptions about the hunting and fishing rights of Chippewa people in northern Wisconsin. Since I knew very little about the issue, I attended a lecture where Pat Sheppo of the Lac du Flambeau Reservation spoke. In her talk, she outlined an agreement—rediscovered by researching students—between the Lac du Flambeau Chippewa (or Anishinabe or Ojibway) and the government of the United States (Doyle 1990). Two students who were very interested in the issue secured more information from her, interviewed several more people, conducted research on their own, and produced an excellent paper on the spearfishing controversy.

American Mosaic precipitated a number of other interesting research efforts as well, including work on the Chinese Exclusion Act and the history of Chinese Americans, research into Columbus's annihilation of the Arawak Indians, a survey of immigrants from Eastern Europe from the turn of the century to the forties, and a look at the Japanese American experience from the Issei days to the present. All this in a composition course! In course evaluations, students remarked over and over that they were glad that we took on these topics. They said that they now had a much better idea of what "equality" does or does not mean for many of our citizens.

Another good text is Sheena Gillespie and Robert Singleton's *Across Cultures: A Reader for Writers*. Shapiro notes that this text is geared toward ESL readers, as it connects students from different backgrounds through readily accessible readings. Several of my colleagues also recommend it for beginning writers. Intended, as Shapiro indicates, for a multiethnic student body, the text's "Preface for the Student" notes:

> When you look around your classes and your campus, you probably see a student body diverse in its many countries, classes, and ages. When *this* inclusive group says, or sings, "We are the world," they are right. This is the world of *Across Cultures*. (xxii)

Across Cultures contains a wonderful variety of myths, folktales, essays, and short stories. The selections are short, interesting, and good sources for both class discussion and writing ideas. The section on education, for example, highlights such diverse pieces as a "Hopi Tale" by Spider Grandmother and Masauwu, Rendon's "Kiss of Death," Norman Cousins's "Confessions of a Miseducated Man," Paule Marshall's "Poets in the Kitchen," Richard Wright's "Discovering Books," Toni Cade

Bambara's "The Lesson," and Gary Soto's "Summer School." And to spur further ideas, each chapter begins with brief, provocative quotations from international figures.

Janet Madden-Simpson and Sara M. Blake's *Emerging Voices: A Cross-Cultural Reader* is also described by Shapiro as a text intended primarily for ESL students and students "not immediately prepared to handle college work." According to Madden-Simpson and Blake:

> Grounded in reader-response theory . . . *Emerging Voices* seeks to involve all readers in a dialectic, not only with the selections, but also with issues arising from the experience of living in a culturally diverse nation. . . . This book focuses on immigrant, ethnic, and minority experiences in the United States . . . to foster an awareness of the diverse forces at work in our society, and . . . to create a sensitivity to the experiences of all Americans. (v)

This text, with its large concentration of narrative pieces, is a wonderful collection of voices from a variety of cultures in American life. Selections include Gloria Naylor's "The Myth of the Matriarch," Vo Thi Tam's "From Vietnam, 1979," Jack Agueros's "Halfway to Dick and Jane: A Puerto Rican Pilgrimage," Maxine Hong Kingston's "Reparation Candy," and many, many others.

Crosscurrents: Themes for Developing Writers, another collection by Madden and Blake, uses much the same approach as *Emerging Voices,* but, as the title indicates, targets "developing writers." Using classroom-tested materials designed for the developmental writer, Madden and Blake arrange pieces thematically and order them from inner-directed topics to outer-directed topics. Readings are drawn from popular culture and from ethnically diverse writers.

Anna Joy's *We Are America* introduces beginning writers to the writing process and reading skills using ethnically diverse points of view. The text begins with "An Overview of the Writing Process." Part two, "A Cross-Cultural Reader," includes a number of excellent readings, complete with questions and writing suggestions. Part three concludes with "Revising Sentences: A Writing Skills Workbook."

Carol J. Verburg's *Ourselves among Others: Cross-Cultural Readings for Writers* is another international treatment, once again with excellent selections. The selections here are perhaps more sophisticated, though, geared for good readers. There is minimal apparatus at the end of each reading.

Henry and Myrna Knepler's *Crossing Cultures: Readings for Composition* is another publication geared for college freshmen. The readings, again, are excellent, a little shorter than the offerings described above and less difficult. Moving from "intra-American issues" to more global subjects, the text deals with identities, encounters, and customs in a new world.

I end this list of intercultural texts with Gary Colombo, Robert Cullen, and Bonnie Lisle's *Rereading America: Cultural Contexts for Critical Thinking and Writing* because I have used it myself several times and love it. A collection of pieces from a variety of American writers, selections range from government documents to poetry. Beginning with the topic "American Dreams," the text calls upon authors such as Thomas Jefferson, Crevecoeur, Langston Hughes, and Louise Erdrich. There are poignant pieces like Tran Thi Nga's "Letter to My Mother," pieces on the changing family, including some written by members of the gay and lesbian community, and pieces on the theme of work, with selections from Erich Fromm and Arlie Russell Hochschild. Indeed, there are some tough essays here, both in terms of content and level of difficulty.

It is frustrating to mention only these few books, but it is clearly impossible to include them all. As I've said several times throughout this book, there's been an explosion of multicultural materials on the market, and professors and teachers have only to ask any major publisher for information about a number of worthwhile texts.

If literature mirrors life, then the choices we make for our students must be consonant with the reality of their environment. We must actively engage in seeking out the best materials we can so that students will be exposed to a true view of our global community. It is no longer enough to seek materials for our own classes. We need to reach across our campuses and enlist the help of others in the pursuit of a truly pluralistic society.

Thank You, Mrs. Coleman, Wherever You Are

There once was a little boy; we'll call him Bennie. He was African American, the middle child of seventeen, and his prospects for an exceptional future—according to statistics—were very slim. But Bennie was ambitious and bright, and he did very well in school, finishing his studies with a doctoral degree from Stanford University. He is presently dean of the college of education at a major research institution on the West Coast.

It must have been very difficult for Bennie to find the motivation and to receive the kind of incentives one needs to succeed educationally and to rise professionally to such a high administrative level. I once asked Bennie if he could identify the motivational forces in his educational past that gave him the wherewithal to get as far as he had. He told me this:

> Of course, I was lucky that my parents supported education and were very strict with all of us about doing our homework, keeping up our grades, and the like. But both my mother and father worked long hours, and when they were home they had their hands full just handling dinners, rides to and from sports and other school activities, and so on. They didn't have much time to read to us or to take us to the library and do all those things we know facilitate children's academic skills.
>
> But Mrs. Coleman, my fourth-grade teacher, recognized that the little black kid sitting in the back row loved to read. So she asked my parents, and they agreed, to let her take me to the library after school. Each Wednesday I'd check out a pile of books, read them all week, and return them and get another pile for the next week. It was a wonderful opportunity. From that experience, I developed the hobby of reading, which, as every student knows, becomes his or her greatest asset later on.
>
> In high school, looking for role models and the chance to identify in an academic world, I was lucky again. Ms. Baher, my English teacher, introduced me to some of the great black writers of the twentieth century—Richard Wright, Ralph Ellison, James Baldwin—and I began to see the great talents of people just like me. These impressions had a significant influence on my development as a young African American in an academic world.

In discussing his youth, Bennie also told me about a lot of unpleasant experiences he endured as a result of racism, such as the time someone spit in his face and called him "nigger." Although well liked at school, he was seldom invited to any of his friends' homes. His high school counselor told him that since he was such a good student, he could become a fireman. He also told me about working after his sports activities so that he could earn extra money and about how little time there was for studying. But somehow he made it through all of the negatives, and he credits the nurturing of his teachers in large part.

All of us face circumstances that make it difficult to meet the needs of our students. Our classes are overcrowded. We have too many curricular restrictions. We have too much material to cover. Our students are mainstream and don't see the significance of multicultural literature. Or, they are from diverse groups and aren't interested in the literature that we choose for them. We have tenure pressures. We don't have adequate time to meet with students or to prepare our lessons.

But whatever the reason for our frustrations, whatever the cause for our despair, we must not forget about the influence that we have on our students. We must take advantage of this influence and use it in a positive way. Perhaps Bennie would have made it without Mrs. Coleman and Ms. Baher, but you'll never convince Bennie of that. Let us seek out the Bennies in our classrooms and provide them with the kind of experiences they can use to build successes. Let us remember how much influence we have on our students. We cannot perform miracles, but— given the expertise and the commitment—we *can* make a difference.

References

Allen, Paula Gunn. "The Sacred Hoop: A Contemporary Indian Perspective on American Indian Literature." In *Literature of the American Indians: Views and Interpretations*, edited by Abraham Chapman, 111–36. New York: New American Library, 1975.

American Alliance for Theatre and Education and the Association for Theatre and Disability. "Theatre: The Art of Inclusion." Conference, Seattle, 6–9 August 1992.

Anaya, Rudolfo. "The Censorship of Neglect." *English Journal* 81 (September 1992): 18–20.

Anderson, James A. "Cognitive Styles and Multicultural Populations." *Journal of Teacher Education* 39 (January/February 1988): 2–9.

Angelou, Maya. *I Know Why the Caged Bird Sings*. New York: Random House, 1969.

———. "An Evening with Maya Angelou." St. Cloud State University, St. Cloud, MN, 4 February 1990.

Anzaldúa, Gloria. "How to Tame a Wild Tongue." In *Borderlands: The New Mestiza*. San Francisco: Aunt Lute Books, 1987.

Applebee, Arthur N. *Tradition and Reform in the Teaching of English: A History*. Urbana, IL: National Council of Teachers of English, 1974.

———. *A Study of Book-length Works Taught in High School English Courses*. Albany, NY: Center for the Study of Teaching and Learning of Literature, 1989.

———. "Stability and Change in the High School Canon." *English Journal* 81 (September 1992): 27–32.

Applebee, Arthur N., Judith A. Langer, and Ina V. S. Mullis. *Understanding Direct Writing Assessment: Reflections on a South Carolina Writing Study*. Princeton, NJ: Educational Testing Service, 1989.

Applegate, Jimmie R., and Michael L. Henniger. "Recruiting Minority Students: A Priority for the '90s." *Thought and Action* 5 (Spring 1989): 53–60.

Asante, Molefi. *The Afrocentric Idea*. Philadelphia: Temple University Press, 1987.

Athanases, Steven Z., David Christiano, and Susan Drexler. "Family Gumbo: Urban Students Respond to Contemporary Poets of Color." *English Journal* 81 (September 1992): 45–54.

Atwell, Nancie. *In the Middle: Writing, Reading, and Learning with Adolescents*. Upper Montclair, NJ: Boynton/Cook, 1987.

Baldwin, James. "Sonny's Blues." 1965. In *The Norton Introduction to Literature*, 4th ed., edited by Carl E. Bain, Jerome Beaty, and J. Paul Hunter, 266–300. New York: Norton, 1986.

Ballinger, Franchot. "*Ambigere:* The Euro-American Picaro and the Native American Trickster." *MELUS* 17 (Winter 1991–92): 21–38.

Banks, James A. "Approaches to Multicultural Curriculum Reform." *Multicultural Leader* 1 (Spring 1988): 1–2.

———. "Multicultural Education: Characteristics and Goals." In *Multicultural Education: Issues and Perspectives,* edited by James A. Banks and Cherry A. McGee Banks, 2–26. Boston: Allyn and Bacon, 1989.

———. "Teaching Minority and Ethnic Culture." Fifth Annual Conference of the Society for the Study of Multi-Ethnic Literature of the United States (MELUS), University of Minnesota, Minneapolis, 13 April 1991.

Barker, Andrew P. "A Gradual Approach to Feminism in the American-Literature Classroom." *English Journal* 78 (October 1989): 39–44.

Beach, Richard, and James Marshall. *Teaching Literature in the Secondary School.* San Diego: Harcourt Brace Jovanovich, 1991.

Bedrosian, Margaret. "Multi-Ethnic Literature: Mining the Diversity." *Journal of Ethnic Studies* 15 (Fall 1987): 125–34.

Bennett, Christine I. *Comprehensive Multicultural Education: Theory and Practice.* Boston: Allyn and Bacon, 1986.

———. *Comprehensive Multicultural Education: Theory and Practice.* 2d ed. Boston: Allyn and Bacon, 1990.

Betances, Samuel. "Multicultural Education." Speech given at St. Cloud State University, St. Cloud, MN, March 1989.

Biklen, Douglas, and Robert Bogdan. "Media Portrayals of Disabled People: A Study in Stereotypes." *Interracial Books for Children Bulletin* (1977): 4–9.

Bischoff, Joan. "Fellow Rebels: Annie Dillard and Maxine Hong Kingston." *English Journal* 78 (December 1989): 62–67.

Bjorklun, Eugene C. "School Book Censorship and the First Amendment." *The Educational Forum* 55 (Fall 1990): 37–48.

Blair, Linda. "Developing Student Voices with Multicultural Literature." *English Journal* 80 (December 1991): 24–28.

Blicksilver, Edith. *The Ethnic American Woman: Problems, Protests, Lifestyle.* Dubuque, IA: Kendall/Hunt, 1978.

Bloom, Allan. *The Closing of the American Mind: How Higher Education Has Failed Democracy and Impoverished the Souls of Today's Students.* New York: Simon and Schuster, 1987.

Buchanan, John H. "The Right to Read: School Book-banning Groups Continue Censorship Crusade." *Star Tribune: Newspaper of the Twin Cities,* 24 September 1988.

Cage, Mary Crystal. "More Minority Programs Now Emphasizing Efforts to Keep Students Enrolled in College." *Chronicle of Higher Education*, 12 April 1989, A1, A4.

Candelaria, Cordelia. "Hidden Complacencies." *American Book Review* 11 (January/February 1990): 1, 13, 15.

Carroll, Joyce Armstrong. "Minority Student Writers: From Scribblers to Scribes." *English Journal* 69 (November 1980): 15–18.

Carver, Nancy Lynn. "Stereotypes of American Indians in Adolescent Literature." *English Journal* 77 (September 1988): 25–32.

Chan, Jeffery Paul, Frank Chin, Lawson Inada, and Shawn Wong. "An Introduction to Chinese-American and Japanese-American Literatures." In *Three American Literatures: Essays in Chicano, Native American, and Asian-American Literature for Teachers of American Literature*, edited by Houston A. Baker, Jr., 197–228. New York: Modern Language Association, 1982.

————, eds. *The Big Aiiieeeee! An Anthology of Chinese American and Japanese American Literature*. New York: Meridian, 1991.

Chapman, Abraham. "Introduction." In *Literature of the American Indians: Views and Interpretations*, edited by Abraham Chapman, 1–23. New York: New American Library, 1975.

Chin, Frank. "Come All Ye Asian American Writers of the Real and the Fake." In *The Big Aiiieeeee! An Anthology of Chinese American and Japanese American Literature*, edited by Jeffery Paul Chan et al., 1–92. New York: Meridian, 1991.

Chin, Frank, Jeffery Paul Chan, Lawson Inada, and Shawn Wong, eds. *Aiiieeeee! An Anthology of Asian-American Writers*. Washington, DC: Howard University Press, 1974.

Christenbury, Leila, and Robert Small. "From the Editors." *The ALAN Review* 18 (Winter 1991): 1.

Christopher, Renny. "The Unheard: Vietnamese Voices in the Literature Curriculum." In *Understanding Others: Cultural and Cross-Cultural Studies and the Teaching of Literature*, edited by Joseph Trimmer and Tilly Warnock, 201–12. Urbana, IL: National Council of Teachers of English, 1992.

Cobb, Martha K. "From Oral to Written: Origins of a Black Literary Tradition." In *Tapping Potential: English and Language Arts for the Black Learner*, edited by Charlotte K. Brooks, 250–59. Urbana, IL: National Council of Teachers of English, 1985.

Colombo, Gary, Robert Cullen, and Bonnie Lisle, eds. *Rereading America: Cultural Contexts for Critical Thinking and Writing*. New York: St. Martin's Press, 1989.

Cook, William W. "The Afro-American Griot." In *Tapping Potential: English and Language Arts for the Black Learner*, edited by Charlotte K. Brooks, 260–71. Urbana, IL: National Council of Teachers of English, 1985.

Corson, Carolyn M. "YA Afro-American Fiction: An Update for Teachers." *English Journal* 76 (April 1987): 24–28.

Coughlin, Ellen K. "Scholars Work to Refine Africa-centered View of the Life and History of Black Americans." *Chronicle of Higher Education*, 28 October 1987, A6–7, A12.

Cox, Mitch. "Revising the Literature Curriculum for a Pluralist Society." *English Journal* 77 (October 1988): 30–34.

Davis, Bonnie. "Feminizing the English Curriculum: An International Perspective." *English Journal* 78 (October 1989): 45–49.

Davis, James E. "Dare a Teacher Disturb the Universe? Or Even Eat a Peach? Closet Censorship: Its Prevention and Cure." *The ALAN Review* 14 (1986): 66–69.

Dean, Terry. "Multicultural Classrooms, Monocultural Teachers." *College Composition and Communication* 40 (February 1989): 23–37.

Dorris, Michael. "For the Indians, No Thanksgiving." In *Crossing Cultures: Readings for Composition*, 3d ed., edited by Henry Knepler and Myrna Knepler, 199–202. New York: Macmillan, 1990. Reprinted from the *Chicago Tribune*, November 1988.

Douglass, Frederick. *Narrative of the Life of Frederick Douglass, An American Slave, Written by Himself.* 1845. In *Blackamerican Literature, 1760–Present*, edited by Ruth Miller. Beverly Hills, CA: Glencoe Press, 1971.

Doyle, Pat. "Term-Paper Research Spurred Treaty-Rights Battle." *Star Tribune: Newspaper of the Twin Cities*, 15 April 1990, A1, A6.

D'Souza, Dinesh. "Illiberal Education." *The Atlantic Monthly*, March 1991, 51–79.

Duff, Ogle B., and Helen J. Tongchinsub. "Expanding the Secondary Literature Curriculum: Annotated Bibliographies of American Indian, Asian American, and Hispanic American Literature." *English Education* 22 (December 1990): 220–40.

Edelman, Marian Wright. Address given at the *Essence* Awards, 29 May 1992.

Elbow, Peter. *What Is English?* New York: Modern Language Association, 1990.

Ely, Robert. "The Philosophy of Teaching Composition through a Cross-Cultural Approach to Interdisciplinary Humanities." Paper presented at the Thirty-First Annual Meeting of the Conference on College Composition and Communication, Washington, DC, 13–15 March 1980. ED185567.

Epps, Janis. "Killing Them Softly: Why Willie Can't Write." In *Tapping Potential: English and Language Arts for the Black Learner*, edited by Charlotte K. Brooks, 154–58. Urbana, IL: National Council of Teachers of English, 1985.

Farr, Marcia, and Harvey Daniels. *Language Diversity and Writing Instruction.* New York: ERIC Clearinghouse on Urban Education, 1986. ED274996.

Fields, Cheryl. "The Hispanic Pipeline: Narrow, Leaking, and Needing Repair." *Change* 20 (May/June 1988): 20–27.

Foster, David. *A Primer for Writing Teachers: Theories, Theorists, Issues, Problems.* Upper Montclair, NJ: Boynton/Cook, 1983.

Fowler, Robert. "An Analysis of the Composing Processes of Three Black Adolescents." Research report for the University of Pittsburgh, 1979. ED188207.

———. "The Composing Process of Black Student Writers." In *Tapping Potential: English and Language Arts for the Black Learner,* edited by Charlotte K. Brooks, 182–86. Urbana, IL: National Council of Teachers of English, 1985.

Frangedis, Helen. "Dealing with the Controversial Elements in *The Catcher in the Rye.*" *English Journal* 77 (November 1988): 72–75.

Frankson, Marie Stewart. "Chicano Literature for Young Adults: An Annotated Bibliography." *English Journal* 79 (January 1990): 30–38.

Gallo, Donald R., chair, and the Committee on the Senior High School Booklist of the National Council of Teachers of English. *Books for You: A Booklist for Senior High Students.* 9th ed. Urbana, IL: National Council of Teachers of English, 1985.

Garcia, Ricardo. "Overview of Chicano Folklore." *English Journal* 65 (February 1976): 83–87.

Garciagodoy, Juanita. "The Wake-Up Call: An Introductory Essay." In *Braided Lives: An Anthology of Multicultural American Writing,* 81–84. St. Paul: Minnesota Humanities Commission; Minnesota Council of Teachers of English, 1991.

Gates, Henry Louis, Jr. *The Signifying Monkey: A Theory of Afro-American Literary Criticism.* New York: Oxford University Press, 1988.

———. "The Master's Pieces: On Canon Formation and the Afro-American Tradition." In *Conversations: Contemporary Critical Theory and the Teaching of Literature,* edited by Charles Moran and Elizabeth F. Penfield, 55–75. Urbana, IL: National Council of Teachers of English, 1990.

Gay, Geneva. "Ethnic Minorities and Educational Equality." In *Multicultural Education: Issues and Perspectives,* edited by James A. Banks and Cherry A. McGee Banks, 167–88. Boston: Allyn and Bacon, 1989.

Gilbert, Sandra M., and Susan Gubar, eds. *The Norton Anthology of Literature by Women: The Tradition in English.* New York: Norton, 1985.

Gill, Glenda E. "The African-American Student: At Risk." *College Composition and Communication* 43 (May 1992): 225–30.

Gillespie, Sheena, and Robert Singleton, eds. *Across Cultures: A Reader for Writers.* Boston: Allyn and Bacon, 1991.

Glancy, Diane. "The Fire Dragon and Sweat: An Introductory Essay." In *Braided Lives: An Anthology of Multicultural American Writing,* 13–15.

St. Paul: Minnesota Humanities Commission; Minnesota Council of Teachers of English, 1991.

Goldberg, Mark F. "Portrait of Shirley Brice Heath." *Educational Leadership* 49 (April 1992): 80–82.

Gómez, Alma, Cherríe Moraga, and Mariana Romo-Carmona, eds. *Cuentos: Stories by Latinas.* New York: Kitchen Table–Women of Color Press, 1983.

Greenberg, Karen L. "Dialect Differences in the Composition Class." In *Nonnative and Nonstandard Dialect Students,* edited by Candy Carter, 106–7. Urbana, IL: National Council of Teachers of English, 1982.

Greene, Brenda M. "A Cross-Cultural Approach to Literacy: The Immigrant Experience." *English Journal* 77 (September 1988): 45–48.

Guild, Pat Burke, and Stephen Garger. *Marching to Different Drummers.* Alexandria, VA: Association for Supervision and Curriculum Development, 1985.

Haberman, Martin. *Recruiting and Selecting Teachers for Urban Schools.* New York: ERIC Clearinghouse on Urban Education; Institute for Urban and Minority Education, 1987. ED292942.

Harris, Muriel. *Teaching One-to-One: The Writing Conference.* Urbana, IL: National Council of Teachers of English, 1986.

Henry, William III. "Beyond the Melting Pot." *Time,* 9 April 1990, 28–31.

Hertzel, Leo J. "Review of *Braided Lives.*" *Minnesota English Journal* 22 (Winter/Spring 1992): 1–12.

Hill, Roberta. Panel discussion participant at the Native American Women's Institute, Augsburg College, Minneapolis, 26–28 October 1989.

Hirsch, E. D., Jr. *Cultural Literacy: What Every American Needs to Know.* Boston: Houghton Mifflin, 1987.

Hodges, Helene. "I Know They Can Learn Because I've Taught Them." *Educational Leadership* 44 (1987): 3.

Hoeveler, Diane Long. "Text and Context: Teaching Native American Literature." *English Journal* 77 (September 1988): 20–24.

Hogan, Patrick Colm. "Mo' Better Canons: What's Wrong and What's Right about Mandatory Diversity." *College English* 54 (February 1992): 182–92.

hooks, bell. "Racism and Feminism." In *Rereading America: Cultural Contexts for Critical Thinking and Writing,* edited by Gary Colombo, Robert Cullen, and Bonnie Lisle, 303–11. New York: St. Martin's Press, 1989. Reprinted from A*in't I a Woman? Black Women and Feminism* (1981).

Hughes, Langston. "Harlem (Dream Deferred)." 1951. In *The Norton Introduction to Literature,* 4th ed., edited by Carl E. Bain, Jerome Beaty, and J. Paul Hunter. New York: Norton, 1986.

Jackson, Jesse. "Why Blacks Need Affirmative Action." In *Emerging Voices: A Cross-Cultural Reader,* edited by Janet Madden-Simpson and Sara M.

Blake, 266–67. Fort Worth: Holt, Rinehart and Winston, 1990. Reprinted from *Regulation*, September/October 1978.

Jay, Gregory S. "The End of 'American' Literature: Toward a Multicultural Practice." *College English* 53 (March 1991): 264–81.

Johannessen, Larry. *Illumination Rounds: Teaching the Literature of the Vietnam War*. Urbana, IL: National Council of Teachers of English, 1992.

Joy, Anna, ed. *We Are America*. San Diego: Harcourt Brace Jovanovich, 1989.

Kiah, Rosalie Black. "The Black Teenager in Young Adult Novels by Award-winning Authors." In *Tapping Potential: English and Language Arts for the Black Learner*, edited by Charlotte K. Brooks, 286–96. Urbana, IL: National Council of Teachers of English, 1985.

Kilborn, Judith, ed. *Kaleidoscope: St. Cloud State University's Multicultural Magazine*. St. Cloud, MN: The Write Place, 1990+.

Kim, Elaine H. *Asian American Literature: An Introduction to the Writings and Their Social Context*. Philadelphia: Temple University Press, 1982.

———. "'Such Opposite Creatures': Men and Women in Asian American Literature." *Michigan Quarterly Review* 29 (Winter 1990): 68–93.

Kirkpatrick, Ken. "Recent African-American Scholarship." *College English* 52 (November 1990): 812–21.

Kissen, Rita M. "Multicultural Education: The Opening of the American Mind." *English Education* 21 (December 1989): 211–18.

Knepler, Henry, and Myrna Knepler, eds. *Crossing Cultures: Readings for Composition*. 3d ed. New York: Macmillan, 1990.

Kolb, David A. *Learning Style Inventory*. Boston: McBer and Company, 1986.

Kondo, Dorinne. "*M. Butterfly*: Orientalism, Gender, and a Critique of Essentialist Identity." *Cultural Critique* 16 (1990): 5–29.

Lake, Patricia. "Sexual Stereotyping and the English Curriculum." *English Journal* 77 (October 1988): 35–38.

Laskin, David. "Gabriel García Márquez." *Literary Cavalcade* 42 (November/December 1989): 4–7.

Lauter, Paul. "Publication of *The Heath Anthology of American Literature*." Fifth Annual Conference of the Society for the Study of Multi-Ethnic Literature of the United States (MELUS), University of Minnesota, Minneapolis, 13 April 1991.

Lauter, Paul, et al., eds. *The Heath Anthology of American Literature*. 2 vols. Lexington, MA: D. C. Heath, 1990.

Layton, Marilyn Smith, ed. *Intercultural Journeys through Reading and Writing*. New York: HarperCollins, 1991.

Li, David Leiwei. "Filiative and Affiliative Textualization in Chinese American Literature." In *Understanding Others: Cultural and Cross-Cultural Studies and the Teaching of Literature*, edited by Joseph Trimmer and Tilly Warnock, 177–200. Urbana, IL: National Council of Teachers of English, 1992.

Lincoln, Kenneth. "Native American Literatures: 'old like hills, like stars.'" In *Three American Literatures: Essays in Chicano, Native American, and Asian-American Literature for Teachers of American Literature,* edited by Houston A. Baker, Jr., 80–167. New York: Modern Language Association, 1982.

Lowe, Lisa. "Heterogeneity, Hybridity, Multiplicity: Marking Asian American Differences." *Diaspora* 1 (1990): 24–44.

Madden, Janet, and Sara M. Blake, eds. *Crosscurrents: Themes for Developing Writers.* San Diego: Harcourt Brace Jovanovich, 1992.

Madden-Simpson, Janet, and Sara M. Blake, eds. *Emerging Voices: A Cross-Cultural Reader.* Fort Worth: Holt, Rinehart and Winston, 1990.

Madhubuti, Haki R. [Don L. Lee]. "Hard Words and Clear Songs: The Writing of Black Poetry." In *Tapping Potential: English and Language Arts for the Black Learner,* edited by Charlotte K. Brooks, 168–75. Urbana, IL: National Council of Teachers of English, 1985.

———. "Exclusion, Intrusion, Infusion: What Do We Do with the Canon?" Annual Convention of the National Council of Teachers of English, Seattle, 23 November 1991.

Margolis, Howard, and Arthur Shapiro. "Countering Negative Images of Disability in Classical Literature." *English Journal* 76 (March 1987): 18–22.

Martin, Reginald. "The New Black Aesthetic Critics and Their Exclusion from American 'Mainstream' Criticism." *College English* 50 (April 1988): 373–82.

———. "Current Thought in African-American Literary Criticism: An Introduction." *College English* 52 (November 1990): 727–31.

Mayher, John. "Interaction with the Local Censor: Moffett's *Storm in the Mountains.*" *English Journal* 79 (February 1990): 83–85.

McCarthy, Bernice. *The 4MAT System: Teaching to Learning Styles with Right/Left Mode Techniques.* Barrington, IL: Excel, 1980.

McDonald, Frances Beck. "Freedom to Read: A Professional Responsibility." Appendix B in *Teaching Literature in the Secondary School,* edited by Richard Beach and James Marshall, 548–58. San Diego: Harcourt Brace Jovanovich, 1991.

McKendy, Thomas. "Gypsies, Jews, and *The Merchant of Venice.*" In *Expanding the Canon: Bridges to Understanding,* edited by Faith Z. Schullstrom, 18–21. Urbana, IL: National Council of Teachers of English, 1990.

McLeod, Susan, with the assistance of Stacia Bates, Alan Hunt, John Jarvis, and Shelley Spear, eds. *Writing about the World.* San Diego: Harcourt Brace Jovanovich, 1991.

McMillan, Terry, ed. *Breaking Ice: An Anthology of Contemporary African-American Fiction.* New York: Viking, 1990.

Meade, Jeff. "A War of Words." *Teacher Magazine* 2 (November/December 1990): 36–45.

Miller, Carol. "Tellers of the Circle: The Novels of Leslie Marmon Silko, Paula Gunn Allen, and Louise Erdrich." Unpublished manuscript, 1989.

Minnesota Department of Education. *A Policy on the Freedom to Teach, to Learn, and to Express Ideas in the Public Schools*. St. Paul: Minnesota Department of Education, 1985.

Minnesota Humanities Commission and the Minnesota Council of Teachers of English. *Braided Lives: An Anthology of Multicultural American Writing*. St. Paul: Minnesota Humanities Commission; Minnesota Council of Teachers of English, 1991.

Mizokawa, Donald T. "The Problem with Lumping Data." Paper presented at the American Educational Research Association Conference, 22 April 1992.

Momaday, N. Scott. "The Man Made of Words." In *Literature of the American Indians: Views and Interpretations*, edited by Abraham Chapman, 96–110. New York: Meridian, 1975.

Moore, Lisa. "One-on-One: Pairing Male and Female Writers." *English Journal* 78 (October 1989): 34–38.

Moore-Foster, Musa. "The Kaleidoscope of Self: An Introductory Essay." In *Braided Lives: An Anthology of Multicultural American Writing*, 141–44. St. Paul: Minnesota Humanities Commission; Minnesota Council of Teachers of English, 1991.

Morrison, Toni. *Playing in the Dark: Whiteness and the Literary Imagination*. Cambridge, MA: Harvard University Press, 1992.

Moss, Anita. "Gothic and Grotesque Effects in Virginia Hamilton's Fiction." *The ALAN Review* 19 (Winter 1992): 16–28.

Mullican, James S. "Cultural Literacy: Whose Culture? Whose Literacy?" *English Education* 23 (December 1991): 244–50.

National Coalition Against Censorship (NCAC). *Books on Trial: A Survey of Recent Cases*. New York: National Coalition Against Censorship, 1987.

Native American Authors Distribution Project. *Fall 1992 Book List*. Greenfield Center, NY: The Greenfield Review Press, 1992.

Native American Women's Institute. Augsburg College, Minneapolis, 26–28 October 1989.

NCTE. "Censorship: Don't Let It Become an Issue in Your Schools." *Language Arts* 55 (February 1978): 230–42.

———. "Statement on Censorship and Professional Guidelines." Urbana, IL: National Council of Teachers of English, 1982.

NCTE Commission on Composition. "Students' Right to Their Own Language." *College Composition and Communication* 25 (Fall 1974, special issue): 5–10.

———. "Teaching Composition: A Position Statement." *College English* 36 (October 1974): 219–20.

Nickolai-Mays, Susanne, and Phyllis Post Kammer. "Non-white Students' Concerns about Attending College." *School Counselor* 34 (May 1987): 379–83.

Norton, Donna E. "Teaching Multicultural Literature in the Reading Curriculum." *The Reading Teacher* 44 (September 1990): 28–40.

Office of Educational Research and Improvement (OERI). *Youth Indicators 1991: Trends in the Well-Being of American Youth.* Washington, DC: United States Department of Education, 1991.

Oliver, Eileen. "An Afrocentric Approach to Literature: Putting the Pieces Back Together." *English Journal* 77 (September 1988): 49–54.

Oliver, Eileen, and Tamrat Tademe. "Students of Color on White Campuses: Building Self-Esteem in a Hostile Environment." In *Proceedings of the Conference on the Troubled Adolescent, 9–11 April 1991*, 118–21.

Pace, Barbara G. "The Textbook Canon: Genre, Gender, and Race in U.S. Literature Anthologies." *English Journal* 81 (September 1992): 33–38.

Page, Ernest R. "Black Literature and Changing Attitudes: Does It Do the Job?" *English Journal* 66 (March 1977): 29–33.

Perry, Jesse. "A Selected Bibliography of Multi-Ethnic Literature." *Minnesota English Journal* 22 (Fall 1991): 32–37.

Peterson, Judith E. "Golden Discoveries: Literature of the Americas." *English Journal* 81 (September 1992): 39–44.

Raines, B. G. "A Profile in Censorship." *Virginia English Bulletin* 36 (1986): 37–45.

Ramsey, Paul A. "Teaching the Teachers to Teach Black Dialect Writers." *College English* 41 (October 1979): 197–201.

Raymond, James C. "Authority, Desire, and Canons: Tendentious Meditations on Cultural Literacy." In *Conversations: Contemporary Critical Theory and the Teaching of Literature*, edited by Charles Moran and Elizabeth F. Penfield, 76–86. Urbana, IL: National Council of Teachers of English, 1990.

Reed, Ishmael. "The History of the Before Columbus Foundation." Speech given at Washington State University, Pullman, April 1991.

Reed, Ishmael, Kathryn Trueblood, and Shawn Wong, eds. *The Before Columbus Foundation Fiction Anthology: Selections from the American Book Awards, 1980–1990.* New York: Norton, 1992.

Reimer, Constance, and Marcia Brock. "Books, Students, Censorship: Reality in the Classroom." *English Journal* 77 (November 1988): 69–71.

Rice, Mitchell, and Bonnie Alford. "A Preliminary Analysis of Black Undergraduate Students' Perceptions of Retention/Attrition Factors at a Large, Predominantly White State Research University in the South." *Journal of Negro Education* 58 (Winter 1989): 68–81.

Rico, Barbara Roche, and Sandra Mano, eds. *American Mosaic: Multicultural Readings in Context.* Boston: Houghton Mifflin, 1991.

Rosenblatt, Louise M. *Literature as Exploration*. 3d ed. New York: Noble and Noble, 1976.

Royster, Jacqueline. "A New Lease on Writing." In *Tapping Potential: English and Language Arts for the Black Learner*, edited by Charlotte K. Brooks, 159–67. Urbana, IL: National Council of Teachers of English, 1985.

Sacco, Margo. "ALAN Intellectual Freedom Committee Report." *The ALAN Review* 18 (Winter 1991): 6–7.

Savery, Pancho. "'Who Was That Masked Man?': Literary Criticism and the Teaching of African American Literature in Introductory Courses." In *Practicing Theory in Introductory College Literature Courses*, edited by James M. Cahalan and David B. Downing, 189–98. Urbana, IL: National Council of Teachers of English, 1991.

Scott, Jerrie Cobb. "Nonmainstream Groups: Questions and Research Directions." In *Counterpoint and Beyond: A Response to* Becoming a Nation of Readers, edited by Jane L. Davidson, 27–32. Urbana, IL: National Council of Teachers of English, 1988.

Shannon, George. "Making a Home of One's Own: The Young in Cross-Cultural Fiction." *English Journal* 77 (September 1988): 14–19.

Shapiro, Nancy. "Textbooks in Focus: Cross-Cultural Readers." *College Composition and Communication* 42 (December 1991): 524–30.

Shaughnessy, Mina. *Errors and Expectations: A Guide for the Teacher of Basic Writing*. New York: Oxford University Press, 1977.

Shirley, Carl, and Paula Shirley. *Understanding Chicano Literature*. Columbia: University of South Carolina Press, 1988.

Simmons, John. "Censorship in the Schools: No End in Sight." *The ALAN Review* 18 (Winter 1991): 6–8.

Slark, Julie, et al. "Learning Assessment Retention Consortium of the California Community Colleges." Research report for the California Community Colleges, Sacramento, Office of the Chancellor, September 1987. ED286566.

Smagorinsky, Peter. "Towards a Civic Education in a Multicultural Society: Ethical Problems in Teaching Literature." *English Education* 24 (December 1992): 212–28.

Small, Robert C., Jr., and M. Jerry Weiss. "What Do I Do Now? Where to Turn When You Face a Censor." Paper presented at the Annual Convention of the National Council of Teachers of English, Seattle, November 1991.

Smitherman, Geneva. "English Teacher, Why You Be Doin' the Thangs You Don't Do?" *English Journal* 63 (January 1972): 59–65.

Smitherman-Donaldson, Geneva. "Opinion: Toward a National Public Policy on Language." *College English* 49 (January 1987): 29–36.

Spurlin, William J. "Theorizing Signifyin(g) and the Role of the Reader: Possible Directions for African-American Literary Criticism." *College English* 52 (November 1990): 732–42.

Staples, Brent. "Night Walker." In *Crossing Cultures: Readings for Composition*, 3d ed., edited by Henry Knepler and Myrna Knepler, 172–76. New York: Macmillan, 1990. Reprinted from *Ms.*, September 1986.

Stensland, Anna Lee. *Literature by and about the American Indian: An Annotated Bibliography*. 2d ed. Urbana, IL: National Council of Teachers of English, 1979.

Stock, William, et al. "A Study of Placement Test Subscores and Their Use in Assigning CSU, Fresno Freshmen to Beginning English Courses." Research report presented to the English Placement Test Development Committee, California State University, Fresno, 15 August 1986. ED289453.

Swing, Georgia Hanshew. "Choosing Life: Adolescent Suicide in Literature." *English Journal* 79 (September 1990): 78–82.

Takaki, Ronald. Workshop on multicultural education. St. Cloud State University, St. Cloud, MN, 30 January 1991.

Tatum, Charles, ed. *Mexican American Literature*. San Diego: Harcourt Brace Jovanovich, 1990.

Taylor, Ethel, and Ernest Bradford. "Using the Oral History Approach to Teach Freshman Writing." In *Tapping Potential: English and Language Arts for the Black Learner*, edited by Charlotte K. Brooks, 214–18. Urbana, IL: National Council of Teachers of English, 1985.

Tchudi, Stephen, and Diana Mitchell. *Explorations in the Teaching of English*. 3d ed. New York: Harper and Row, 1989.

Thompson, Julian. "Defending YA Literature against the Pharisees and Censors: Is It Worth the Trouble?" *The ALAN Review* 18 (Winter 1991): 2–5.

Trevino, Consuelo, and Bette Wise. "Summer Acceptance Programs: A Viable Option for Provisional Students Entering a Private University." Paper presented at the Thirteenth Annual Meeting of the Western College Reading Association, San Francisco, 27–30 March 1980. ED188118.

Truth, Sojourner. "Ain't I a Woman?" 1851. From "Reminiscences by Francis D. Gage of Sojourner Truth, for May 28–29, 1851." In *The Heath Anthology of American Literature*, edited by Paul Lauter et al., 1: 1911–13. Lexington, MA: D. C. Heath, 1990.

Turner, Darwin T. "Black Experience, Black Literature, Black Students, and the English Classroom." In *Tapping Potential: English and Language Arts for the Black Learner*, edited by Charlotte K. Brooks, 297–307. Urbana, IL: National Council of Teachers of English, 1985.

Verburg, Carol J., ed. *Ourselves among Others: Cross-Cultural Readings for Writers*. New York: St. Martin's Press, 1988.

Villegas, Ana Maria. *Culturally Responsive Teaching*. Princeton, NJ: Educational Testing Service, 1991.

Wagner, Dori, and Rick Coe. "Multicultural Perspectives and Development of Writing Abilities." *Working Teacher* (1982): 17–22.

Walker-Moffatt, Wendy. "The Hmong Paradigm." Paper presented at the American Educational Research Association Conference, 22 April 1992.

Warner, J. Sterling, Judith Hilliard, and Vincent Piro, eds. *Visions across the Americas*. San Diego: Harcourt Brace Jovanovich, 1992.

Washington Center for Improving the Quality of Undergraduate Education. "Core Curriculum Profile: Washington State University." *Washington Center Newsletter* 7 (Fall 1992): 11.

Wells, Ida B. "Lynching at the Curve." In *Rereading America: Cultural Contexts for Critical Thinking and Writing*, edited by Gary Colombo, Robert Cullen, and Bonnie Lisle, 168–74. New York: St. Martin's Press, 1989.

Whetten, Clifford L. "Culture and Learning Styles." *Community Education Journal* 18 (1991): 17–19.

wiger, flo. "Native Americans and Curriculum Change." Native American Women's Institute, Augsburg College, Minneapolis, 27 October 1989.

Wiget, Andrew, and Carla Mulford. "Native American Traditions." In *The Heath Anthology of American Literature*, edited by Paul Lauter et al., 1: 22–24. Lexington, MA: D. C. Heath, 1990.

Williams, Carole A. "Studying Challenged Novels: Or, How I Beat Senioritis." *English Journal* 77 (November 1988): 66–68.

Williams, William F. "Teaching Literature, Canon Formation, and Multiculturalism." *English Leadership Quarterly* 13 (1991): 2–3.

Winkler, Karen J. "A Scholar's Provocative Query: Was Huckleberry Finn Black?" *Chronicle of Higher Education*, 8 July 1992, A6–8.

Wright, Richard. *Black Boy.* New York: Harper and Row, 1945.

Yep, Laurence. "A Garden of Dragons." *The ALAN Review* 19 (Spring 1992): 6–8.

Youdelman, Jeffrey. "Limiting Students: Remedial Writing and the Death of Open Admissions." *College English* 39 (January 1978): 562–72.

Zeichner, Kenneth M. "Educating Teachers for Cultural Diversity." Unpublished manuscript, University of Wisconsin–Madison, 1992.

Author

Eileen Iscoff Oliver is assistant professor of English and coordinator of English education at Washington State University. She has taught in high schools, continuation and correctional schools, community colleges, and university programs in California, Texas, New York, Minnesota, and Washington. Her interests in composition, English education, literature, and multicultural studies are reflected in articles and book chapters that have appeared or are forthcoming in *English Journal, English Leadership Quarterly, English Quarterly, Arizona English Bulletin, Expanding the Canon: Bridges to Understanding, Teaching Culturally Diverse Populations: From Theory to Practice*, and *Whole Language in the Secondary and Post-Secondary Classroom*. She received a B.A. from the University of California at Berkeley in 1965, a Secondary Teaching Credential from California State University at San Francisco in 1967, and a Ph.D. from the University of Texas at Austin in 1984.